MANN
FOR
ALL
SEASONS

" 'Cagney & Lacey' was just another television series . . . a hopeful gleam in this Producer's eye . . . until Judy Mann brought us to the attention of the nation in *The Washington Post*. The rest, as they say, is herstory."

—BARNEY ROSENZWEIG, Executive Producer of
"Cagney & Lacey"

"Judy Mann's observations on the dilemma of American family life in the '90s are keen and forceful. They will make you think and act."

—REPRESENTATIVE PATRICIA SCHROEDER,
United States Congress

"In *Mann for All Seasons*, Judy Mann raises the voice of the ordinary woman in an extraordinary way. As I read, I found myself nodding in agreement. No matter what our career choices, because of our gender, we face common problems from infancy to old age. Judy Mann allows us to discover we are not alone."

—GERALDINE FERRARO, author and speaker

"Judy Mann's columns propel even activists like myself to further action. Empathetic but clearheaded, her writing draws an issue into relief so that the clear injustice at its core evinces itself. Action, not just anger, is what she provokes through her work."

—IRENE NATIVIDAD, consultant and former
Chairperson of the National Women's
Political Caucus

"Judy Mann's columns are always a good read, and all of her fans probably have their favorites. For me, the raising-the-kids pieces are classics and worth the price of admission all by themselves."

—HERB BLOCK, award-winning syndicated
cartoonist

"Judy Mann is right on target: it's high time this nation came to grips with the realities of family life in the 1990s. Women and families need maximum flexibility to combine work and family life in a healthy, productive mix. That means, among other things, more good-quality child care, increased parental leave options and work schedules that accommodate family responsibilities. Mann's thoughtful analysis of the changes and challenges facing today's women and families is useful to all of us who are committed to creating, in Mann's words, a more 'family friendly' environment."

—MARIAN WRIGHT EDELMAN, Executive Director
of the Children's Defense Fund

"Judy Mann was the first columnist in the nation to zero in on the gender gap in national politics. She is without question insightful, courageous and on the mark with her analysis and commentary on women and politics and society as a whole. Cutting edge and thoughtful—a must read for feminists."

—ELEANOR SMEAL, women's rights advocate and
President of the Feminist Majority

MANN
FOR
ALL
SEASONS

MANN
FOR
ALL
SEASONS

Wit and Wisdom
from
The Washington Post's
Judy Mann

JUDY MANN

MasterMedia Limited
NEW YORK

Published by MasterMedia Limited

MASTERMEDIA and colophon are registered trademarks of MasterMedia Limited.

10   9   8   7   6   5   4   3   2   1

Library of Congress Cataloging-in-Publication Data

Mann, Judy (Judy W.)
   Mann for all seasons: wit and wisdom from The Washington Post's
Judy Mann/by Judy Mann.
      p.   cm.
   Includes index.
   ISBN 0-942361-22-9
   I. Title.
PN4874.M4767A3   1990
814'.54—dc20   90-39907
                                                     CIP

Designed by Stanley S. Drate/Folio Graphics Co. Inc. for Martin Cook Associates, Ltd.

Manufactured in the United States of America

This book is dedicated to my children:
Devin,
Jeffrey
and Katherine Mann
and to my husband,
Richard Starnes,
who have all given me the joy of love.

Contents

INTRODUCTION

What do women want?

In the sixties and seventies, women rebelled against what they had, which was essentially a life of domesticity and dependency. It was a life anchored in the needs of children, parents and husbands. Women were dependent financially and emotionally on their husbands. They were set up on a pedestal—but it was a trick out of a Saturday-morning television cartoon. They were knocked down one after another—until an entire generation of women stood on the wings of the stage like a Greek chorus warning the next generation of women: Don't let it happen to you.

The next generation paid heed: they saw their mothers, their mothers' best friends, discarded in mid-life and shelved with the label "displaced homemaker." These were the women of the sixties. They got caught in the middle. They came ahead of the women's revolution and during the divorce revolution. They went into the marketplace—because they had to go to work—with less education and far fewer skills than the generation of women to come.

But the next generation didn't enter the job market with degrees in raising children. They left college and graduate schools with M.B.A.'s and law degrees and Ph.D.'s in everything from engineering to medicine. They thought they could manage career, marriage, children and family life by turning the sequence that had tripped up their mothers upside down. They would work in their twenties and create their families in their thirties.

Some of them overstayed the biological clock. Some ran into the physical and emotional impossibilities of doing it all at the same time. Supermoms brought us quality time, but by the end of

1

the eighties, they were talking more and more about personal time, as in "I never have any time for myself." And they did not. Many, in fact, were holding two full-time jobs. They were working full-time outside the home and full-time inside the home. Just as their own mothers had done. Only their own mothers did not work full-time outside their homes as well.

Unfortunately, women are no good at putting their own self-interests first. We find compromising between what we expect of ourselves as mothers and what we expect of ourselves as career-women difficult. So we juggled and balanced—and lived our lives on the ragged edge of exhaustion.

There seemed to be no ideal way for a woman to conduct the various aspects of her life. Once she married and began a family, her life became complicated beyond measure and often difficult beyond endurance. Ellen Futter, the president of Barnard College, who is a lawyer and mother of two, says the question of how to do it all remains one of the questions most frequently asked her by young women today. "I talk a lot with them," she told me. "And it is still my most disappointing answer. They say what's the formula? I tell them there is no formula."

The Lessons to Be Learned

But there are some lessons that this pathfinding generation of women, now in their late thirties, forties and fifties, can pass along to younger women and, yes, to men that can help them sort out ways to reconcile the primary tasks of life in a more humane and less stressful fashion. Probably the single most important thing we need to do is to be a great deal less judgmental of how different men and women, couples and families go about their business of reconciling work and family life. If there is no formula—and Ellen Futter is right, there is none—then there is no right and wrong way of blending these elements of life together. Ellen Futter speaks of a generosity of spirit and of flexibility: "If we can be as women and as men and women more generous of spirit in understanding that there are different routes from here to there, and if our institutions could respond to that, we'd be more flexible." We would create communities in which working parents had a range of choices about how to manage their careers and family obligations and could choose what was best for their particular family.

Generosity of spirit. Flexibility. Choices.

What women of my generation have learned is that what we really need is an environment in which we are free to make choices. And that was what this second stage of the women's movement, which began with the publication in 1963 of Betty Friedan's *The Feminine Mystique,* was really all about: women did not want to be confined to the domestic life. They wanted to be able to make a choice about whether to work or not to work outside the home. Friedan made the case against the rigid confines of home-making and housewifing. She made the case for women to be able to maximize their productivity and potential by working for money if they wanted to. Choice was an essential part of that argument, but it got lost in the controversies about rights that have dogged the women's movement for two and a half decades. Nevertheless, in that time millions of women were able to make the choice to enter the workforce. They won the right to equal credit, which is to say they got the right to go into debt. They secured the right to enter professional schools that had been closed to them and to enter fields that had excluded them. The earnings of working mothers have kept real household incomes from sinking since they peaked in 1973.

Despite this contribution to their families, however, women found themselves in the midst of a great social backlash in the eighties. They heard a president whose mind belonged to another century blame them for high unemployment—women were taking jobs that belonged to men. Working mothers were blamed for everything from the drug epidemic to the pregnancy epidemic among teenagers to the poor performance of American high school students on standardized tests. Women were not at home in the afternoons to supervise the children, and the children were getting into trouble. Studies found that latchkey children who came home from school to empty houses instead of milk and cookies served by an adoring mom were more fearful and apprehensive than children whose mothers were at home. Another study found that younger children who were cared for by older siblings in the afternoon were often beaten up by resentful older brothers or sisters. Still another study found more experimentation with drugs, alcohol and sex by teenagers who were home without adult supervision for several hours in the afternoon.

Common sense should have told us that when adults are not

around, children will get into trouble. But common sense has never been a strong suit in America's dealings with its families. We tend to romanticize and fantasize about our families much the way we do about the Wild West. And when realities don't meet our fantasies, we find it hard to adapt. We feel resentful. So instead of adapting to the changes in American families that occurred in the seventies and eighties, and instead of honoring the contributions working mothers were making, America laid a guilt trip on them. Reaganesque America said women were breaking up the American family. Working mothers were blamed for everything from the rising divorce rate to inflation. Instead of developing day care (the way we did when we needed American women to work in the factories in World War II), we developed studies showing that children in day care got more colds than children who were at home. We pressed the hottest button there is for a mother: you are harming your child by your actions, and therefore you are not a good mother. But why blame mothers? By the time the eighties rolled around, a lot of women were saying, why not blame the fathers?

New Solutions to New Problems

But the question that ought to be asked is: why blame anyone at all? Why not figure out new solutions to new problems instead of trying to fit old solutions to new problems? Why not lengthen junior high and high school days, for example, with after-school study halls and library periods? We must make our institutions more flexible and more responsive to family needs. Communities across the country are lengthening school days in an attempt to reverse declining achievement by students. Longer school days and longer school years are likely to benefit students by exposing them to more teaching and less trouble. And it is a far more productive social response than to blame women who are working to support their families. We don't need any more guilt and blame. We need to offer women and parents more choices about the best way to function as a family.

The nineties should be the decade in which women consolidate the gains of the women's revolution of the sixties. But women can't do this alone. They are going to have to persuade the men they work with, love and live with that it is in their best interests to make women full partners. This means equal pay in the workplace and equal sharing of burdens at home.

Every American family in which the wife is cheated out of her full paycheck will be helped financially and in many other ways by enforcement of laws banning discrimination in pay. Every American family that has a female worker who is underpaid is operating at a lower standard of living than it would if women were not consistently paid a third less than men are. At no juncture is this more keenly felt than by divorcing families, and particularly the women, who usually are awarded custody of the children. Automatically, most of them drop into poverty because their own incomes are low and the child support awards are insufficient or not paid. Families headed by women would be significantly better off if laws banning discrimination in pay were enforced. This would not just help these families: the fathers could probably reap benefits in the form of more equitable sharing of the cost of rearing children and a diminished burden of child support on their own shoulders.

Women who choose to stay home and raise children are doing valuable, honorable work. That choice must be respected, and I believe it is. I think this business of women who stay at home feeling put down by women who have careers is more media myth than anything else. And if anyone doubts that the media are capable of mythologizing when it comes to modern women, let me remind them of the phony story current a few years ago about career women who did not marry before they were in their thirties. "Are These Old Maids?" shouted *People* magazine from a cover adorned by Diane Sawyer, Donna Mills, Sharon Gless and Linda Rondstadt.

Come on, fellas, give us a break.

That same summer, *Newsweek* did a story on what it called the marriage crunch. It cited the same study (by two Yale sociologists and a Harvard economist) that offered grim predictions about the statistical probability of unmarried women of certain ages ever getting married. *Newsweek* came up with this classic: "Forty-year-old [women] are more likely to be killed by a terrorist" than to get married. "They have a minuscule 2.6 per cent probability of tying the knot." Professional women who had heard plenty about the biological clock striking midnight for them at forty were now being told that a statistical crunch would ambush them at thirty.

It took a woman reporter, Susan Faludi, of the Sunday magazine of the *San Jose Mercury News,* to blow the study and all the spin the media were putting on it out of the water. Turns out that Harvard-Yale study was based on a model never before used to predict human behavior. Turns out the authors were distancing themselves as far as possible from the media hoopla. Said one of the study's authors: "The underlying message of many of these stories on the study is a very sexist position implying women should be married, that a woman's best place is in the home. It's saying you women have gone out and gotten careers and asked for too much and look what you got. This is what you deserve."

Turns out also that a Census Bureau study based on a time-tested model that polled one out of every six households came to a dramatically different conclusion about what happens to women who don't go the ring-by-spring route. The Census Bureau found that women at the age of forty have a 23 percent chance of marriage, not a 2.6 percent chance.

The Media and Women

The media, which until this decade were very much in the grip of white men whose wives had stayed at home, have been notoriously unfriendly to modern women. Men who run newspapers, television stations and other news organizations have been just as frightened of the profound changes brought on by the women's movement as men running every other institution. Newspapers, for example, have been slow to advance women into management and slow to respond in their coverage to the changing interests of women readers. The results were predictable: daily newspapers have lost a quarter of their women readers. The conventional wisdom in the industry is that women readers don't have the time to read newspapers anymore. That's nonsense: women's magazines are among the fastest-growing segment of the magazine industry. We make time for what's relevant.

Media corporations have been slow to respond to the family pressures of both their male and female employees. When corporations do nothing to help working mothers balance family and career, they lose talented women who could have someday entered management. But significant improvements are coming. At *The Washington Post,* for example, employees can use sick leave to stay home and care for a sick child. We don't have to get on the phone and fake bronchitis. This policy costs the company very little and makes a tremendous difference to working parents whose child care arrangements fall apart when a child comes down with a cold. The *Post* has been able to keep reporters with newborns on the payroll by offering them the option of working part-time, and reporters and editors have developed a variety of part-time arrangements that best fit job and family. A decade ago, this would have been unheard-of at a major daily newspaper. Reporters and editors have also been given extended leaves of absence to stay home and care for babies—not just for writing books and taking professional fellowships.

The *Post* understands that to compete and retain workers it must adapt to the new exigencies of workers' lives. And that means acknowledging that people must have choices about whether to have children, when to have them, how best to care for them and who will mind them. The *Post* also has a dependent care assistance program that lets us shield from taxes a portion of the money we spend on the care of dependent children and adults.

We Need Choices

Very slowly, we are developing a range of choices for taking care of children as businesses across the country realize that they must get involved if they are going to retain workers. But the task of developing affordable, safe child care is far from done. We are far behind many of our trade competitors, and certainly far behind Europe. Perhaps at some point our policymakers will make the obvious connection between lower productivity and the fact that we do not have the family support systems that we need in order to make American working women and men as efficient in the workplace as they should be.

For more and more families, this is going to mean much more than child care. It is going to mean help with elderly parents, a job that falls primarily on women. A typical American woman can expect for some period of her life to be responsible for the care of a parent, one or more school-age children, as well as handling a full-time job. If the elderly parent lives with her, it might mean taking the parent to an adult day care facility or hiring a home health aide during the day. It might mean coordinating physical therapy for a relative who has had a stroke. It might mean putting the elderly relative in a nursing home and overseeing her care and the financing of it.

It will almost certainly—until we get a more rational form of health care—mean the kind of bureaucratic paper nightmare that can drive the most resilient human being mad. The paperwork from medical insurance companies and from Medicare compounds the difficulties of the primary caretaker beyond reason. The complete absence of the endless forms and bureaucratic bedevilment of already overburdened relatives is one of the most appealing aspects of Canada's national health care system—from which this country ought to learn a great deal. Absent universal health care, however, we must provide as many other choices as possible to help families manage the care of their elderly and infirm. Many working women quit their jobs to stay home and care for elderly relatives. Since most women make less money than their husbands do, the family takes less of a financial jolt when the wife's income stops than when the husband's does. More often than not, the wife—not the husband—will quit work to care for her husband's parent. But professional women who have invested decades in their careers are going to be loath to drop out of the workforce in order to care for elderly parents. For one thing, families of professional women can ill afford to lose that kind of income. For another, the professional woman may feel she has invested too much for too long to take such a setback to her career. And she may well be a single mother who cannot afford to quit her job. She needs options—options that will include the right to take a leave of absence, the ability to hire home health care workers that are licensed, competent and reliable or the choice of being able to put the relative in a nursing home that is close by and affordable.

There is no reason why we should not have enough nursing homes in every community. We are going to need to do this, and we should do it right. The fastest-growing segment of our population are the very old, those who are over eighty-five. While some remain vigorous and well, many are frail and in need of constant care. For the last six months of her life, my mother was in a nursing home five minutes away from my house and five minutes away from my father's home. Not a day passed that someone from the family did not visit her. The proximity of the home made an enormous difference: my grief-stricken eighty-eight-year-old father was not driving long distances in the car—and courting accidents—to visit her. I was able to stop by frequently. These are details that seem relatively unimportant—until you begin managing the care of an elderly loved one who is dying.

My generation has been exposed to the prolonged death of elderly relatives like no previous generation in history. Experts in the business of labeling trends call it "previewing." My generation has previewed life in nursing homes and the anguishing descent into dementia of aged parents, and we hope desperately that this will not happen to us. More and more of us are realizing that our parents said the same thing. We see that an active, energetic, involved life is no guarantee against a bedridden decline in which we are helpless, out of it and a terrible burden to our families.

More and more of us are seeing firsthand how the medical profession can keep people alive long after there is any quality of life remaining. Pneumonia, once called the old man's friend, is no longer allowed to take its course. Doctors routinely prescribe antibiotics when people in a vegetative state get pneumonia. Often the person responds, and stays alive until the next onset of pneumonia and the next round of antibiotics. Who profits from this? Nursing homes and doctors and hospitals, of course. The agony of families is simply prolonged, as is the life of the elderly victim who probably wished to avoid this fate as much as any of us.

Many of us have told our spouses and children that we don't want heroic measures used to keep us alive if we become hopelessly debilitated. But our legal definitions of heroic measures are so narrow and our own legal authority to enforce our wishes is so fragile that far more often than not we and our families are at the mercy of doctors who make life and death decisions for us with malpractice suits, or profits, in the forefront of their minds. They tell us the dynamics of the medical and legal systems force them to prescribe whatever they can to keep people alive, rather than letting people go. Maybe. But for a century or so, good doctors have been gently helping hopelessly ill old folks cross the final threshold. It's a pity more do not.

We hear more and more stories from friends and contemporaries about elderly relatives who have lived for years in vegetative or comatose states following strokes or who are in the final despairing stages of brain diseases. And as more and more of us experience the impact of modern medicine on the American way of aging and death, we will be willing, and probably anxious, to develop more options for our own care—much the way women have insisted on more options for the care of breast cancer. Living wills in which we forbid the use of heroic measures now have the force of law in some places. "Heroic measures" need to be more broadly defined so that people can choose to forbid the use of antibiotics and feeding tubes to keep them alive long after their conditions are irreversible. These are life-prolonging methods commonly used now. Who knows what will be available twenty or thirty years from now, when the generation that is now middle-aged is very old, and our children will face the same life and death questions with us that we have so painfully previewed with our parents? We are capable of keeping people alive for years, but we are not capable of letting them go. We must start talking about this private anguish in public if we are to secure better choices about how we are cared for in our own final days.

My generation of women has flexed its muscles on every major institution in society—with the exceptions of the Catholic and Mormon churches. We demanded—and secured—more humane treatment of pregnant women by doctors and hospitals, of rape victims by legal authorities and hospitals, of breast cancer patients. We took on a hostile workplace and as more and more women entered it, we reached critical mass and have now become numerous enough and powerful enough that we can stamp our own ethic, priorities and values on the way America works. And we should. We do not have to accept the old models. They were tailored to one-worker families, and the workplace was tailored by and for men. Women now comprise 54.2 percent of the workforce. Fifty-six and a half million of us are working full- or part-time. We should no longer have to be the second sex—the "other"—in the workplace. We should no longer have to feel like strangers working all of our lives in a foreign culture, trying to find safe harbor in a foreign land.

We can be willing to do things our way, and we can learn from those who have gone before us who have themselves rejected the old conventions about work and linear careers and become pathfinders in the second and third stages of their lives. The generation now in its sixties and seventies has given us the concept of second careers. Men and women are retiring from corporations or government and taking up entirely new fields—an engineer becomes an artist, a bureaucrat a lawyer, a politician a cleric. What they have really introduced is the notion of sequencing our lives. It is a pattern that we can adapt to help some of us sort out the competing demands of family and work. Do we really have to do it all, all at the same time?

Who says?

Our obsession with youth is going to diminish very rapidly as the baby boom generation ages. Middle age will be the prime of life, and we aren't going to trust anyone under thirty. After all, those were the get-rich-quick schemers who helped bring down the House of Drexel Burnham Lambert. Businesses aren't going to be nearly as enchanted with young workers as they have been in the past. There won't be that many of them. This means that businesses can no longer afford to discriminate against mature workers or people who have stayed out of the workforce to raise children. In the past, women felt they had to go to work straight out of college, or be left far behind. But changing demographics will make women who have stayed at home to raise children very attractive job candidates. It is no longer an employer's market: it is an employee's market and that means more choices and more options for tomorrow's working parents.

Neither political party understands the importance of giving people choices beyond the narrow implications of the abortion debate. The Democrats have become identified as the party that favors reproductive choice—yet the House of Representatives, which the Democrats control, has for years passed some of the most restrictive antiabortion legislation on the books anywhere in the country. The Republicans were identified as the party that wanted to restrict abortions—that is, until the U.S. Supreme Court said the state legislatures could do it. Only once before in the history of the republic has a right that Americans have come to regard as fundamental been taken away from them. That was the right to drink alcohol and the Prohibition era, which most of us have come to view as one of the most misbegotten political episodes in our history. The whole history of this country has been one of expanding rights and freedoms, not of curtailing them. And while the debate rages, it is inflaming political passions and arousing deep sentiments that are going to be felt throughout the social fabric. Women who assumed that legal abortions were a matter of right are feeling threatened and deeply resentful. Who decides? is the battle cry of the resurgent pro-choice movement. And that question is resonating within women on a lot of different levels. Who, indeed, decides? And who decides what?

Women have come out of this phase of the women's movement with prizes that cannot be measured by pollsters and politicians. Women in their thirties, forties, fifties and sixties who have survived the past two and a half decades of working and raising families have come out of the turbulence with a sense of self-worth, confidence, self-esteem and a rock-solid belief in our judgment and good sense. Women don't need anybody telling us what to do.

Vince Breglio, a Republican pollster, found this out when he was doing focus groups and polls for Republican congressional candidates who were trying to prepare their positions on abortion as they headed into the 1990 election cycle. "The issue of choice over abortion is related to a more fundamental issue of trust to make the correct decisions in a whole variety of areas," he said. "It is so much on the minds of so many people, but the underlying driving force is often only partially related to whether or not you can abort a fetus. It does reflect an essentially fundamental sense of self-worth and trust and importance in the whole decision-making framework which has been denied women over time. It is: Trust me to make good decisions, trust me to take care of my life, trust me that I won't do anything stupid."

The breakup of totalitarian regimes in Eastern Europe and the evolving of more democratic forms of government throughout the world are reflections of that same sentiment at the ballot box, he thinks. "It can be a very positive thing for this country. Allowing people to have agency, to make their decisions, is a positive step in the right direction. That is happening around the world. I think the extent to which politicians echo this sentiment they will gain votes. The extent to which they do not, they will lose votes. My sense is anytime you attempt to limit a person's freedom to decide, you end up with political difficulties."

Family Issues Matter

History has a warning here for women. After World War II, the women who manned the factories were dispatched out of the manufacturing sector and either into the homes—with the admonition that they should be full-time homemakers—or into the offices and schools, with the admonition that secretarial and teaching work were the only becoming jobs for them. We are at a similar historical juncture: the Cold War is over and we are looking at the probability of an enormous adjustment in all parts of the economy that have been driven by unslakable needs of the defense establishment. Men and women, both, are going to be facing shutdowns in everything from assembly lines that manufacture weapons to consulting companies that grind out proposals. It is inevitable that there will be fewer jobs linked to military needs, unless the sector of the economy is artificially propped up. It was in a similar climate of declining military jobs that Rosie the Riveter got sent home. And for a few years after World War II, the march into the workforce by women which had been going on for two centuries since the beginning of the Industrial Revolution briefly reversed itself in the United States. The day care centers that had allowed women to work in the factories were swiftly dismantled. Men were given the higher-paying jobs in the manufacturing sector, the GI bill sent them to college, the Highway Act sent families into the suburbs, the husband became the breadwinner and the American housewife got set up on her shaky pedestal.

Could this happen again? You bet it could.

We are entering a period that requires vigilance but that also holds great promise. But they will be empty promises if men and women simply sit around waiting for good things to happen. There are too many well-entrenched interests who will be looking for ways to manipulate tax monies and public policies for their own benefit. Nothing made this clearer than the bailout of the savings and loan industry—at a time when America could not find money to bail out its own children. For the peace dividend to arrive in the mail some sunny morning, men and women who genuinely care about America's families must learn how to make the political system work to their advantage and those of their families.

Family issues such as day care, care of the elderly, long-term health care costs have for years taken a backseat to such issues as defense spending, foreign affairs, the economy and taxes. With the Cold War over, however, these problems that can have such devastating implications for families have a better chance of getting the public's attention and developing widespread public support for some solutions. Says Breglio: "One thing I believe the George

Bush candidacy has cultivated out there is the expectation on the part of a large segment of the electorate that this administration and those who support it are going to do something positive for the American family—whether it is the environment, education or health. We have a certain obligation to step up to those expectations." As long as the economy and foreign affairs remain stable, he predicts that these family issues, and he includes the environment in that group along with long-term health care, will come to the fore.

Congress has been put on notice that family issues matter to voters. There is, for the first time in nearly a decade, a president in the White House who seems ready to listen and to learn about the cares and crises that can engulf the most well-intentioned families. President Bush is not the captive of the right wing on family policies, and he may turn out to be capable of vision and leadership. He has repeatedly told Americans that on child care he wants to offer families choices about what is best for them. And that is what they need. They do not need to be told that mothers should stay at home or that day care centers are better than family care centers. They need to be able to make their own decisions about what is best for their family. More than any president in recent memory, George Bush seems to respond to this.

But whether he will be overwhelmed by pressures from a shortsighted business community remains to be seen. As this book went to press, the White House had decided to veto the Family and Medical Leave Act, which would give workers unpaid leave to handle family crises. This legislation has been adamantly opposed by the U.S. Chamber of Commerce, which claims it is a mandated benefit that will set a precedent for the government to require businesses to provide health insurance. What the business community fails to understand is that our top trade competitors, such as West Germany, Canada and Japan, all have comprehensive health care systems and family support systems that include paid leaves for such family obligations as the care of newborns.

Linda Dorian, executive director of Business and Professional Women, says that the Bush White House has developed a much better dialogue with women and given women's organizations much greater access than did the Reagan administration. She gives substantial credit for this to Bobbie Greene Kilberg, Bush's public liaison director, who is one of the most energetic, bright and thoughtful women in Washington. "NO women's leaders went to talk to the Reagan administration," says Dorian. "That was beyond the pale. What was the point? The Bush people are receptive to the dialogue. What remains to be seen is what action they will take to help women."

And what remains to be seen, as well, is what political action men and women will take to help themselves.

We are entering a period in which we can turn our attention back to our communities and our homes. These are golden times for working men and women to use their political muscle to secure policies that will assist them in doing the best they can for both their families and employers. This means paying more than lip service to the American family, something both political parties have been doing without producing much in the way of results. Above all, it means doing something we have never done in this country: that is, to create an environment that is genuinely family friendly. That would be the ultimate prize of the modern women's movement.

1

The War Between
the Sexes

It's gotten worse. The Cold War may be over, but the battle between men and women seems destined to go on forever, with victory for neither side. Sure, one sex will win a little territory for one decade and then lose it over the next, but it's trench warfare—slow, brutally indecisive, and with casualties far disproportionate to any gains. Peaceful coexistence has been achieved with the Evil Empire, but men and women cannot even establish workable ground rules for marriage or divorce. The savagery with which Drs. Elizabeth Morgan and Eric Foretich have fought over Hilary Morgan is the kind of epic struggle that is rarely waged in a vacuum. In nearly twenty-five years as a reporter, it is the most sordid and tragic example I've ever witnessed of the wrongs and abuses men and women inflict on each other when love turns to hate. Civility goes out the window, and the courts go out to lunch.

Lawyers, judges, marriage counselors and most people who've been there know there's no such thing as a civilized divorce. That's because too many people stand to make money when their clients decide to go to the mat. The result: wife and

17

husband are beggared by legal bills and children are forever caught in the fallout of the marital explosion. It need not be that way: civilizing divorce, making both parties abide by simple rules of fair play, can be done and it ought to be one of the most important social goals for the decade. We insist on civilized standards of behavior for every other form of social, legal and business enterprise. There is no reason why divorce should be exempt. And parents who fight over their children, who use them as weapons in their deadly battles, ought to be held up to the scorn society saves for those who abuse their children—for that is exactly what those parents are doing.

Of Men and Nasal Spray
NOVEMBER 21, 1986

Tuesday's *Washington Post* brought some truly fascinating news on the latest scientific findings about sex. It turns out that sex is not only good for men—a theory initially advanced by the first male *Homo sapiens* to reach puberty—it is also good for women.

A suspicious female reader might leap to the conclusion that this research was quickly cooked up to counter fear of sexually transmitted diseases, which recent surveys tell us has radically altered the availability of willing female partners. But a careful reader of Boyce Rensberger's story cannot escape the conclusion that there is, indeed, sound scientific evidence that heterosexual sex is healthy for women's reproductive cycles. We're not talking base gratification here; we're talking general health. This could put a whole new spin on the fitness craze. "Aerobics" could get a new meaning.

And the word "pheromones" could gain currency no one ever dreamed of.

Pheromones, according to the story, "are special aromatic chemical compounds discharged by one individual that affect the sexual physiology of another." Pheromones have acted as "sex attractants" in animals, but now researchers at the Monell Chemical Senses Center and the University of Pennsylvania medical school have established that they exist in humans. They don't act as "sex attractants" (didn't these used to be called "aphrodisiacs"?), but over a period of weeks, they can influence women's menstrual cycles.

In studies done over thirteen years, researchers found "that women who have sex with men at least once a week are more likely to have normal-length menstrual cycles, fewer infertility problems and a milder menopause than women who are celibate or who have sex in a sporadic 'feast-or-famine' pattern." The male chemicals, which are released by sweat glands under the armpit, apparently are not effectively transmitted except during intimate contact.

Ingenious researchers, however, found that they could extract what they called "male essence" with alcohol and absorbent pads that male volunteers held under their arms. Women volunteers had the pads rubbed under their noses three times a week, and within months found their cycles normalized.

Winnifred B. Cutler of the Monell Center, who led the research, said: "A very clear pattern has been emerging and it all confirms that a woman's optimal reproductive health is a part of a finely tuned system and that a man, on a regular and sustained basis, is an essential part of it." And, she added, "You might say that exposure to pheromones is the essence of sex."

Research showed a link between delayed beginning of sexual activity and subsequent infertility problems, leading Cutler to believe that there is yet another connection between sexual contact with a man and a healthy reproductive system.

These findings could add a whole new channel of communications in the ongoing efforts at coexistence between the sexes. A great deal of current research into men's and women's perceptions of that behavior is coming to the conclusion that one of the women's major complaints is that men are selfish.

A creative adolescent male, armed with the new research, has a new talking point besides his libido with which to pursue the girl of his dreams. Instead of "You'd do this if you really loved me"—which is getting a little trite after all these centuries—he could say something along the lines of "Honey, this is for your own good. You don't want to grow up to be thirty-five and suddenly find you can't have children, do you?"

Husbands of women who have a lot of headaches at night, or who are chronically tired when their husbands are wide awake, now have the scientific evidence with which to assure their wives that regular sexual contact will spare them the heartbreak of menstrual irregularity and the horrors of hot flashes. It may not be the most romantic overture, but it may beat hot flashes.

This would not be America if researchers couldn't assure us that they are hoping the pheromones can be synthesized into such things as nasal sprays to help correct reproductive problems, make the rhythm form of birth control more reliable and alleviate difficulties of menopause. With the current fears about sexually transmitted disease, it's a great relief for single women, at least, to know that they may not always have to have sex regularly in order to protect their reproductive systems. On the other hand, you can understand why modern American men are running scared. Who else is faced with the prospect of having his essence turned into a nasal spray?

The War Between the Sexes
NOVEMBER 18, 1987

One of the nice things about writing a newspaper column is that you get free magazines so you don't have to spend a lot of extra money at the supermarket to find out what's on America's mind, or at least the part of it that's on the rack. My own recent informal survey of articles shows that we are fascinated by money, frightened by sex and deeply worried about relationships.

Relationships are, in fact, becoming big business. Bookstores now devote full blocks of shelves to books about what's wrong with male-female relationships, and authors are earning permanent seats on the best-seller lists by discovering new ways of analyzing why we fall in love with various losers. (Actually, people don't fall in love with losers anymore. They have addictions.)

Intimacy has replaced real estate as the topic du jour at dinner parties, which would have been understandable had the interest rates remained high, but is especially revealing of a deep malaise when interest rates are comparatively low. One can only conclude that investments in real estate must carry a lot less risk than investments in relationships, and thus make for less compelling conversation.

The war between the sexes goes back to the beginning of time, of course, but we seem to be studying it and analyzing it as

archers advanced several theories for their findings: mar-
are less lonely; if their wives work, their household
o up dramatically; they don't have the constant pressure
o find a female companion, and when they are married,
s often protect them from life's troubles. After divorce,
to other research, men are at much higher risk of serious
d physical troubles, and even death, than are divorced

amuel Johnson, upon learning that a friend was about to
remarked that a second marriage was a triumph of hope
rience. This dim view of the institution is reflected in the
e that married men don't live longer, it just seems longer.
anymore.

still may fear commitment, but with all this new informa-
nd, it seems almost irrelevant to ask why. One thing you
d a study to prove is that anything that can get men to live
el better and get richer is a surefire bet to succeed.

ionaire Marriages
BER 21, 1988

Mike Tyson and Jack Kent Cooke have in common? What
in common is a lot of woman trouble.
n't generally go misty-eyed over the amorous misadven-
millionaires. As a matter of fact, when their marital
nes do become public, it serves to reinforce the adage
us learned at our mother's knee, namely, that money
uy happiness. To those of us who are innately skeptical of
think it is really a bromide to make up for the shortage of
res, it's always reassuring to hear that all is not smooth
the lifestyles of the rich and famous.
c'mon. What's going on in the Cooke and Tyson ménages
, so incredible—so, well, bizarre—that, let's face it, you
sorry for a couple of rich guys who look like they got
a real ride. At the very least, nothing in the modern
f male-female warfare could have prepared them for the
undering of their marital troubles that their mates have
in.

never before. This may be a luxury of an advancing society or it may be the frantic rethinking of a polarized society. In any event, it would be a grave mistake if we approached those matters as though we were the first generation or the first society to find sexual cohabitation even more impossible than sharing the planet with the Russians.

The emotional minefields of relationships have always been the special province of women, probably going back to the hunter-gatherer cultures. (Jean Auel got herself at the top of the best-seller lists three times with her Earth's Children series of books, and the hunting scenes in those were not the best parts.) Men and women, according to prevailing wisdom, are driven by different elemental forces that are connected to the perpetuation of the species. Thus, men do not want to commit monogamously, they want to perpetuate pluralistically. Women, wishing to protect themselves and their young, want monogamy. In modern times, this has boiled down to women wanting marriage and men wanting freedom. The two are irreconcilable, and thus the battle is joined.

Shere Hite, the pop sex researcher, has recently reentered the scene with a tome that is essentially a compilation of every female complaint ever uttered toward the male of the species. Her book has been roundly criticized as thoroughly unscientific. Hite took voluntary responses to a mailed questionnaire, stuck some percentages on the responses and called it research. She's also been making funny phone calls and acting strange on her book tour, which hasn't helped her credibility. Nevertheless, the inescapable conclusion one has to reach from browsing through the book is that there are a lot of women out there who are deeply unhappy and who are retreating from men and relationships.

Now, the Sunday New York Times Magazine has weighed in with an article in which the author traveled around the country interviewing several dozen men in their thirties and forties who have never married. The article, entitled "Why Wed? The Ambivalent American Bachelor," was written by Trip Gabriel, who summed up his findings this way: "Grown-up American men in the full swim of life say they're scared stiff of getting married."

Gabriel came up with some startling observations. The men he interviewed were not obsessed with chasing women, and a number were leading almost chaste lives. Some were deeply involved with sports: "Some bachelors seem to have effected a simple exchange: the vicissitudes and uncertainties of a single man's sex life for the known payoffs of athletics."

Some of the men felt they were still growing up, all of them worried that they had not married and many wondered about being alone in their old age. They had been hurt in past relationships, and many he talked with are "simply shutting down emotionally, not so red hot to risk it with someone new."

Sound familiar? Women, cast early as the keepers of the hearth, have been talking along these lines for a good while. What is changing is that men are talking, too. They are choosing alternatives and wondering out loud if they're being wise. They're retreating, perhaps, but they are also revealing fears, ambivalence, pain and unrealistic expectations. Who knows? We may be entering a period of glasnost in the epic struggle between the sexes.

New Weapon to Hold a Man
MARCH 2, 1988

Last year was the year of "commitment." That is not to suggest that people were actually making commitments in record numbers. But it is an incontrovertible fact—that's a fact you can bet the mortgage on—that they were discussing commitment in record numbers. And one of the major themes in last year's marathon analysis of the ongoing war between the sexes had to do with the axiomatic belief that men fear commitment and the only real question is why.

The underlying assumption for this line of inquiry is that if somehow females can figure out the mystery behind the males' fear of commitment, they—that is, the females—can help them see the error of their ways and turn them into creatures who not only no longer fear commitment, but also will actually embrace it.

In ancient times, women resorted to feminine wiles and various other forms of witchcraft in order to get men to do what they wanted them to do. Whether the goal was obtaining a new, improved cave or a winter's supply of frozen mammoth steaks, this goal invariably boiled down to men making a commitment to provide and protect the hearth. I am aware that there is extensive mythology about races of warrior women, but I suspect these women didn't have kids at home to take care of, which is why they

were able to go out and play wa
don't hear much about them any

Witchcraft, hexes and love
where along the way—perhaps I
tive—so women had to develop
ments to ensure the propagation
human evolution, tribes had bro
had been replaced by castles an
family fortunes or augmentation
if not more importance than tl
survival. Obtaining commitment
lenge. Moral support came from
and what was then known as "
principle in that era was that wo
making their own commitment.
person to exhort the youth of Am

Moral standards fell apart in
struggling to find new ways of s
Sexual permissiveness may have
titude toward sex, but the fact is
Until quite recently, the most
securing commitment from men
disease.

Thanks to USA Today, howev
to women's arsenal for obtaining
talking about sharing a one-year l
We are talking about marriage. "A
line, "adds satisfaction to a man'
line said: "Husbands live longer,
get more raises."

Students of human behavior I
men do better than single men o
and financial measures, but US.
number of recent findings and the
ler, a University of Michigan socio
couples in the Detroit area, told U.
men improves unbelievably when t
in the article found that married n
outlive a man who never married,
to live longer than divorced men.

Rese
ried men
incomes
of trying
their wive
according
mental a
women.
Dr.
remarry,
over expe
old whee
Not true
Mer
tion at ha
don't nee
longer, fe

Mill
OCTO

What do
they hav
I do
tures of
misfortu
many of
doesn't
that, wh
milliona
sailing i
Bu
is so wil
gotta fee
taken fo
annals
public
engage

Do we care? You might ask. The answer: You betcha. Every word being written about the Robin Givens–Mike Tyson fiasco is being devoured by millions of readers. This is the stuff of pop history. Also the stuff of big bucks. Think of the possibilities: *The Robin Givens Story* by (who else?) Robin Givens and a ghostwriter (although she went to Sarah Lawrence and may have delusions of being a writer, so she may have a go at writing Her Story herself). To be followed by *The Mike Tyson Story* by Mike Tyson and the top collaborator currently working in New York, personally hand-picked for Mike by Donald Trump. Next season, ABC could air a feature-length movie, *The Robin Givens Story,* starring (who else?) during the fall ratings sweep. By then, Mike Tyson will either be getting ready for another zillion-dollar payday in Vegas or wrapping himself around another tree.

Suzanne Martin Cooke is no Robin Givens, but there are similarities. Both women were raised by their mothers, in the absence of fathers. Both latched onto men who had vastly more money than they did. It is not clear whether Givens was pregnant when she married Tyson, but Cooke most assuredly was when she married Cooke. She signed a prenuptial agreement, and by her own account agreed to have an abortion the day after she wed the billionaire Redskins owner, who was then seventy-four. She was thirty-one, and had already had two abortions. She reneged on the deal and Cooke, by her account, was furious. He filed for divorce on October 5, and four months later, Jacqueline Kent Cooke weighed in at eight pounds, thirteen ounces. As all of Washington knows, the Cookes' domestic drama has been played out in a cover story in *Washingtonian* magazine, in TV interviews and in *The Washington Post.* Jack Kent—"no more Mr. Nice Guy"—Cooke has never seen his daughter or acknowledged her existence.

Givens, according to the latest news accounts, which could change at any moment, is now saying she doesn't want any of Tyson's money. Since she was looking like an emasculating gold-digger, and rapidly losing in the court of public opinion, this was the smartest move she could have made to salvage what's left of her reputation—and thus her career. A gorgeous woman wronged by the heavyweight champ cuts a lot more sympathetic figure in the public mind than a conniving witch.

Besides, there are very real legal questions about what she would have been entitled to. The women's movement has fought hard to promote the idea that marriage is an economic partnership and that wives are entitled to an equal share of the marital assets. The premise behind that is that wives make a nonmonetary contribution to the economic partnership in the form of child-rearing and emotional support for the wage earner. There's nothing in the public record, at least, to indicate that Givens provided Tyson with anything more than a huge headache.

Cooke, on the other hand, provided her husband with a daughter, and the last thing we're going to hear from her are Givens' immortal words: "I will not seek nor accept any money for myself." Cooke signed a prenuptial agreement that provided her with $50,000 a year for three years if the marriage ended, plus use of Cooke's pad in the Watergate for five years and a new Jaguar. Her divorce became final this week, but not her property settlement. She's not about to undergo postpartum depression. She's asking for a $15 million lump sum settlement, spousal support of $10,000 a month and $8,000 in child support. For seventy-three days of marriage?

The hope here is that she draws a judge who'll tell her what her mother obviously never told her. Money doesn't buy happiness.

Women Who Kiss and Tell
MARCH 3, 1989

Rich and famous people, which most of the time means rich and famous men, used to be able to get away with just about everything short of murder when it came to the opposite sex. Wives tolerated infidelities, mistresses went away quietly. Sexual shenanigans were either ignored by those in the know or viewed as some benign personality quirk. The women involved, above all, didn't talk. Now you can't pay them to be quiet.

Margo Adams, erstwhile traveling companion of Boston Red Sox batting champion Wade Boggs, did not go gently into that good night reserved for the tossed-over lovers of married baseball players. Maybe she thought the place was too crowded. When the couple ended their relationship last year, after four seasons and sixty-four road trips, Adams filed a $12 million lawsuit against the third baseman claiming breach of contract and emotional distress. While the California courts have whittled her claim down to the

$500,000 range, Adams has also turned to the court of public opinion, and Wade Boggs never is going to be the same.

Adams chose *Penthouse* as her vehicle, saying that *Playboy* wanted only her pictures, not her story. *Penthouse* is paying her $100,000 for a two-part chronicle of her relationship with Boggs, how her underwear or lack thereof affected his batting average, and various insights she has to offer about baseball players on the road.

You might wonder why *Penthouse* paid her $100,000 for her observations of baseball players' lives on the road and did not pay some veteran sportswriter who could have used the money to put his kids through college. The answer to that question comes next month when *Penthouse* publishes the second part of the Adams Chronicles: "The Pictures." Margo told a news conference in New York on Wednesday that she's seen them and they are "fabulous." Veteran sportswriters are rarely paid to take their clothes off.

Adams is the latest in a growing list of women who have bedded rich and famous men and made a temporary living off telling their tale. She says she never asked him to leave his wife, but she ended the relationship in part because she discovered that she was not The Other Woman but merely another woman. Adams didn't just get mad, she got even.

She is not only telling all about Boggs' sexual practices—he liked her to serve him double anchovy pizzas while wearing a garter belt and stockings—but also she is betraying all manner of pillow talk confidences about what he thinks of other Red Sox. She is also telling stories about what other players do on the road. That's the kind of inside baseball that veteran sportswriters don't tell their wives.

Blowing the whistle on rich and famous men, at least in modern times, began when Michelle Triola Marvin hauled actor Lee Marvin into court in 1971 after he tossed her out. She claimed that for seven years she'd done everything for him a wife would do, that she'd given up her career to help him, that he'd made a lot of money and that she was entitled to a portion of it. The California Supreme Court upheld the validity of such arrangements outside of marriage and thus gave a legal stamp of approval to palimony claims.

Suddenly, a scorned woman had somewhere to turn for solace: the courts. Over the years, women have filed suits against actors, athletes and just plain folks who've done them wrong. And, in the course of time, women such as Margo Adams have carved out a new ethic for the woman who is dumped, whether it is the wife— Shari Theismann comes to mind—or the mistress.

These women are no longer afraid to talk, not just to their lawyers, but to the world. Shari Theismann took to the pages of *Washingtonian* magazine and then to the airwaves to tell everyone who would listen that Joe was an egocentric lout. Joe left Shari, his college sweetheart and the mother of his three children, for Hollywood personality Cathy Lee Crosby—but by the time Shari finished sacking him in print, you got the feeling that Cathy Lee wasn't walking off with any prize.

Kiss and tell is no longer a high crime, a violation of some primitive code imposed by men upon women to protect men. It has standing in the court, and, God knows, it sells magazines and books. And while it is hard to feel sympathetic toward Margo Adams, she and her fellow whistle-blowers are performing a valuable service in the war between the sexes. They are making it much harder for rich and famous men to walk off and discard women—and get away with it because of the power of their names. People with money and fame, who are vulnerable to having their pockets picked and reputations ruined by angry, scorned women, are going to have to be much more careful than ever before.

Capitals Incident Raises a More Basic Question
MAY 23, 1990

A seventeen-year-old girl has accused four members of the Washington Capitals hockey team of sexually assaulting her in the back of a limousine outside a sports bar in Georgetown. The key legal question in this mess seems to be did she consent or not.

The key social question we should be asking ourselves, however, is what on earth kind of society do we live in in which it might be remotely acceptable for men to engage in group sex with a teenage girl, or with any woman for that matter?

Even if the young woman agreed to this kind of activity— which is by no means certain—do we want the young people who look up to sports figures as role models to be looking up to men who engage in group sex in the back of cars? With role models like this, who needs role models?

Exactly what happened on the night of May 12 in the alley behind Champions sports bar is something that a grand jury is investigating.

No charges have been brought. Whatever the outcome of the investigation, and whether the sexual activity was consensual or not, the incident can serve as an opportunity to remind and educate women about the perils they face.

The girl involved has told police that four players participated in raping and sodomizing her. A fifth player has told police that he stepped into the limo but left when he saw the girl struggling with his partly clad teammates.

The driver of the rented limo has told investigators from the U.S. Attorney's Office that he did not see any sexual activity. He said the girl got into the limo voluntarily and that when she got out she said, "Thanks, guys, see you later."

The driver has said that he was not in the limo for some of the time and that the privacy screen separating the front area of the vehicle from the back seat was raised at times.

The girl has told a friend who was with her and her boss that night at another sports bar that she got into the limo because the players offered her a ride and that she trusted them because they were friends with a player she had dated.

Denise Snyder, executive director of the D.C. Rape Crisis Center, says that 60 to 80 percent of all rapes are committed by an acquaintance of the victim.

Studies done over the last fifteen years have concluded that one of every three women can expect to be raped in her life.

"One of the issues that make acquaintance rape so traumatic is the issue of trust violation," says Snyder. "You have the sense of who can I trust now?"

Snyder says it is similar to domestic violence. "Men do it because it works and they can. It gives them the sense of power and domination they are striving for when they engage in this activity. They can because the reaction of society is not one that chastizes them, that ostracizes them. There are no significant ramifications for most men who rape."

She says that the most important thing women can do to

protect themselves from acquaintance rape is "trust your instincts. We are very much trained not to trust our instincts, not to trust women's intuition or to respond to it. In an acquaintance rape a woman will almost always say afterwards, when she calls a hot line, something felt weird.

"Something was going on and it felt bad. What they do in the middle of a situation is they discount their gut level reaction. We think we don't want to hurt his feelings. I don't want to embarrass myself. I don't want to draw attention to myself.

"What you have to do is weigh off the fact you may draw attention to him, you may embarrass yourself, but if you don't you may be raped. Hurting his feelings is not a larger concern than preventing yourself from being sexually assaulted.

"The issue of victim blaming is very heavy around acquaintance rape," says Snyder. "What was a seventeen-year-old doing at the party anyway, what was she doing in the car? Those very questions are victim-blaming and put the responsibility on her. Men rape and men are solely responsible for rape. Women may exercise bad judgment, but bad judgment is not a rapable offense."

Athletes, for better or worse, are esteemed by young men and held up as role models. If they were not, corporations wouldn't be spending millions of dollars a year on getting them to endorse everything from soft drinks to designer sneakers.

The influence they have on young men compounds the destructiveness of the incident, as does the thundering silence we are hearing from the Capitals' management, which has not uttered a peep about the right or wrong of its players getting into such a compromised situation with a teenage girl.

Snyder puts it well: "What we don't need is role models going around displaying aggressive sexual behavior that's not based on a healthy moral code, that is not based on respect for other people."

The Art of the Divorce
FEBRUARY 14, 1990

If Ivana Trump has her way, they're going to have to rewrite the *Guinness Book of World Records*, which once listed Washington's own Jack Kent Cooke as the co-holder of the world record for the most costly divorce settlement. He got out of his first marriage for about half of his $100 million fortune. The year was 1979, the state was California. The legal concept was fair and modern. It was called "community property."

Ivana Trump, whose husband, Donald, walked out on her last week, reportedly wants somewhere between $150 million and half a billion dollars of the estimated $1.7 billion in the Trump empire. She is going to be advancing another fair and modern legal concept, which is that she was a business partner as well as a marital partner.

Prenuptial agreement? What prenuptial agreement?

The Divorce of the Decade may break new grounds in the ever-shifting trends of marital dissolution. "IVANA BETTER DEAL" was the headline on yesterday's New York *Daily News*, which proved once again that its headline writers have no match. The *New York Post* hit the streets with news that Ivana wants the Plaza hotel, which she has been in charge of refurbishing, the jet and $150 million.

Her attorney, Michael Kennedy, called the prenuptial agreement signed by the couple thirteen years ago and updated at least twice "unconscionable and fraudulent." Under its terms, Ivana would get the couple's Connecticut home and $25 million. The agreement was originally drawn up by Roy Cohn, who may have been the sleaziest lawyer ever to practice in New York—which is saying a lot. Trump once called Cohn, who died in 1986, his mentor.

The *New York Post*'s Cindy Adams wrote that Donald Trump "is auditioning lawyers even as we speak. He has attorneys in New Jersey and New York. He has real estate specialists, gaming specialists, sports specialists. He has not yet hired a matrimonial expert but he was moving in that direction yesterday." In the immortal lyrics of Lorenz Hart, "when love congeals it soon reveals the faint aroma of performing seals."

Dr. Ruth call home. Donald Trump Needs You. The diminutive counselor of love would be a lot less pricey than the army of experts Donald Trump plans to field to protect the empire.

Donald Trump's camp is already trying to tear down the carefully erected public image of Ivana Trump, the career woman who ran his Atlantic City casino. Turns out, according to them, that Ivana wasn't a career woman after all. One Trump associate told *The Washington Post* that Ivana "is like a figurehead. She makes no financial decisions. It's strictly PR. She's done the wallpaper in the suites at the [Trump] Plaza. That's what she does."

Later on in that same story, however, we find that in the first thirty days of her reign at the Plaza, Ivana fired thirteen key staff people. Donald Trump has gone on record on talk shows about what a great job his wife did managing the casino in Atlantic City. Those appearances may have been designed for PR, but if Ivana can establish that she was a partner and executive in the Trump business empire, Donald Trump may find that it costs him a lot more to fire his wife than it does to fire a contractor.

The *New York Post* on Monday quoted Donald Trump saying to an unidentified friend: "I like Ivana, but we've grown apart. Her level of arrogance has grown steadily worse in recent years. The bottom line is I don't want to create another Leona Helmsley." This from a man who names everything he buys after himself.

Donald Trump may discover that wives aren't people you put on retainers, and that the bottom line isn't a prenuptial agreement when wives get involved in their husbands' business—not an unusual occurrence these days. What did Ivana contribute to the business to help it grow? All those charity dinners and fund-raisers she attended and led—what value to the Trump empire were those? What business decisions did she make? Why did Trump compare his wife to Helmsley, who ran her husband's hotel empire? Were their roles similar, or merely their attitudes?

The prenuptial agreemeht calls for her to get custody of the couple's three children and for him to get custody of more than $1.5 billion. Donald Trump is quoted in the *New York Post* as saying to "intimates" that the prenuptial agreement is "airtight, fair and modern."

How airtight it is remains to be seen. Trump accumulated the bulk of his fortune during his marriage to Ivana. In most states, that would make her eligible for a large chunk of the couple's community property. The prevailing idea is that marriage is an economic partnership. Ivana also is claiming that theirs was a business partnership. To her, it isn't PR.

As for fair and modern, the prevailing trend is not just that couples split their assets. They also share custody of the kids.

The Children of Divorce
FEBRUARY 7, 1986

> *"The problem, of course, is that fathers who might be very willing to give generously of their good fortune to their children are probably going to be much less willing to share with their former wives. That's understandable. Unfortunately, it is impractical to have her live in the doghouse while the children enjoy the main house. . . ."*
> —"MORE THAN A MATTER OF MONEY"

True or false: Nearly half of all children whose parents have divorced and who are living with their mothers have not seen their fathers in more than a year.

You don't have to turn your newspaper upside down for the answer. It is true, according to research published in the *Journal of Marriage and the Family*. The article, written by Frank F. Furstenberg, Jr., professor of sociology at the University of Pennsylvania, and Christine Winquist Nord, a sociologist and demographer with Child Trends, Inc., a private firm in the District, is based on research that was done as part of the National Survey of Children. That survey to study children's well-being was first done in 1976 with a nationally representative household sample of 2,300 children, according to Nord.

A second survey, upon which this research is based, was conducted in 1981 on a subgroup of 1,423 children to look at the effects of marital disruption. The children ranged from eleven to sixteen years of age and included children from the first survey who were in high-conflict families or broken marriages, as well as children whose biological parents were still married.

One of the most striking findings of the research was that 49 percent of the children of divorced parents had not seen the nonresident parent for more than a year. Only one child out of every six had some form of regular, weekly contact with his or her father.

"It amazes all of us," says Nord, but why it is happening is not clear. "Part of it is if people have moved away, there is going to be less contact. Also . . . as kids get older, there might be less reason for the fathers to see them. Obviously, child support has some effect. If there's no support, there's no contact, but you don't know which came first. The longer the separation, the less the contact.

"It's not clear how much the fathers are dropping out from their own desires to do so, or how much the mother doesn't want them. She's trying to avoid conflict by avoiding contact with him. She ends up with most of the responsibility, and inevitably she ends up with most of the decision-making. Once the father has less direct responsibility for the child, he adopts more of a friendship role."

Most of the children lived with their mothers, although a small sample lived with their fathers. The children saw the absent parent an average of 7.4 days a month in the first two years after separation, but that dropped off dramatically to an average of two times a month after two years of separation. Fifty-five percent said they never saw the absent parent in separations that had lasted two to nine years. After ten years, 74 percent of them said they never saw the parent. The majority said they had never slept over at their parent's new home during the first two years of separation, and 42 percent said they'd never been in it. Only 14 percent said they had a place to keep their things at the absent parent's home, although that figure rose to 25 percent in the two to nine years following separation—and then dropped back to 14 percent when the separation had gone on for ten years or more.

"Contact with the outside parent, if it occurs at all," the researchers wrote, "is usually social or recreational. Among the minority of children who had seen their parents during the past week, only a tenth had been given assistance with schoolwork; slightly more than a fifth had worked on projects together, such as making something, cooking or sewing; about a fourth had played some game or sport."

The researchers noted that the children were generally unwilling to be critical of the outside parents. But some patterns emerged clearly: "Children with fathers living outside the home are decidedly more discontent with their paternal relationship than those residing with their father. More than half say that they do not get all the affection they need, and nearly as many say they are only fairly close or not close at all to their fathers. Outside fathers are also faulted for not making clear and consistent rules and for not being firm enough."

The researchers also found that remarriage and stepparents did not complicate relationships with the nonresident parent and they concluded that children's abilities to deal with the complexities of expanded families were "impressive." These children seem to do better than children whose parents have dropped out of their lives, they found. Yet it is the latter that is happening as fathers move from one household to the next. Biological parenthood is becoming as impermanent as marriage, they conclude—a troubling finding, indeed.

More Than a Matter of Money
OCTOBER 28, 1987

Money has a way of generating considerable controversy between those who have it and want to keep it and those who don't have it and want to get it. So it is no wonder that guidelines about child support awards—which have been put into place in most states this month—are prompting lively debate about what standard of living a child should aspire to once his parents divorce.

At the nerve center of this debate is how much noncustodial parents—usually the fathers—should be required to pay the custodial parents—usually the mothers—at a time when they usually can't stand each other.

For decades, these decisions were usually left up to judges and they did, by and large, an abysmal job. Sometimes they awarded the custodial parents too much money, beggaring the fathers, but much more often they awarded far too little and then did not enforce the awards, beggaring the mothers and children. Studies have shown that 87 percent of the children on welfare rolls are there because of insufficient child support.

The situation became scandalous and costly enough to taxpayers that Congress passed the 1984 child support enforcement law that required each state to set up guidelines for judges to use in setting child support awards. The guidelines were supposed to achieve uniformity and to raise the level of the awards. Congress left it up to each state to devise its own guidelines and gave them nearly three years to do it. All but five met the October 1 deadline, the exceptions being Maryland, Virginia, Idaho, New Mexico and

New Hampshire, according to Diane Dodson, counsel for family law and policy of the Women's Legal Defense Fund.

The formulas vary considerably. Massachusetts, she says, assumes the noncustodial parent should pay 25 percent of his gross income in support for the first child. Texas, on the other hand, assumes he should pay 19 percent of his net income for one child. Some states have developed guidelines that provide for lower percentages of the income as the income goes up. States that have followed this course include Colorado, New Jersey and South Carolina. The District's formula takes into account the number and ages of the children, the income of the custodial parent, her child care payments and the income of the noncustodial parent up to a maximum of $75,000 of the gross.

The controversy has arisen over the amount of money the children are entitled to when the fathers have money. "What we hear again and again from fathers' groups is this is hidden alimony, we shouldn't have to pay any more than what the child is going to eat or wear," says Dodson. Carl Friedman of Arlington, writing a letter to the editor in Monday's *Washington Post*, put it this way: "Children do not eat twice as much food when their parents' income doubles, nor do they normally buy twice as much clothing merely because their parents are earning more money." He favors support standards that are based "solely on the actual cost of raising children."

That misses the point of what children are entitled to, entirely.

Children, in a divorce, are in all probability going to have their standard of living eroded, but the socially desirable course is to have their lives and standard of living altered as little as possible. They are entitled to have their fortunes rise and fall with their parents', just as they would had the family remained intact. This means that if the father loses his job, they are going to have less, and if the father has a big score, they ought to have more. This might put them in a nicer house, or a newer car, or private schools and it could mean filet mignon on Friday nights instead of hamburgers. Children do not cost a fixed amount. They cost what a family can afford, and they are entitled to that, whether the father lives with them or not.

The problem, of course, is that fathers who might be very willing to give generously of their good fortune to their children are probably going to be much less willing to share with their former wives. That's understandable. Unfortunately, it is impractical to have her live in the doghouse while the children enjoy the main house and a standard of living comparable to their father's.

What makes this a little fairer is that the guidelines make no provision for the many hours the custodial parent spends each week on the caring for and raising of the children, usually on top of a full-time job. She contributes money and uncompensated time and, as Dodson put it, "if her lifestyle benefits from some of these monetary benefits coming in, there's nothing wrong with that."

Nothing at all.

The H-Bomb of Divorce
MAY 26, 1980

Courts have historically had a terrible time sorting out domestic disputes and determining child custody. The trends toward no-fault divorce, equal division of property, joint custody and guidelines for child support awards reflect attempts to bring some sense of economic fairness to those proceedings and to protect the best interests of children.

That trend toward civility has deprived enraged spouses of some of the economic weapons they could formerly use against their mates. Courts have little interest in finding fault or in being used as tax-supported battlegrounds for continued domestic wars. Judges are using 50–50 formulas for distributing marital assets and following guidelines for child support awards that reflect local economic conditions.

Against that backdrop, there has emerged what the experts are calling the "nuclear weapon" of divorce: the claim by mothers that the father has sexually abused the child or children during visitations. The remedy mothers usually seek is a halt to visitation or severance of parental ties.

When the children are very young, it is often impossible to determine what really happened. Sorting out those cases has become one of the most difficult tasks confronting judges, most of whom are male, and most of whom—like the rest of us—would rather not think a father is capable of such heinous behavior. Judges view those claims with great suspicion.

In the last few years, stories have surfaced about women being ordered by courts to send children on visits with fathers the mothers claim are abusive. Women who have violated court orders have been jailed for civil contempt in Oregon, Washington, Texas and in the District. Others, faced with contempt, have taken the child and disappeared.

Last June, *U.S. News and World Report* did a cover story on the emergence of an underground railroad that helps parents and children flee and rebuild their lives elsewhere. No one knows how many mothers have used that network, but the article quoted sociologists and children's advocates as estimating the number to be in the thousands.

The best-known of those civil contempt cases involves Dr. Elizabeth Morgan, who has spent twenty-one months in D.C. Jail rather than turn over her daughter for unsupervised visits with Dr. Eric Foretich, whom Morgan asserts repeatedly sexually abused the child. Foretich, a McLean oral surgeon, has vehemently denied that. Morgan sent her daughter into hiding and her whereabouts are unknown.

Representative Frank R. Wolf (R-Va.), a member of the Select Committee on Children, Youth and Families, is sponsoring a bill to put a limit on the length of time people can be jailed for civil contempt in child custody disputes. As drafted, his bill would limit the time to eighteen months and it would be retroactive, freeing Morgan if passed.

"The issue is whether a person who's never been tried can be held for twenty-one months and the answer is no. Enough is enough," he says. He is amenable to shorter periods, which exist in Wisconsin (six months) and California (twelve months), with a provision that once the limit is reached, the person could be charged with criminal contempt and get a jury trial and specified sentence.

While he hopes his bill will help break the stalemate in the Morgan situation, Wolf's larger concern is with the untold number of other parents around the country who are forced into jail or hiding, neither of which is good for the child. Wolf hopes Congress can be a pacesetter for the rest of the country. "The alternative is the mother goes underground and takes the child away and the child doesn't get an education and it's crazy," he says.

Howard Davidson, director of the child advocacy unit of the American Bar Association, said a study by the ABA and the

Association of Family and Conciliation Courts found that court personnel believed that in the overwhelming percentage of cases, the parent alleging sexual abuse made the accusation in good faith. "The best data we've seen on willful or false reporting is in the range of 3 to 8 percent," he said. He stressed, however, that in a large number of cases, court personnel said they could not determine what had happened.

Those allegations were made in only about 2 percent of the six thousand cases in the study. They are, however, among the most destructive cases ever to come along in the unhappy history of American divorce. Wolf's efforts to limit despotic powers of the courts bring the focus of those cases back to where they should be, and that is what is in the best interest of the child. It is a rare child who will flourish on the run or with a mother in jail.

Short End of the Stick
JANUARY 31, 1990

The squire of Middleburg got a big, big break from a country judge in Fauquier County last week, proving, once again, that it pays to be very rich and very mean. It also pays to do your dirty business in your own backyard.

For the record: there is no sympathy or fondness here for the erstwhile Mrs. Jack Kent Cooke, née Suzanne Martin. This is a woman who met and married a multimillionaire under a sordid series of circumstances, not to mention the false pretense that she had gotten an abortion, a peculiar condition of their marriage. Suzanne Cooke didn't get an abortion, Cooke locked her out of his Middleburg estate in August, filed for divorce in October, and Suzanne gave birth on January 25, 1988, to a daughter whom she named Jacqueline Kent Cooke.

If Jack Kent Cooke thought that Suzanne was going to fade away like some wronged heroine in a Victorian novel, he had another think coming. She was just getting started.

Jacqueline may not have been to the manner born, but her mother was going to do her very best to see that she lives like it.

Cooke acknowledged paternity after a court-ordered blood test last spring. He has never seen the child, which tells you everything you need to know about Jack Kent Cooke. He is paying $6,000 a month in alimony through 1993, but he refused to make child support payments until a judge set the amount.

Cooke's lawyers have tried to portray Suzanne Martin Cooke as a golddigger, and she played right into their hands. This woman has about as good a sense of public relations as Marie Antoinette. She asked the court for $11,640 a month in child support—$1,650 for vacations, $600 a month clothing and money for riding lessons and everything else the properly equipped daughter of a multimillionaire needs.

In the end, Judge William Shore Robertson awarded $29,040 a year in child support, and denied Suzanne Martin's request that Cooke be ordered to pay her attorney fees. He also refused to order Cooke to make a lump-sum payment, which would have ensured support for the child in the event Cooke dies before she reaches the age of eighteen. He is seventy-seven years old now, so that is not an insignificant consideration. Both sides put his worth at $500 million, and the lump sum he would have had to pay would have been under half a million, small change for him.

Robertson, under Virginia law, had enormous discretion in this case. Ed Walinsky, who specializes in Virginia divorces for Feldesman, Tucker, Leifer, Fidell and Bank, one of D.C.'s preeminent divorce law firms, says that the state's child support guidelines do not cover income that exceeds $10,000 a month. "Once it goes beyond here it is up to the discretion of the judge. With a child of this age you have the overlay of the judge's mindset. It focuses more on the parent. Some of the money is going to slough off on the parent, as it should. It is intended to cover some of the housing costs, car costs, insurance costs. It's a referendum on the parents and whether or not they want to penalize one parent or the other for their perfidy."

Suzanne Cooke may have gotten what she deserved, but the child of this ill-fated union deserves much better than she got. A judge ought to be thinking about the welfare of a child and not the perfidy of the adults. This child is the daughter of a multimillionaire and there is no money provided for her college education. If Cooke *père* drops dead tomorrow, the child will get no more support.

Walinsky says that judges' hands are tied to a large extent by what the legislatures say they can do. He says that it is common in divorce agreements to set up a life insurance provision that would provide support if the parent dies. Judges can't order the parties to do this, however. Nor can they order the person paying child support to pay for the child's college education, or set up trusts, although the parties can agree to this.

The Cooke divorce, and all the attendant publicity, ought to make the legislature sharply aware of large holes that continue to exist in the fabric of legal protections designed to safeguard mothers and children in divorces. At the very least, Judge Robertson should have made Cooke pay lawyers' fees for his former wife, because he has been the party who refused to pay child support. At the very least, judges should have the power to order wealthy parents to pay for children's college education and to set up life insurance provisions that would cover child support in case of their deaths.

As things stand now, a two-year-old who should not have a financial worry in the world will probably have lots of financial worries unless Jack Kent Cooke takes better care of her in his will than he has in his life.

And nobody should bet on that.

The Missing Truth
FEBRUARY 28, 1990

There have been at least two victims so far in the Elizabeth Morgan–Eric Foretich war. The first, of course, has been the child of their ill-fated union, Hilary, and the second has been the truth.

Morgan and Foretich each has a good deal to account for in this mess, but so does the legal system that failed utterly to protect a little girl who was caught in the middle of a titanic struggle between two strong-willed, moneyed people who obviously hated each other.

To this day, after nearly five years of litigation in the most papered child custody case in history, the truth of what happened to a two-and-a-half-year-old child remains unknown. Her mother says she was repeatedly raped and abused by Foretich. He denies all the allegations. D.C. Superior Court judge Herbert Dixon's response to all the conflicting testimony was to disallow much of it and not believe the rest of it. And then toss the mother in jail for more than two years when she refused to turn the child over for extended, unsupervised visits with a man she says was raping the child.

It is, of course, infinitely easier on a judge's stomach to digest the notion that a former spouse is lying about her ex-husband than to believe that a father routinely sexually abused his infant daughter during visitations. Ex-spouses, or about-to-become ex-spouses, have been known to commit all kinds of perjury out of vengeance or greed or both, so it is understandable that a judge will view a former wife's accusation of child molestation by her former spouse with a high degree of suspicion.

But as this case has unraveled in court hearings, appeals court rulings and countless investigative newspaper and magazine articles, it has become clear that witnesses who should have testified didn't and testimony that should have been admitted wasn't. So-called expert witnesses testified with little or no experience in child abuse cases. Testimony alleging sexual abuse of an older half-sister to Hilary wasn't admitted. News accounts have quoted a D.C. police detective, now retired, who investigated abuse allegations as saying he was not asked to testify. Hilary's nanny, Fran Walton, who might have been a source of information, was deposed only in a civil case in Alexandria and not in the case in D.C. Superior Court.

The Washington Times also reported this week that a report done by Elissa P. Benedek for the U.S. District Court in Alexandria found that Elizabeth Morgan came from a home in which the father was abusive toward the mother and children and had a violent temper.

The *Times* quotes that report as saying Morgan had a "very disturbing relationship" with her father and that Benedek believes Morgan has a "mixed personality disorder." Benedek is a former president of the American Psychiatric Association. The report was based in part on an extensive interview with Antonia Morgan, Elizabeth's mother, who told Benedek that her husband, William Morgan, had been physically abusive to her and threatened and berated their children, the *Times* reported. The psychiatrist's evaluation not only raises questions about Morgan's emotional stability, but that of the family system from which she came. It becomes all the more meaningful with the revelation that those are the grandparents who spirited Hilary into hiding after Dixon ordered that she be turned over to her father for visits.

The court in Alexandria as well as the court in the District had paramount obligations to ensure that the health and safety and well-being of a minor child were being protected. Instead, the child ended up in hiding with a couple who might not have passed muster had they applied to become foster parents. Their age alone would have disqualified them in most jurisdictions.

The Hilary Morgan case, no matter how it ends up, can serve as a textbook example of how not to handle sexual abuse allegations. It ought to put an end to the practice of jailing parents who don't obey judges' orders to turn over the child. Judges who can do that have no incentive for getting to the truth. As Dixon demonstrated repeatedly, it is far easier to jail a parent for contempt than to try to sort out what really happened, listen to all the painful testimony and try to protect the child.

If the case is retried in New Zealand, Hilary may get a better break. The legal system there may do a better job of protecting children. In the end, however, she may have to make her break herself: she is seven and old enough in most jurisdictions to have her testimony admitted into evidence. If she can tell what really happened, the truth may finally be known—and the legal system that failed her can begin the process of helping her live the life of a normal little girl.

2

Women in the Media

Women will never become full partners in any society as long as they are regarded as the second sex, or the other sex, by the media that chronicle and reflect the culture they live in. If we are what we eat, we are also what we read and watch and hear. The American media are owned, dominated and run by and for men. White men. For decades, news about blacks was excluded from newspapers. Police reporters didn't even bother to tell their city editors about crimes that involved black people. When the riots broke out in cities across the country after the assassination of Dr. Martin Luther King in April 1968, editors everywhere were scrambling to find black people to go into the ghettos to cover the mayhem. White reporters and photographers couldn't get near the story. That was an eye-opener for newsroom managers, and in the years that followed, many newspapers and broadcast outlets made an effort to recruit and hire black reporters and photographers. There has been much soul-searching about the way the media cover news about black families and cultural institutions—and there has emerged a long-overdue recognition that the media must nurture, promote and respect black reporters and editors if we are to do an effective job of covering the news of interest to members of the black community.

Unfortunately, the media have yet to reach a similar age of enlightenment in the way they deal with women both as news-makers and as members of the media. The stranglehold that white men have on our information outlets is evident in every news meeting held every day around the country: a group of white men gather around a table or in a managing editor's office once or twice a day at every major media outlet to decide what you will hear on the news or what you will read in the following day's paper. That same group decides how the company's budget is allocated every year. These are subjective decisions that are made on the basis of the background, prejudices and interests of the men who are making them. They decide what is news, and what is not news. And where it is played. These prejudices were baldly evident in the front-page play given to the dismissal of CBS sportscaster Brent Musburger and the Style section play given to the departure of Jane Pauley from the "Today" show. Susan Miller, director of editorial development for Scripps-Howard newspapers, prepared a report in 1989 that showed how newspapers allocate their re-sources versus what readers read. More than 80 percent of the readers read local community news and less than 55 percent read sports. Yet sports had by far the largest number of beat reporters.

Women working in the media have a stake in how they are treated—studies have repeatedly demonstrated that women work-ing for newspapers earn a third less than men do, about par with women in other sectors of the economy. Black women are at the bottom of the newsroom pay scales. Other studies show that women comprise a tiny fraction—less than 5 percent—of top manage-ment. But the general public has an even more important stake: we use the media to find out what is going on in the world around us, and if half of us are not covered, we are all ill informed.

The University of Southern California's Media Watch: Women and Men, an industry monitor founded by Betty Friedan, has done two annual surveys of how women are represented in the news that amply document how we remain the second sex in news coverage. The survey released last April, which was done in conjunc-tion with the American Society of Newspaper Editors, showed that the number of women quoted as sources in front page stories and the number of female bylines on the front pages of twenty of the nation's newspapers surveyed had actually declined from 1989 to 1990. "This glass ceiling that keeps women from positions of defining and assigning creates a blind spot in newspapers and accounts for a slightly dinosaurish quality in the ways newspapers are covering American life today," said Betty Friedan at the press conference where the survey results were released.

The result of all this is women readers are canceling their connection with their newspapers. Readership among women has declined more rapidly than any other demographic group—and yet the big concern in the industry these days is that newspapers are not reaching young people. Some bright newspaper editor may realize that half of those young people are women—but don't bet on it. What is equally revelatory about the blind spot in the media is that the advertising that supports newspapers is overwhelmingly targeted at women consumers. With the exception of the tire ads that support the sports sections, every other major category of advertising is aimed principally at women: the children's toys and clothing ads, the display advertising for garments, the weekend real estate sections and the supermarket supplements. You would think that people who own and manage newspapers would create a friendly environment for their ads, but they do not. Reid MacClug-gage, editor of *The Day* in New London, Connecticut, and the chairman of ASNE's Human Resources Committee, said at that same press conference that readership by women has been taken for granted by newspaper editors. "Fifty-three percent of women read newspapers at least once a week, compared to 47 percent of men. As women become more and more active in the workplace and their time is more constricted they are turning away from papers. The decline is steep and the industry is facing a crisis."

William Woestendick, head of the University of Southern California's Journalism School, and one of the best-known and respected newspaper editors in the country, blamed the current state of the media in part on "the arrogance of editors who think they know what's important and not the readers." The result, as Friedan put it, is that "papers are behind the development of American women. That's why they are losing readers. They are not addressing the concerns of women who have less time."

Women on TV
JANUARY 7, 1983

There she was, the one and only Suzanne Somers (the one with the big teeth), cavorting for ten thousand leering American servicemen in West Germany, proving once again that nothing is too bad to be put on television. Instead of "Cagney & Lacey," a show of contemporary interest that portrays women as human beings, CBS inflicted on America last Monday evening a tasteless anachronism that had only one thing to sell: Suzanne Somers, sex object.

She slinked and wiggled and shimmied and jiggled her way through a collection of songs while the camera focused either on her or on the GIs in the audience who got right into the spirit of things by ogling her like they were watching a strip show. There were no redeeming displays of talent, funny jokes or skits to distract the viewers from the principal product. Unlike the great sex symbols of the past, Somers left little to the imagination. At one point, she appeared in a skimpy black costume wearing something that looked like a dead black bird in her hair and hollered into the microphone: "Is there a man out there who needs a good woman? Let me tell you I am a good, good, good woman."

The high point of the special came when she bounced onto the stage wearing a Big Bird costume. The low point came when she and other women performers appeared on the stage doing a burlesque number, wearing costumes that were, in a word, unbelievable. They were poured into purple outfits shaped like merry widow corsets, with ornaments resembling piano keyboards affixed to their bustles. Each performer, including Somers, appeared with two bells dangling from the center of the fabric that covered their breasts, which they shook to create bell sounds. After this, the divine Suzanne delivered herself of some patriotic remarks and then tortured "America, the Beautiful."

In fairness, I should confess a certain bias: "Cagney & Lacey," which is about two women police officers, is fast becoming one of my favorite shows. The heroines look and talk like real women and they have real working women's ambitions and problems. One of them has a terrific husband who cooks dinner and picks up children from the baby-sitter's. It may not sound terribly exciting, but when you figure it is one of the few shows on television that portray working women in a way that remotely resembles reality, then you can see its appeal. That is why its replacement with something like the Suzanne Somers show was even more annoying.

Last fall, the National Commission on Working Women released a ten-year study of how television has portrayed women who work outside the home. While the study concentrated on working women, it offered some telling insights into how television has treated women in general. It found that Hispanic women were invisible on television. So were working couples. In the decade the commission studied, there were only eleven two-income couples in prime-time series and of those, only four had children; and most of the TV wives held traditional jobs.

More than half of all adult women are working, an enormous change of the last three decades with innumerable ramifications as to what interests women, what conflicts and problems dominate their lives and how they perceive themselves. "TV has not caught up with this reality," noted the report. "Like advertising, it is still presenting an image of a woman whose role hasn't changed in 20 years.

"Stretching a paycheck, getting to work when the kids are sick, or trying to get promoted to a better job, rarely preoccupy women TV characters. In fact, they seem to have no financial worries at all."

The commission pointed out that networks have experienced a 10 percent decline in viewers in the last three years, with further declines expected as communities gain access to cable and pay TV. And it suggests that the new technologies—including cable, which is rapidly coming to the Washington area—can offer working women the kind of quality programming that the networks won't.

Television can entertain, it can teach, it can influence opinions and perpetuate stereotypes. It can also, as CBS demonstrated Monday night, offend. "Amos and Andy" is off the air. It is a testament to how far behind the times CBS is—and to the enormous vacuum cable and pay TV can fill—that the Suzanne Somers special was on.

Neuharth's USA *of Yesterday*
AUGUST 2, 1989

> *"The most ridiculous, not unexpected, was from that Palace of Malice east of the Potomac.* Washington Post *columnist Mann and her chauvinistic boss, Ben Bradlee, who sicked her to 'get' me, well know that my record on equal opportunity is unassailable. I've not only preached it but practiced it for a lifetime."*
> —AL NEUHARTH, *USA Today*

> *"I can tell you I never discussed the column I wrote with Ben or anybody else. To me, the question that still isn't answered is, Why on earth did he write that kind of column?"*
> —JUDY MANN, *USA Today*

The founder really stepped in it this time. Al Neuharth, owner of one of journalism's largest egos—and, it appears, smallest intellects—took to the pages of *USA Today* on Friday to lament the sad state of aviation. He ended up giving an object lesson in the sad state of journalism.

Neuharth retired in April as chairman of the Gannett Company, the nation's largest media conglomerate. He has continued, however, to write a column called "Plain Talk" in *USA Today,* which he founded. Lest anyone forget that, the photograph that accompanies his column identifies him as *USA Today* Founder. An enormous bust of Neuharth graces the entrance to *USA Today*'s headquarters in Arlington, Virginia. Neuharth is working on his autobiography, whose working title is *Confessions of an S.O.B.*

During his nearly two decades in the gilded stratosphere of corporate barony, Neuharth was spared the agonies of most Americans who travel on commercial airlines. He led a cosseted life of corporate jets.

When Neuharth stepped—or stumbled, more accurately—back into the real world, it was like some poor Rip Van Wrinkle awakening to find himself twenty years older, in a world that had passed him by. This is what he saw:

"Most of the young, attractive, enthusiastic female flight

attendants—then called stewardesses—have been replaced by aging women who are tired of their jobs or by flighty young men who have trouble balancing a cup of coffee or tea."

He went on:

"I understand why so many older attendants aren't very peppy or happy after 20 or 30 years at the same job. If they're good, they should have been promoted to better positions with the airlines."

Not everyone can become CEO, although you might argue that some of these aging flight attendants could have done better than the CEOs who have overseen record numbers of strikes, bankruptcies and crashes. But, then, would you trust Frank Lorenzo with your dinner tray?

Neuharth wants to ease "the cabin pressures," as he so coyly put it, by bringing back "sky girls." What he really yearns for is some young thing to whisper "Coffee, tea or me?" into his ear, but he attempts to legitimize this by leaning on the job description used for the first flight attendants. "Wouldn't you fly more and enjoy it more," he asked his readers, "if your cabin had at least one sky girl who is a nurse, under age 25, not over 5 feet 4 inches tall and weighed less than 115 pounds?"

Neuharth's column outraged readers and more than 175 *USA Today* staff members who signed a letter published in the paper on Monday calling his column "bigoted and insulting—not only to flight attendants and nurses, but also to the women and men who work for Gannett Co. Inc."

USA Today also interviewed Susan Bianchi-Sand, president of the 29,000-member Association of Flight Attendants, who outlined the legal and economic progress flight attendants have made while Neuharth was living in la-la land. She also pointed out that safety is the flight attendants' major responsibility, not fulfilling passengers' fantasies.

USA Today has done more than most newspapers to court women readers. Reporters are urged to include women and minority experts in news and feature stories and readers' opinion columns. Stories of particular concern to women are prominently played on section fronts.

The Gannett Company leads the industry in the number of women publishers and top editors, and *U.S.A. Today* has more high-ranking women executives—and more women's bylines on its front page—than any other mass circulation daily. Gannett executives have been at the forefront of industry efforts to improve opportunities for women in the news business. The Gannett Foundation sponsored a well-publicized conference this spring, "Women, Men and the Media."

Neuharth established himself as such a progressive force in these matters that he was honored by the National Women's Political Caucus, which gave him one of its ten "Good Guys" awards in 1986.

What got into the founder last week? Did he succumb to the Pete Rose syndrome that he is so big he plays by different rules? Was it too much Cocoa Beach sun? Neuharth, who is traveling, isn't talking. It doesn't much matter. What does matter is that someone who seemed to be such a leader in the newspaper industry turned out to be nothing more than a wolf in sheep's clothing. His commitment to women in the business and to women readers was a cynical ploy to grab circulation, not a genuine personal commitment to enhance the status of women in the business or in society—or, for that matter, in his own mind.

While he's digging up antiquated terms like sky girl, Neuharth ought to research a term that surfaced just about the time he went corporate. In plain talk, it's male chauvinist pig.

The Great Pretender
AUGUST 18, 1989

By late Wednesday afternoon, enough of my female colleagues had voiced objections to a recent column that appeared in this newspaper that I went back into the library, made a copy of it and read it. The bad news is that Morton Downey, Jr., appears to have resurrected himself as a columnist for *The Washington Post*.

I speak, for others who missed it, of a column that appeared in the Sunday magazine by Richard Cohen titled "Fakin' It."

What set him off was a scene in the movie "When Harry Met Sally . . ." in which a woman demonstrates to a man—with considerable histrionics—how she fakes an orgasm.

"Women are not laughing just at what's on the screen," writes Cohen. "They're laughing at all men."

Hell hath no fury like a male ridiculed.

In the finest spirit of getting even, Cohen reveals to the world that men fake it, too. "We pretend to listen. Mostly we pretend to listen to women, to open our eyes wide in totally insincere interest, nod our heads occasionally and say at appropriate intervals, 'Right, honey.'"

As a result of the women's movement, he writes, men now have to pretend to listen all the time, lest they be "accused of not being sensitive."

The faking by men, he writes, "is not limited to listening. They pretend to see women colleagues as persons. . . . They pretend not to notice other women. They pretend to be interested in parenting, in housework, in, of all things, relationships (even their own)."

As for the movie scene, Cohen concludes: "Harry, to his credit, makes his eyes bulge and has a look of absolute shock on his face. It's very funny. But the laugh's on you, ladies.

"He wasn't even listening."

So there.

Insulting to women? You bet. When you tell half of your audience that they aren't worth listening to, that's about as nasty a put-down as there is.

What's the point? Well, August is a slow month for columnists. Step out on a limb and say something outrageous and you're sure to generate some hate mail, get a little personal publicity, make a little rep for yourself.

Folks in the media business might pretend to be above such crass self-aggrandizement and commercialism, but don't let them fool you.

Across the Potomac, *USA Today* founder Al Neuharth got himself back into the headlines by insulting flight attendants and wishing for a return to the days of postadolescent "sky girls."

William Randolph Hearst started the Spanish-American War to sell newspapers. We come from a somewhat tainted tradition.

Columnists are supposed to be opinionated, thought-provoking and sometimes outrageous. Unfortunately, they are also supposed to be—dare I say it?—a little sensitive.

Thus, it would be poor form for a columnist to write an anti-Semitic diatribe, to indulge in an anti-Catholic screed or to mount a full-scale attack against Hispanics or blacks.

Newspaper editors are loath to censor columns, and good

editors encourage columnists to be as freewheeling in their writing and thinking as they can be. But there are limits—and no editor in his right mind is going to want his newspaper labeled anti-Semitic, anti-Catholic, anti-Hispanic or racist.

They don't have the same reservations, however, about printing stuff that is patently sexist and as offensive to women as a polemic against blacks.

Would we have published a white columnist making light of whites not listening to blacks? Would *USA Today* have printed a column wishing for a return to the days when servile black bellmen eased the travel of white train passengers?

Hardly.

The media have failed to develop the same level of sensitivity—or plain good sense—when it comes to writing about women. Or not, in another case, writing about women.

An obituary that recently ran in this newspaper described Nobel laureate William B. Shockley as the "son of a consulting mining engineer and grandson of a whaling captain." No mention of his mother or grandmother. Was his a reverse immaculate conception?

Newspapers aren't alone. "Rhymes with Rich" was the headline on a recent *Newsweek* cover story on Leona Helmsley—who hasn't been convicted of anything.

From 1982 to 1987, the number of women who read a newspaper four days out of five declined by 26 percent, according to the Newspaper Advertising Bureau.

This decline is sometimes explained by the theory that women have less time. Men have more? Hardly. They are busier than ever (pretending to be busy with parenting, housework and relationships).

Women would read newspapers if they were vital to them and served their needs. Women have money now and they need information.

What has happened is that their need for newspapers has declined, and insulting them is not the way to bring them back.

Is anybody listening?

Ms. *Dead; Women Bashing Isn't*
NOVEMBER 15, 1989

The demise of *Ms.* magazine deserves better than the sophomoric treatment it received recently in this newspaper. *Ms.* was the magazine of the women's movement and it would have been the first to point out that male columnists who think that woman bashing is the way to get rich and famous aren't being very original.

Robert Ruark, the late Scripps-Howard columnist who wrote *Something of Value*, got his first real notoriety when he wrote pieces for *The Washington Daily News* shortly after he came back from World War II contrasting the accommodating European and Asian women with American women.

Servicemen in the trenches, he wrote, were sustained by thoughts of coming home to "wonderful American women." But, "what we find shouldn't happen to a war criminal. Our girls who kept our souls alight when we were sleeping in mud or being ill on destroyers looked like something Salvador Dali might muster up after a midnight snack of Welsh rarebit." Ruark went on about women's hairdos, shoes and clothes for a few paragraphs and then:

"When God made little girls and little boys he made the boys wide on top and narrow on the bottom and the girls vice-versa. So it is shocking to observe the trends in ladies' suit, shoulders padded, so that the slightest of females resembles a professional football player in battle dress. . . . It won't be surprising if the boys start remembering Australia, England and even Germany overfondly. Over there, at least the women look like women."

Hugh Foster, Ruark's biographer, says the pieces "ostensibly generated 2,000 pieces of mail." They led to Roy Howard's offering Ruark a column, which he wrote almost until his death in 1965. Was Ruark merely insecure about women? "Certainly the conversations I've had with other people who knew him suggest he was," says Foster. "But I sensed more he used his relationship with women as a vehicle to achieve notoriety, to achieve success as a columnist."

This sad commentary on American journalism—then, as now—is one of the things that made *Ms.* magazine necessary and so beloved by its readers. It did not pander to the lowest common denominator. Unlike Ruark and the litters of clones he spawned,

Ms. magazine offered serious, contemporary commentary. It helped define and shape the issues for the most significant social movement of the late twentieth century. It promoted women's sports as a profitable venture and women's history as an academic discipline. It helped break stereotypes and sponsored speak-outs on sexual harassment that helped define it as discrimination and not, as editor Mary Thom wrote, a dirty joke. Readers used the letters to *Ms.* column as a forum to talk to each other and to reveal their most private agonies, including incest.

In her preface to a collection of such letters, Thom wrote: "Most movingly, *Ms.* readers look to the Letters column as a caring community to share their reactions to national events that affected them, whether it was despair over the defeat of the Equal Rights Amendment, horror at the New Bedford rape trial, euphoria over the tennis Battle of the Sexes between Billie Jean King and Bobby Riggs, or excitement over the vice presidential campaign of Geraldine Ferraro. And on the occasion of our anniversaries . . . readers joined us in assessing their own personal progress as they struggled to make change in their lives. . . . And always, letter writers felt a strength in community with other readers. As one wrote us in 1982, 'In 1972, I asked, "What's wrong with me?" Now, at thirty-three, I ask, "What the hell is the matter with them!"' "

When publication was suspended in October, *Ms.* had 550,000 subscribers. In its seventeen years, however, it never showed a profit. Unlike other women's magazines, it did not push advertisers' products in the news columns so it did not get the big cosmetic ad dollars. It spawned imitators that were not so pure. And it hauled the traditional recipe-pushing women's magazines into the new reality of women's lives, which was that most of them were working inside and outside the home and they cared deeply about such things as reproductive freedom and equal pay. *Ms.* magazine's new owner, Dale Lang, who is also the owner of *Working Woman*, has not said what he plans to do with the magazine. There is talk of a newsletter and talk of a black-and-white edition that would be supported by subscribers.

In any case, *Ms.* as we knew it won't be here for back-slid sports columnists to kick around anymore. Age is a radicalizing experience for women, and for the women who applauded Gloria Steinem when she turned fifty and said it was like turning forty used to be, there are many battles still to be won. It will be a lot harder without *Ms.*

Television Makes a Discovery
NOVEMBER 17, 1989

The soap opera at the "Today" television show continues. The latest word from New York on this riveting melodrama is that the morning show is going to get ready for the nineties by discovering that women watch women. Somebody up there is finally making some sense.

I do not watch TV in the morning. I tried to look at "CBS Morning News" a few days ago after reading about some woman television critic taking shots at Kathleen Sullivan's appearance. My few contacts with Kathleen Sullivan have left me with the impression that she is a nice and decent person so I tuned in to see what was going on with her, but, alas, she was not on. Instead, I saw Brooke Astor being interviewed in her library—not exactly a rumpus room—and talking about how much she enjoyed giving away money. My kind of woman.

I did watch a few minutes of the "Today" show recently while waiting for an airplane to take off. Jane Pauley was talking about something forgettable, and the flight attendant assured me that it would be turned off as soon as we started moving. If something went wrong, at least I wouldn't be spending my last moments on earth listening to Jane Pauley or Bryant Gumbel or any of the other members of that happy family.

This incident occurred after those smoothies who run NBC presided over the diplomatic debacle of the year: the Norville-Pauley imbroglio. It was enough to make us all forget Nancy and Raisa. By the time it was over, Deborah Norville, Jane Pauley and Dick Ebersol, the NBC News executive vice president who is in charge of the "Today" show, were all blaming sexism for the fiasco. It sounds better than managerial incompetence.

Whatever happened, neither Norville nor Pauley came out very well and the men pulling the strings didn't either. After all the explanations, hypes and denials, you couldn't figure out whom to believe, and so it is much easier to believe no one. For a show that's supposed to give its viewers reliable information, the credibility gap is going to be no small handicap.

Ebersol has said on several occasions that he wants to make "Today" more appealing to women. "Women watch women," he said in an interview after the goopy show in which Pauley announced her departure plans. "Getting more women to watch the 'Today' show became very important to me." In an interview this week with *USA Today*, Ebersol repeated that theme, and added: "There used to be this adage that women watch men. I don't believe that."

At some point, Ebersol may realize that pitting women against each other in humiliating public spectacles is not the way to get women to watch the "Today" show. But however maladroit he may be as a manager, it appears he may be in the forefront of media executives who are realizing that it is good business to go after women consumers of news and information.

Women don't have time to waste, but they do have money to spend, they need information that is relevant to their lives and they will go to the medium that delivers the most for their time. Chances are that this will be a medium where women are reporting stories and making decisions on what to cover—a medium that is user-friendly to women. So far, that field is wide open.

Studies that were showcased at April's conference in Washington on "Women, Men and Media" found that the percentage of women correspondents reporting network news had risen only slightly in 14 years—from 9.9 percent to 15.8 percent, with CBS leading with 22.2 percent, ABC following with 14.4 percent and NBC trailing with 10.5 percent. The percentage of stories in which women were the subjects went from 13.7 percent at ABC, to 10.2 percent at CBS and 8.9 percent at NBC.

Another survey found that only 27 percent of the front page bylines on ten major newspapers belonged to women and only 24 percent of the photographs included women, usually in family groupings. Only 11 percent of the people mentioned by name were women. In 1982, 61 percent of women were frequent readers of newspapers. By 1987, only 45 percent were—a 25 percent drop in readership in only five years. When women are asked how they spend their leisure time, the top activity is television.

There appears to be a gradual awakening in the media that an important market is slipping away. In the stiff competition for circulation and advertising dollars that exists in most markets, this development can only be good news for women consumers of information. Networks that are losing viewers will court them, as will newspapers trying to win circulation. Ebersol's belated discovery that women watch women, that we want to get our information from women, suggests that the media may finally be catching up to the marketplace.

Milestone in Presenting Raped Woman as Victim
APRIL 6, 1990

Geneva Overholser, editor of the *Des Moines Register*, has raised one of the most important questions about the media and society to come along in many years: Do newspapers and broadcast operations perpetuate the stigma of rape by their traditional practice of withholding the names of victims?

And in so doing, do the media contribute to shielding the crime, and thus the criminals? Is what we think of as an act of compassion really an act of complicity?

The *Register* gave its own answer to those questions in February when it ran a five-part series on an Iowa woman who was abducted and raped. The woman, Nancy Ziegenmeyer, now twenty-nine, a wife and mother who runs a small child-care center in the bucolic town of Grinnell, allowed the *Register* to identify her so that her story could put a name and face on a crime whose victims are usually invisible.

Ziegenmeyer came to Overholser a year ago after she had written a column questioning whether newspapers were, in effect, part of the problem society has had in combating rape. "As long as rape is deemed unspeakable—and is therefore not fully and honestly spoken of—the public outrage will be muted as well," Overholser wrote.

"It's always troubled me that we would treat this crime differently," she said at a news conference during the annual meeting of the American Society of Newspaper Editors this week. "This woman came to me and said use my name. I think openness will help." The series, written by staff reporter Jane Schorer, graphically detailed the crime, Ziegenmeyer's treatment by medical personnel and the legal system, and the impact of the crime on her family. Her assailant, whom she testified against, was convicted and sentenced to life without possibility of parole. He is appealing the case.

Betty Friedan, who is running the University of Southern California's Media Watch: Women and Men project, praised Overholser's courage at the news conference. She called it a breakthrough in eradicating the shame and guilt with which society has conspired to taint rape victims.

"The courage," responded Overholser, "came from this woman. . . ." She said she was able to break with tradition much the way Richard Nixon broke through on our anti-China policy. As a woman, she was in a stronger position to challenge the conventional wisdom that the media are protecting women by withholding their names. The fact that she was a woman editor also made it easier for Ziegenmeyer. "Nancy said she would not have felt comfortable had that not been the case."

The reaction of the *Register*'s readers was intense and positive. "America seems to be ready to look at this," says Overholser, who will not change the paper's policy of withholding the names of women who do not want to be identified. "It is not for the newspaper editor, eyes fixed on distant virtue, to sacrifice today's unwilling victims," she wrote in her column last year. "If I seek a world in which newspapers routinely print rape victims' names, it is also a world in which rape victims are treated compassionately, the stigma eradicated."

Hers is probably the most balanced and thoughtful position there can be in the slow and painful evolution that the crime of rape is going through. It is not unlike evolutions that newspapers have gone through, along with society, as we have struggled out of abysmal ignorance about other human tribulations. Cancer, for example, was never mentioned in obituaries. People died from "lingering illnesses." Tuberculosis bore the same stigma, so did venereal disease and, most recently, AIDS. The recognition that these were public health problems and not moral problems did not come until people were able to talk openly and in an informed manner about them.

Rape is now recognized in enlightened circles for what it is: a brutal crime of power, not one of sex. No woman is immune. Victims range from babies to the most elderly women in the population. It happens to rich women and to those who are poor. It is a fear that has touched every woman who has had to walk on a dark street at night and heard footsteps. But there are still plenty of benighted judges, police officers and lawyers who will blame the woman for being in that street. And as long as there is that kind of blame-the-victim thinking in the land, it is wrong for newspapers to arbitrarily print the names of victims. It will drive some women back into secrecy and shame.

But Overholser, a feminist, wants those women who can to identify themselves as a means of forcing society to come to grips with the rampage against women it has tolerated far too long. She has provided the next step in consciousness-raising about how rape is treated by the media and society. She wants women of courage, such as Nancy Ziegenmeyer, to take the next step, too.

3

First Ladies

"*I was particularly hurt by a column by Judy Mann in the* Washington Post, *who wrote that instead of helping all Americans, 'Nancy Reagan has used the position, her position, to improve the quality of life for those in the White House.*

"*This was so completely different from how I viewed my work that I was devastated. All I could think of was Clare Boothe Luce's famous line that no good deed goes unpunished.*"

—NANCY REAGAN, *My Turn*

"*Safire had gone so far that even Judy Mann, a columnist in the* Washington Post *and normally a critic of mine, was moved to defend me. Describing Safire's article as 'vicious, below-the-belt commentary,' she wrote . . .*"

—NANCY REAGAN, *My Turn*

People say it's the hardest unpaid job in the world, but think of the perks: a house to die for, the most fabulous passenger jet in the world at your command, a husband who wouldn't dare leave you, at least not while he's in office, and you get to meet anyone in the world you want to. Plus, you don't have to cook when your husband entertains business associates. But to do the job right, you must have class, style, a keen sense of tact and diplomacy, and if you display any hint of humor, America will love you. Warning: If you meddle, you'll be criticized. If you don't, you'll be criticized, too. It's the ultimate high-wire act for a woman, being First Lady, and as women around the world begin pushing at the boundaries of their traditional roles, so will the world's First Ladies. Nancy Reagan caught a lot of heat at first for frittering away time and money on brain-dead enterprises such as redecorating the family quarters of the White House and buying expensive new china. But by the end of the Reagan years, she was getting criticized for a far different role—booting out White House chief of staff Donald Regan and for pushing her husband into peace negotiations with the Soviet Union. Of course, she had the help of her astrologer—but, hey, it's a tough job.

Below the Belt
MARCH 6, 1987

First Lady Nancy Reagan managed to do what nobody else was able to do—namely, rid the administration of someone who was literally crippling the presidency. White House chief of staff Donald Regan hung on and on in an unprecedented display of supreme arrogance, placing his own self-interest above that of President Reagan and, certainly, above the welfare of the country. Calls, pleas, messages through the media, personal visits from Republican leaders could not move the president to replace him.

The gentlemen who could exercise the greatest influence on the president couldn't do the job. Mrs. Reagan did the dirty work for them, and now they are out to get her.

The Republican and conservative power brokers ought to be sending her bouquets of long-stemmed red roses. Instead, she's being depicted as a power-hungry dragon lady.

The men and women of the press, who failed by the power of the pen to persuade President Reagan that he had to replace Regan, are behaving like bullies toward the person who did the job.

New York Times columnist William Safire led the pack.

In a vicious, below-the-belt commentary that appeared the Monday after Regan cleaned out his desk, Safire began:

"At a time he most needs to appear strong, President Reagan is being weakened and made to appear wimpish and helpless by the political interference of his wife.

"Nancy Reagan's campaign to force her husband to fire [Regan] has been crowned with success. With extraordinary vindictiveness, the First Lady issued a gleeful victory statement when her target was brought down.

"Donald Regan's sin, in her eyes, was to have joined the Vice President and C.I.A. director in supporting the President's decision to trade arms for hostages; when that Regan decision turned out to be a disaster, the chief of staff had to suffer a scapegoat's humiliation.

"His more immediate sin, in the view of the power-hungry First Lady, was in pressing the President of the United States to get off his duff and show the people who elected him that he was on top of his job.

"The First Lady, being advised on matters of credibility by a foreign agent about to be indicted on four counts of perjury . . ."

You get the picture.

Safire also referred to Mrs. Reagan as being "at the top of the henpecking order" and an "incipient Edith Wilson, unelected and unaccountable, presuming to control the actions and appointments of the executive branch."

What really seemed to get Safire's goat, however, was that "Mrs. Reagan has a coterie of media biggies in whom she regularly confides," and he isn't one of them.

The Los Angeles Times portrayed Mrs. Reagan as a "political strategist with influence far exceeding that of most presidential wives." *The New York Times* reported that she has told friends "she plans to focus her attention on seeking an arms control agreement with the Soviet Union." Cartoonists depict her in a variety of power-grabbing scenarios, and news columns chronicle public concern about her growing power and influence.

All of this has opened up the old debate about just how a First Lady is supposed to do her job.

Which is what it is: an unpaid and, if done responsibly, a very tough job. In Mrs. Reagan's case—besides her other duties—she has taken on a personal campaign against drug use that has taken her across the country for speeches, visits to schools and rehabilitation projects. She has given enormous visibility to a deadly epidemic and probably done more to generate public concern about this than any other single human being.

That's okay. That's a good social cause, a proper thing for a First Lady to do. But when it comes to exercising real power on policy and appointments, the questions get asked: who elected her? To whom is she accountable? Who is she to interfere?

By contrast, former senator Paul Laxalt, often identified as the president's closest friend, and now a mere Washington lawyer, lobbyist Michael K. Deaver and political consultant Stuart Spencer are called in to help the administration straighten out the mess and nobody raises an eyebrow. Laxalt shoots arrows through the press about the president's grasp of the deteriorating situation and no one suggests that he is making the president look like a wimp.

The First Lady is the only one on the White House team who can't be fired. That put her in a position to do something that no one else was able to do: get the presidency back on track.

The president didn't look like a wimp. He had a wife who understood what had to be done and was willing to do the dirty work. That makes him a pretty lucky man.

The Summit's First Ladyfest
DECEMBER 9, 1987

When Nancy Reagan and Raisa Gorbachev get together for coffee and the White House tour today, they'll have something in common to talk about, and it won't be their recipes for bread pudding. Tips on keeping your balance during a high-wire act would be more like it.

Both First Ladies have become controversial in their homelands. Both, it would appear from news reports, are functioning against a backdrop of resentment, jealousy and pettiness. And both are emerging as people who wield enormous personal power in cultures where the very notion of powerful women is an oxymoron. As wildly different as the histories of the Soviet Union and the United States are, both societies are lurching along awkwardly toward a more egalitarian accommodation between the sexes. But neither is the least bit comfortable yet with having First Ladies who are overtly, visibly, out-of-the-closet powerful influences on their husbands.

Nancy Reagan is a veteran of the balancing act that U.S. First Ladies are faced with. Traditional older women gave her high marks when she arrived in Washington and devoted her considerable energies to redecorating the family quarters and getting new china. She set a lot of other people's teeth on edge. She played the role of traditional wife and swiftly became one of her husband's political liabilities. In more recent times, another Nancy Reagan has emerged: this one is the all-powerful woman running the show while a confused and enfeebled president dodders around the White House looking for his slippers.

Open season got declared on this Nancy Reagan when she did what nobody else seemed able to do, namely engineer the coup de staff in which Donald "Throw Weight" Regan returned to his first love, the private sector. *New York Times* columnist William Safire called her a "power-hungry first lady," and wrote that the president was being "weakened and made to appear wimpish and helpless by the political interference of his wife."

On the eve of the signing of the Intermediate-Range Nuclear Forces Treaty, apoplectic conservatives, who are turning purple over the possibility that something was about to happen that might prevent Armageddon, took up the Safire refrain. That great American, Howard Phillips, who is chairman of the Conservative Caucus and co-chairman of something called the Anti-Appeasement Alliance, offered this insightful analysis of how Reagan came to sign the INF Treaty: "Ronald Reagan is a very weak man with a strong wife and a strong staff. He becomes a useful idiot for Kremlin propaganda." The very thought of a strong First Lady short-circuited the sector of Phillips' brain that controls his manners.

Right about the time that Regan was returning to the private sector, *The New York Times* reported that Nancy Reagan had told friends "she plans to focus her attention on seeking an arms control agreement with the Soviet Union." That is precisely what is happening nine months later.

According to the manuscript of a book by former White House aide and Reagan confidant Michael K. Deaver, Mrs. Reagan pushed her husband into his first summit with Gorbachev. She was also the force behind a purge of hard-liners.

The evidence is mounting, in other words, that Mrs. Reagan can do a great deal more than pour a cup of tea.

Now comes the news that the same applies to Raisa Gorbachev. Her husband told the entire world (the entire world, that is, except the Soviet Union), via American television, that he discusses "everything" with his wife. The Moscow censors apparently thought that this was simply too much for the folks at home in the motherland to handle so it was deleted in that broadcast. Glasnost has its limits.

But the damage has been done. Both women have been revealed to be real wives—the kind of people their husbands confide in and trust—and that gives them enormous influence and power. It goes with the territory. Pretending otherwise is hypocritical or naive—or both.

There can't be a much lonelier job than being a head of state. In the United States, for example, anyone close to a head of state automatically qualifies for a six-figure advance on a tell-all book. The First Lady is the one person the president can trust to be always on his side. She's not thinking about her next job and she's not beholden to special interests that got her a Cabinet post. She's the one person who can be a critic without getting fired. She can be a stabilizing influence.

Mrs. Gorbachev and Mrs. Reagan seem to be very much part of a team. Their husbands not only acknowledge this, but they also appear to treasure what their wives do for them. Their countrymen ought to, as well.

Some Kind Words for a Class Act
JANUARY 18, 1989

Nancy Reagan, who brought adoring wives back into fashion, managed one of the more remarkable turnabouts of the Reagan presidency. Severely criticized at the beginning of her husband's first term for her extravagances, she has emerged in the end as one of the most popular and highly regarded First Ladies in history. She's worked hard.

The debate about the proper role of First Ladies will go on as long as the republic endures, which is a good thing. Everyone has firm opinions about this matter—everything from "The First Lady should have no voice in policy at all" to "Put her on the payroll and at the Cabinet table."

A great many of those who say the First Lady should have no voice in policy got their noses stuck out of joint when Mrs. Reagan engineered the ouster of White House chief of staff Donald Regan. A great many of those who would roll their eyes at the notion of her influencing policy breathed an enormous sigh of relief when she did the dirty deed. She may not have saved the presidency, but she steadied it at its rockiest moment.

A First Lady can be an enormous asset to her husband, or she can swiftly become a liability. That is one of the enduring lessons of Mrs. Reagan's experience. Badly advised at the beginning, she set about refurbishing the White House in royal fashion at the very time her husband was cutting social service programs for the poor. It didn't sit well with the public. Opponents of President Reagan's programs quickly seized on Nancy Reagan's spending habits. Polls showed her popularity plummeting to record lows for First Ladies. New advisers were brought in. Soon enough, a new Nancy Reagan emerged.

She found a serious and meaningful cause—her war on drugs. Nancy Reagan has endured considerable criticism for her slogan, "Just Say No to Drugs." It's been derided as simplistic public relations and as naively insufficient. She has been saying "Just say no" to kids who never had a chance to just say yes to three square meals a day.

If she has developed a deep understanding of the social chaos in America's neglected underclass—and its extraordinarily vulnerable youth—she's kept it to herself. She has not used her position as First Lady to champion the cause of poor single mothers and their children, nor has she taken up the cause of infant mortality, which reaches Third World levels in some parts of the nation, including the capital.

There was much there to be done had she been another Eleanor Roosevelt. But she was not and clearly had no desire to be. Nevertheless, Mrs. Reagan has crisscrossed this country with a simple and very clear message that must have reached a great many young people. She has probably done more than any other person to keep the drug epidemic at the top of the nation's agenda. She's done it by using the White House as a bully pulpit to raise funds for private drug rehabilitation programs and to remove the stigma from rehabilitation. She has probably done more than any other person to underscore for parents the enormity of the risk their children face daily, to push parents into getting themselves educated about drugs and alcohol, and to understand the impact their behavior has on their children. In all, she traveled nearly 200,000 miles to sixty-five cities in thirty-three states, the Vatican and eight countries, giving ninety-five speeches and 135 media interviews on drugs.

Nancy Reagan has made a large and important contribution and her public standing reflects it. She is at the very top of the lists of America's most admired women. Recent revelations that she was still borrowing thousands of dollars' worth of designer clothes caused only the most minor flap, and within hours, she was being defended as the leading champion of the nation's fashion industry. Nancy Reagan may be an unreconstructed clothes horse, but she has built up such a reservoir of goodwill that her borrowing is being viewed as a quaint personality quirk and not as a violation of ethical guidelines. Besides, she always looked as good as Raisa Gorbachev, or better, and if you don't think that's important, then you lose the debate about what we expect of our First Ladies.

Nancy Reagan understood that, and much more, and history ought to judge her kindly not only for the crucial role she played in ousting Regan, but also for her war on drugs. She was given an opportunity to do something extraordinarily valuable for her country. And she did.

4

Women at Work

Unlocking the Room at the Top
OCTOBER 31, 1986

Denise Cavanaugh, who runs a management consultant company, tells the story of an organization that held its annual executive staff meetings in Florida and chose for its social activities heavily competitive, individual sports. It was supposed to be fun.

The men endured it and kept their mouths shut. The women, however, said the entire thing was sexist. Then the men admitted the so-called social activities weren't fun. Cavanaugh told them to create a coalition and "go to the boss and say we want a great outing." The next year, they created a circus theme with team games that helped develop a cooperative spirit the company needed. Men and women who shared similar ideas worked together to change the management style of the company, says Cavanaugh. Neither group could have done it alone.

Cavanaugh's firm, Cavanaugh, Hogan & Rossman, Inc., specializes in helping companies go through periods of rapid transition. She has repeatedly run into the problem of women managers being unable to move up to the top tier of company executives and she is convinced that they are overlooking some problems and some solutions.

"There is a transformation going on in the work world. Women are a part of it. They represent the new values that are emerging in the workforce, but when a woman articulates them, they are denigrated. When a man articulates them, he is humanistic, the wave of the future.

"When women use this consensus-building, value-oriented style of management, they are perceived as being less effective than are men who use it. They are not getting rewarded for using their skills. Women can't change the management style in this country. We need to join with men who share our vision.

"Some women are struggling so hard to make it that they don't consider reshaping the way the top functions. You don't confront it; you create a coalition and that coalition reshapes the top.

"The other issue is that women who are at the top are not very insightful about the implications of the gender differences. Women at the top need to understand that part of what distinguished them is their different psychological perspective of the world." If four of the top five executives of a company are men, she says, the fifth stands out as different. "A lot of top women think that it's their degrees, their personality," that may be holding them back, "rather than that they're an 'only' in a group of 'others.'

"At the top, you have to have a lot of loyalty, a lot of trust. They know Charlie's mettle. That kind of connection is difficult for men and women to build together. Why women don't get picked for the top five is the bonding issue, the male perception of the team, of being able to negotiate the takeover deal, being able to hang out together, have a drink, swear, kick your shoes off in a hotel room after a tough day."

She spoke of one company headed by a man who articulates his commitment to women advancing in the corporate structure, but who promotes the kind of woman who can never break into the top. "They are promoting unidimensional women who are specialists. They are promoting men who are specialists and generalists." They are the ones who ultimately will make it to the top, she says, and "then the women get angry.

"At the top, you have to have a lot of social skills. You have to be able to fly in on the company jet, make people feel excited about the company, get on the plane and leave. A lot of top women haven't learned those skills. A lot say, 'I don't want to go on a boat and go fishing with the boys.' I say, you get your Dramamine and sun screen and go. Women also have to set up social things that men will enjoy."

A number of books and articles have drawn attention to the different management styles women have, and to their inability to break into top management. "The management books are teaching men our skills," says Cavanaugh. "The trouble is there's no place for women to go to learn men's skills." The top business schools "reflect the ultimate of that old line, male culture," she says, and set women up to fail. They don't encourage them to reshape the business world and to build on the continuum of male and female strengths.

Advancing women into higher positions is no longer something corporations need to do simply to improve their images. Women have established themselves as important consumers of everything from automobiles to Xerox equipment. "The demographic changes in the marketplace are going to put at risk the ability of white men to run companies," says Cavanaugh. This is the most compelling reason of all for men who run companies to begin learning what is keeping women out.

Out in the Middle
JANUARY 16, 1987

An item in this month's *Glamour* magazine suggests yet another squeeze play being run on women in middle management: takeovers, mergers and corporate consolidation are forcing female middle managers, who have the least seniority, out of their jobs. One executive placement firm reports a quadrupling in the past five years of women managers who are looking for new positions.

Alice Sargent, author of *The Androgynous Manager* and a consultant to a number of *Fortune* 500 companies and the federal government, agrees that the trend toward bigger conglomerates, fostered by the laissez-faire attitude of the Reagan administration toward antitrust considerations, is creating a business climate in which women are feeling uncomfortable, at best. "I have run into some women who have been part of organizations taken over who have felt very alienated," says Sargent.

She cites the case of a female vice president of a high-tech company in California's Silicon Valley that was taken over by a Chicago-based company. "She doesn't feel part of anything. She'd been with a growth company where she'd had some influence. You just feel you're there to earn money for some conglomerate." The woman was thinking of quitting.

Sargent recalls the remark of a TWA stewardess who described corporate raider Carl Icahn as being "into it for the money. He doesn't have a long-term view of developing a corporation. His short-term view is to take the money and run and sell it to somebody else.

"The oil companies," says Sargent, "as they diversify, there isn't the same kind of meaning [in one's work], and women who have a particular kind of loyalty to an organization feel the disenfranchisement, the alienation, the lack of identification.

"You used to stay in areas you knew something about. Now you have businesses with a little of this, a little of that. Somebody called it PacMan management. You gobble up different organizations."

Add to this new kind of robotization of middle management the increasing frustration women are feeling at their inability to break into the upper levels of management, and you get a bleak picture indeed—particularly if you consider the personal toll women managers have paid.

"When I interviewed women for *The Androgynous Manager*," says Sargent, "the number-one finding was that they'd stopped feeling. Feelings of love, fear, pain we don't allow in the workplace. We taught women to express more anger and close off some of the more tender things. We taught women in organizations to step back a little. My feeling about a lot of women in Washington is that they have streamlined themselves and made themselves very professional. You can know a woman a long time before you get to closeness, affiliation, the showing of vulnerabilities. You hear women talking about this now a lot. We learned to package ourselves very well, but the sad cost is there's a distance you have to get through."

Now, she says, the members of this first generation of successful women professionals are "bumping their heads on the glass ceiling. Women are looking up at the top and not making it into the boardroom or the executive suites. The first-generation affirmative action was getting women into the door; the second-generation affirmative action is retention. I get invited into high-tech companies and they want to know how to hold on to these women. The women are frustrated because they are not moving as fast as the men.

"I look around at women in government, and I think you can say women stay in grade three years longer than men," Sargent adds. "Only 2 percent of the executives in the country are women. In manufacturing, it's 6 to 10 percent, in the service industries it's 25 percent women in management. Women are moving more slowly. Nobody's opening their arms and saying, 'I want you in here.' There is still the clonal effect," a term describing the tendency of managers to hire and promote in their own likeness. "There is still a discomfort level. You still hear men saying, 'I don't feel as comfortable having her around. I don't want to be drinking coffee with her. If we don't have to let them in, then let's not.'

"Without targets and numerical goals and accountability, people do whatever they want. In the old days, there was a system in some of the corporations I consulted to, in which every time you put a white male in a position you had to justify it. That's not the case now."

Small wonder, given the climate, that women managers are looking for better opportunities and that women are starting their own businesses at five times the rate men are. The sandbox may be smaller, but it's likely to be a lot more fun.

The Masculine Style
MARCH 4, 1987

There are two things that the *Challenger* disaster and the White House disaster have in common: both operations were run exclusively by men and both exemplified the worst of the masculine style of management—hierarchical, authoritarian, excessively competitive and ruinously uncommunicative. Among the lasting, useful lessons to be gained out of both situations is that this style simply doesn't work anymore. The world that shaped the Ronald

Reagans and the Don Regans has become too complex; nobody has all the right answers, and nobody who thinks he does should be put into a policy-making position.

The Tower Commission report provided devastating insights into a White House that betrayed and misled the American people. The betrayal came at the very top in the form of a person who ran for the highest office of this land, won it and then proceeded not to work at the job. That has been described as a failure of management style; it was not. It was a sickening demonstration of laziness that showed the most profound disrespect for the office and for the people who elected him. No one expects a president to be right all of the time; the doctrine of infallibility resides in Rome, not in Washington. But people do expect, at the very minimum, that presidents will work hard, make the tough decisions and have a very clear idea of what is going on in their administrations.

The failure of management style came not in the president but in Donald Regan, his underlings and in the operations of the Cabinet. Dissent was stifled and ignored. Winning became the only thing. When a policy, such as selling arms to Iran, failed to gain full support, it was carried out in secret anyway. The atmosphere did not encourage openness, dissent and consensus. The Tower Commission report, for example, found that Secretary of State George P. Shultz and Secretary of Defense Caspar W. Weinberger "distanced themselves from the march of events." It said "they protected the record as to their own positions on this issue. They were not energetic in attempting to protect the president from the consequences of his personal commitment to freeing the hostages."

Marilyn Loden is among a growing number of management experts who have identified these traits as typical of the masculine leadership style. In her book, *Feminine Leadership: How to Succeed in Business Without Being One of the Boys,* she described the differences in the two styles as follows:

"While some male members [of a management group] compete for control, female members are more likely to aim for compromise or consensus-building. They are more often the members who poll the group for ideas, who support the right of all members to express their opinions, and who are more willing to modify their own views based upon the evidence presented during the discussion. While males tend to control and maneuver within the group in order to satisfy their own self-interests, females demonstrate less vested interest in proving that they are right and more interest in maximizing the chances for an outcome that is satisfying to everyone within the group."

Consensus, communication and cooperation are at the heart of the feminine style of management; competitiveness, hierarchical structure, with the aim being to win, are at the heart of the masculine style. It is a style that has its roots in the military, and out of the need for tight control flows an authoritarian management style. In Donald Regan, an ex-Marine, it bubbled over into an extreme form of arrogance. This is a man who hung up on the First Lady, badly underestimating her power. "More than almost any chief of staff of recent memory, [Regan] asserted personal control over the White House staff," the Tower Commission wrote, "and sought to extend this control to the national security adviser."

The Rogers Commission blamed the *Challenger* disaster in part on a management and communications breakdown rooted in the same authoritarian style of management. People didn't share information and they didn't speak out forcefully enough to avert disaster.

Of the White House mess, Senator Nancy Landon Kassebaum (R-Kans.), a member of the Foreign Relations Committee, said: "The underlying problem in all this is a lack of respect for dissent. The president has not been able to hear all sides of an issue. And we saw the same thing on SDI [the Strategic Defense Initiative], contra aid, South Africa and, of course, the budget. People in the administration who challenge policy are just shunted aside. That's the basic flaw in the process."

And twice, now, this management style has led to disaster.

New Form of Sexual Harassment
MARCH 18, 1987

Elizabeth A. Reese, an attractive, thirty-four-year-old marketing specialist, recently collected a $250,000 check from her former employer after winning a unanimous jury verdict that she had been a victim of sex discrimination and sexual harassment. Her lawyers believe that what happened to her is an emerging form of sexual harassment to which successful women—particularly those in sales and marketing fields—may be especially vulnerable.

In a nutshell, according to testimony, Reese was told by her supervisor to prostitute herself for her firm to get business. She refused, but later when she landed a big contract, he told colleagues she had used sex to win it. She then was subjected to an unrelenting pattern of raw language and sexual innuendo that undermined her professionalism. Reese repeatedly complained to superiors in the firm about her supervisor's conduct and they did nothing about it. She finally quit and filed suit under the D.C. Human Rights Act against Swanke Hayden Connell Architects, one of the largest architectural design firms in the country, and her supervisor, Bruce Schafer.

According to the plaintiff's court documents and interviews with Reese and her attorneys, Bruce A. Fredrickson and Susan L. Brackshaw, the pattern began on March 21, 1984, when Reese, employed as a marketing coordinator in the Washington office, was in a business meeting with a principal of the firm and Schafer. Using a crude term, he asked her whether she prostituted herself for the firm and stated that her predecessor had.

"I was shocked," Reese said in an interview. "I didn't really know this man. I said that's not in my contract, and I left the room."

That was only the opening salvo. Schafer, according to the court documents, "made suggestions that she behave inappropriately to advance business on a number of occasions," including suggestions that she date leasing agents and well-connected real estate people.

"Schafer's obsession with Ms. Reese's personal life and sexual activities continued through 1984 and into 1985," according to the documents. "In April 1984, Ms. Reese was explaining an absence from work to her supervisor, Schafer. She told Schafer she had been hospitalized for endometriosis surgery. Schafer responded by insisting that Reese suffered from endometriosis because she did not get" sex "enough. A few months later, in July 1984, Ms. Reese phoned into the office while on vacation. Schafer suddenly got on the line and blurted out" a coarse question. According to the documents, the head of the firm's Washington office testified at the trial that at a September 1984 staff meeting, Schafer commented in front of a principal in the firm and "five or six other Swanke employees that business was slow and that Ms. Reese ought to be" using sex "for the firm.

"Shortly after the firm was awarded a lucrative [contract], Schafer interrogated Ms. Reese about her role in the award, and insinuated that she had done something inappropriate. [The head of the Washington office] testified at trial that Bruce Schafer had stated that she had provided sexual favors to get the firm short listed on the project."

At a Board of Trade dinner, according to the documents, in front of a partner in the firm, and others, Schafer stated that Ms. Reese was a "bitch," and said women "are good for nothing but" sex.

The documents show that he made insinuations about other female employees' activities on behalf of the firm. In March 1985, with a wire in his hand, he approached an employee who was six months pregnant and said: "Well, I guess I'm a little late for this, aren't I?"

Reese quit her job on March 11, 1986. The trial, in October, lasted ten days before a jury of seven women. On the last day, according to court documents, Schafer admitted making anonymous phone calls to Reese at night, which he had previously denied. Gerald Fogerty, attorney for the defendants, said in an interview that the defense in the case was that "it didn't happen, that her charges are without merit." He said the case turned on Schafer's reversal. "Once he admitted lying to them the case was over." The jury also awarded Reese legal fees, for a total of $489,437.01, according to Brackshaw.

"I worked very hard and my work was good," said Reese in an interview. "That's the thing that makes it so outrageous. The stress became so unbearable I found myself in my office, the door closed, and I couldn't cope. It came to my sanity or my paycheck."

"This is not a quid pro quo suit where the harasser says, 'Sleep with me or you're fired.' This is a new genesis of sexual harassment," said Brackshaw.

The implication was that Reese was successful not because of her skills but because of her sexual favors. Her career was undermined, and more than two years of her life were enormously strained. That her supervisor's behavior was tolerated in a business environment is extraordinary—but the jurors made it clear that it is also very costly.

Sweet and Sour Fare
MAY 15, 1987

Almost 1.5 million people make their living waiting on tables in the United States. Eighty-six percent of them are women. Only 5 percent of all waitresses are black. In 1984, waiters earned an average of $237 a week, according to the Department of Labor, while waitresses earned an average of $168 a week—or $69 a week less. Obviously, women don't wait on tables as well as men do.

This, despite our extensive backgrounds in serving breakfast, lunch and dinner to our families.

The food service industry is one of those truly clear-cut situations in which women are patently discriminated against because of their sex. It is also one of those industries in which women dominate numerically—a factor that helps explain the low pay in certain industries—and yet the men who enter the industry are paid substantially more than women. The secretarial and clerical fields are another: male secretaries earn an average of $119, or 30 percent, more than female secretaries each week.

Pay discrimination has been justified in numerous industries on the grounds that women are relatively late entrants into certain fields, and therefore have less experience and less seniority. That doesn't wash in the food service industry or the clerical fields.

The Women's Legal Defense Fund targeted the food service industry several years ago as an industry in which women were discriminated against in hiring and salaries. It negotiated an out-of-court settlement with Ridgewell's Caterers, one of the city's best known, which went into effect in March. In that class action suit, the defense fund represented more than five hundred waitresses who charged that they were not allowed to serve food at Ridgewell-catered events, but had to work in the kitchen instead. The suit was brought by two former Ridgewell employees who said kitchen work paid $1 an hour less than work performed by waiters.

Under terms of the settlement, Ridgewell's agreed to assign men and women to jobs without regard to gender. It also agreed to pay any present or former waitress back pay of $1 an hour for any time worked since February 1982. At the time, sources close to the settlement said it could reach as high as $1 million in back pay, although because of the part-time nature of work at the catering firm, it was difficult to estimate.

The Women's Legal Defense Fund has now negotiated a second settlement, this time with a Georgetown restaurant, Martin's Tavern. The defense fund had received a tip in early 1986 from a former employee of the restaurant who said that the management had told him it would not hire waitresses and would allow blacks to work only in the kitchen. The defense fund encouraged three experienced waitresses who were looking for jobs to apply at the restaurant. None was hired. One of them filed a complaint with the D.C. Office of Human Rights and a charge with the federal Equal Employment Opportunity Commission in October.

Jeffrey Huvelle and Jane Howard-Martin, volunteer lawyers from the prestigious firm of Covington & Burling, represented the waitresses and reached a settlement with the restaurant in April. The settlement includes cash awards to each of the three waitresses and implementation of an affirmative action plan. The plan calls for the restaurant to make a good faith effort to recruit and hire no fewer than seven women or blacks in filling its next ten vacancies in jobs waiting on tables.

The Women's Legal Defense Fund contends that one reason waitresses average so much less pay than waiters is that they often are not hired to wait tables in the more expensive restaurants where salaries and tips are higher. The defense fund has collected an impressive list of public statements from the people who run some of Washington's most pricey eateries. They may not have male chauvinist pigs on the menu, but they have them in management. Comments range from women not being able to cope with the pressures of a French restaurant to women not having the strength to carry serving trays to simply not having had any women apply. One owner said: "We prefer men." Another said he didn't think women need waiting jobs as much as men do—this in an age when one-quarter of all households are headed by women.

What this boils down to, very simply, is that the restaurant industry has managed to ignore the fact that Title VII was passed twenty years ago and that discrimination on the basis of race and sex is illegal. The successful litigation of the Women's Legal Defense Fund in Washington should serve as a prototype for similar litigation across the country—and it should serve notice to the industry that any restaurant that has only male waiters is a potential target for legal action.

Paying for Profits
JULY 15, 1987

The Service Employees International Union and 9to5, the National Association of Working Women, have put together a grim portrait of what has happened to American families as poorly managed industries have tried to compete by cutting wages, benefits and workplace standards instead of through technological advances and maximizing the value of the workforce. If the Democrats are looking for an issue, this is it.

The bottom line—or where the stock is trading—is taking a terrible toll on the nation's workers and their families. People, it would seem, are no longer our most valuable resource. Profits are.

Some of the figures and economic conclusions that SEIU and 9to5 have pulled together have appeared before. Taken together, however, these figures tell an alarming story of the rapid economic erosion of the workforce and the middle class. It is alarming not only for the future, but also for the present.

The union also has conducted a poll that shows overwhelming support among voters for parental leave legislation pending in Congress, as well as for raising the minimum wage and expanded employer health insurance. The poll shows that voters are hurting badly enough now to vote for candidates based on where they stand on these issues.

Three out of every four jobs are now in the service sector, and these jobs pay less than manufacturing jobs did. The standard of living peaked in 1973 and has subsequently declined so that it is now 6 percent less, adjusted for inflation, despite the fact that many more families now have two earners. About 5.7 million people work at more than one job, a 24 percent increase since 1980. One of every four full-time American workers does not earn enough to keep his or her family out of poverty.

The study predicted that young men and women can expect to earn an average of 25 percent less during their lifetimes than the generation of workers that started out a mere ten years earlier. Meanwhile, 37 million workers have no health insurance, double the figure only six years ago. More than 80 percent of those people are employed adults or their dependents.

More people are working on the margins of the workforce in

part-time, temporary or contract jobs, often with no benefits. The 2 million manufacturing jobs lost since 1979 paid an average of $20,846 a year. Nearly half of the full-time jobs created since then paid below the poverty level, which is $11,400 for a family of four. Ten percent of the workforce is now under a two-tiered wage structure.

The service economy has produced industry giants that are often paying poverty-level wages that the taxpayers subsidize through public assistance programs, the SEIU report said. In economic performance, profits and wealth, *Fortune's* Service 500 now rival the *Fortune* Industrial 500. Beverly Enterprises, which runs nursing homes, has 116,000 employes, more than Chrysler's 115,074. McDonald's sales of $4.1 billion are almost as much as Bethlehem Steel's $4.3 billion.

The report documents the bleak erosion of family life as well as the ability of families to maintain a decent standard of living. "The U.S. economy depends on these same men and women to improve productivity, to learn new skills and to work harder to keep pace in a world economy. Yet U.S. institutions, unlike their counterparts worldwide, have not put in place even minimal family leave or child care supports for families.

"Thus, on top of declining incomes, benefits and job security, families face a work place with no provisions for raising children or caring for dependent adults.

"Fifty years ago and more, the widespread failure of corporate policies to put the economy to work for its people brought about a revolution in social and economic policies." These included the minimum wage, child labor laws, Social Security and the rights of workers to organize into unions. The SEIU report calls for changes now that would include wage and benefit policies that can support families, leave policies to balance work and family, education and training policies that conserve human capital rather than trash it, community- and workplace-based child care and guaranteed health care for all workers.

Perhaps the most important message in the SEIU and 9to5 report lies in its call for a "new set of standards to put corporate policy on the side of families and to reflect the needs of the new work force." It's a call to remember what's important and to back off from the paganistic worship of the bottom line that has blinded corporate managers. It's a message the Democrats ought to run with.

The Salary Gap
OCTOBER 14, 1987

I have in front of me a check—or, more accurately, the facsimile of a check—made out to the working women of America and issued on the account of the National Federation of Business and Professional Women's Clubs. The check is for the pay period beginning September 5 and ending December 31. The paycheck amount is $0.00.

The pay stub puts the message another way: "Working women in this country average only 68 cents for every dollar a man makes. If a working woman's paycheck was equal to that of a man's, her salary would last only 68 percent of the year.

"September 4th is the last payday for the average working woman compared to a man. Her salary would have run out. From September 5–December 31, 1987, working women in this country really receive no pay for the work they do, while men still get paid."

That may be one of the most provocative ways developed for putting the salary gap in perspective. It is one thing to hear government figures about how women earn 68 cents for every dollar that men earn, and it's quite another to think of working for nearly a third of the year for nothing. Perhaps we could start writing off our parking and transportation costs on our income taxes under the section where you deduct the costs of volunteer work.

The Census Bureau announced shortly before Labor Day that the gap between men's and women's earnings had narrowed to 68 cents on the dollar, based on hourly wages. Wages are measured in different ways by different agencies of the federal government, such as the Labor Department and the Census Bureau, and the hourly and weekly earnings ratios have generally shown women to be doing better than have the annual earnings measurements.

The Census Bureau's September announcement that women's wages had increased to 68 percent of men's wages in 1986 from 62 percent in 1979 received considerable attention. The news appeared to be one of the biggest breakthroughs in the wage gap, which has remained relatively constant despite the dramatic increase in the number of working women and despite the fact that half of professionals are women.

‾The National Committee on Pay Equity has analyzed the Census Bureau's report, however, and concluded that the news is not as good as it originally appeared to be. The group has been in the forefront of efforts to use comparable worth as a method of improving the wages of working women in the United States. It prepared a briefing paper clarifying some of the confusion that surrounds the salary gap and the various figures that are often cited in discussion of it. The paper, using census and other government data, was prepared with the assistance of Heidi Hartmann, director of the Institute for Women's Policy Research and former study director on women's employment issues at the National Academy of Sciences.

Based on annual earnings, the female-male earnings ratio rose from 59.7 percent in 1979 to 64.3 percent in 1986 for full-time workers. Three-quarters of the improvement in women's wages versus men's wages came from growth in women's earnings, but a quarter represented a drop in men's earnings, largely because of declining employment in higher-paying manufacturing jobs. The pay equity group traced the annual earnings ratios and found that the figure has hovered around 60 percent since 1955, dropping to a low of 57 percent in 1973 and 1974 and rising to highs of 64 percent in 1955, 1957, 1983 and 1984. From 1975 to 1981, it was 59 or 60 percent. After 1981, it climbed steadily to a peak of 64.6 in 1985.

"This slow climb in the past few years does represent progress for women," the report found, "but it is important to note that the ratio has been nearly as high several times in the past." Whether the ratio continues to improve depends on a number of factors, including the strength of the economy and the willingness of employers to eliminate wage disparities based on sex.

As has been the case in the past, young women are doing better in the female-male earnings ratio than women over forty-five. Education and training are contributing to their improved earnings, says Hartmann. "College majors are more similar to men's than they were 20 years ago. There are fewer education majors among women, and more business and science majors."

What is not known, she says, is whether this younger group of women will be able to command a higher earnings ratio relative to men than their mothers have been able to manage. What is known, however, is that for women taken as a whole, the salary gap—no matter which numbers you use—remains an intransigent economic barrier. Chances are that from Labor Day on they're working for free.

The Demeaning "Mommy Track": Separate and Unequal
MARCH 15, 1989

One of the things that women and minorities have in common is that when society has tried to make them separate but equal, they have historically ended up separate and unequal. Protective labor laws that restricted women's participation in the labor force were about as beneficial as laws that restricted blacks' access to education.

Track systems have been thrown out of schools for the same reasons they were thrown out of the workplace—they end up discriminating against women and minorities. This is the inherent danger that feminists sense in the current debate over Felice N. Schwartz's article in the January-February edition of the *Harvard Business Review*. This is the article that midwifed the most lamentable term to come along this year: "the mommy track." Let the record show that nowhere in her ten-page piece does Schwartz use that trivializing term.

Schwartz is president and founder of Catalyst, a New York firm that has for years provided first-rate research and training on women's career issues. She has laid out in a thoughtful article some of the well-known problems that people who have families often face when they work for corporations that demand their undivided attention.

She focuses almost exclusively on women who confront that, ignoring the fact that there are men who have equally keen senses of family responsibilities and could be valuable allies in changing corporate cultures. This is a bow to the reality, however, that women still feel the family imperative more keenly and constantly than do men. And more and more, as their numbers in middle management increase, women are willing to voice that and to seek an accommodation between their two sets of responsibilities.

The most controversial statement in Schwartz's presentation comes right at the beginning when she writes: "The cost of employing women in management is greater than the cost of employing men. This is a jarring statement, partly because it is true, but mostly because it is something people are reluctant to talk about."

She then describes two studies, one of a multinational corporation that shows that turnover among top-performing women managers is two and one-half times that of men, and another study of a consumer goods manufacturer that showed that half the women who took maternity leave returned late or not at all. The studies are of unnamed companies, by unnamed researchers, and nothing further is said to allow the reader to determine their validity. This is a serious flaw of scholarship.

Nevertheless, Schwartz goes on to address the problems of balancing work and family with the proposal that companies sort out early what women are "career-primary" and which are "career-and-family." Because of the coming shortage of management women, those women are "about to move from a buyer's to a seller's market," she writes.

The secret to dealing with women who put their career first, she writes, "is to recognize them early, accept them and clear artificial barriers from their path to the top."

The secret to dealing with—and retaining—women who are career-and-family, she writes, is for companies to plan for and manage maternity, and that doesn't stop at birth, to provide flexibility "that will allow them to be maximally productive," and to take an active role "in helping to make family supports and high-quality affordable child care available to all women."

"Part-time employment," she writes, "is the single greatest inducement to getting women back on the job expeditiously and the provision women themselves most desire." She predicts job-sharing will be the most widespread form of flexible schedule in the future. "It is feasible at every level of the corporation except at the pinnacle," she writes. She believes women will accept lower pay as a trade-off for flexible schedules.

Schwartz's article has come under criticism from working mothers who say that it reinforces the stereotype that women can't have demanding careers and families at the same time. Other working mothers are saying it is simply realistic.

It is unfortunate that Schwartz did not expand her concept of career and family to include fathers who want to give as much to their families as to their corporations. Working mothers are right to sense clear and imminent danger in any talk of separate tracks—

and nothing illustrates this better than the fact that this was instantly given the dead-end name "mommy track." The benefit that can come out of this debate, however, is that it can set the stage for talking about a respected and rewarded career and family track that is not limited to women. That's the only way that separate can ever be equal.

Making Tracks
MARCH 24, 1989

You can't open a newspaper or turn on a talk show these days without seeing or hearing the words "mommy track." At the very moment that we are all ruminating over the fate of working mothers, however, two of the more visible achievers in America are packing it in to spend more time with—what else?—their families.

Neither of them is a working woman.

Both of them are working men.

As odious as the term "mommy track" is, if you can use it in connection with the work lives of women, it's only fair to use the term "daddy track" in connection with the work lives of men. Personally, I'd vote for civilizing the workplace so that there's no need to distinguish between one-dimension careerists and balanced, well-rounded people, but failing that, I'd vote for a more dignified term such as "family track," if tracks we must have.

On Wednesday, two fathers made headlines by opting for the family track, though neither, of course, used that term. National Football League commissioner Pete Rozelle, a young sixty-three, announced that he is retiring "to enjoy free time, stress-free time" with his family. Rozelle has headed the league for twenty-nine years, ushering in and overseeing football's enormously profitable marriage with television. Between these two high-stakes worlds, Rozelle is a guy who knows stress.

NBC News Capitol Hill correspondent Ken Bode announced that he is leaving the pressure cooker of television news to become the director of DePauw University's Center for Contemporary Media. He told *Washington Post* television columnist John Carmody: "The point is, it's really for my family. I've missed the last 10 years but I've bought maybe the next 10 . . . I learned over the last year that it's time to give up some of the money and get back some of the time." Bode, who turns fifty next week, has two daughters, eleven and nine years of age.

The response Bode received from NBC president Michael Gartner was interesting. He praised Bode's work and then wrote: "I understand, though, the personal toll that a network job such as yours takes on a person and his family. *Thus, it was with understanding and admiration* [my italics], as well as a sense of loss, that I read your letter. . . ."

Feminist leaders fear that the mommy track controversy will signal corporations that they can assume working mothers want to be on a less-demanding track with lower pay. They see inherent· danger in anything marked "for women only." Bode, particularly, is a splendid example of a father who is willing to trade in big bucks for more time with his family.

The same day Bode and Rozelle announced that they were getting off the fast track for family reasons, leaders of forty-nine women's organizations held a news conference to set forth the agenda they want Congress to address this session. Career and family issues were the hot topics. Irene Natividad, president of the National Women's Political Caucus and the mother of a four-year-old, said the organizations want to put "all opponents of work and family legislation on notice—particularly the Chamber of Commerce—not to try to turn mommy track stories into mommy track legislation."

Specifically, she and other women leaders are trying to protect the Family and Medical Leave Act, which would permit working people to take job-guaranteed unpaid leave to care for newborns, seriously ill children, spouses or parents. The bill has aroused tremendous opposition from the U.S. Chamber of Commerce, which has taken the stand that Congress would be mandating benefits by passing the bill. Advocates of the measure say it is a minimum labor standard, not a benefit.

"We will not accept a 'mothers-only' bill," said Donna Lenhoff of the Women's Legal Defense Fund. She is heading the coalition backing the bill.

Coalition members fear that a bill that would merely guarantee women maternity leave, for example, would end up working against women because employers would be more inclined to hire men, who would not need such leave. The Family and Medical Leave Act was designed from the beginning to provide job protection for men who have heart attacks as well as women who have babies.

This family track legislation is on the fast track in the House, and it deserves not just the support of women's groups but also of employers and others who want to make it easier for parents to balance their work and family obligations. Mothers, as we saw this week, are not the only ones who are concerned with their families, and who want to be with them

The House leadership wants the act passed for Mother's Day, and that would be nice. Father's Day is only a month later, and the wait would be worth it to make the point that the family track legislation is for them, too.

Mixing Families, Business
NOVEMBER 24, 1989

The *Harvard Business Review*, which made a big splash by publishing the article that led to the "mommy track" flap, has waded into the work and family debate again, this time with a call to the American business community to adapt itself to the changes in the family out of enlightened self-interest.

In the November-December issue, it features an article by Fran Sussner Rodgers and Charles Rodgers, principals of Work/Family Directions, Inc., which argues that businesses must give up such cherished notions as the sanctity of the forty-hour workweek and the belief that productivity is measured by hours spent in the office if they are to compete successfully for workers in a diminishing workforce.

The U.S. is third, behind Scandinavia and Canada, among Western democracies in its dependence on female workers, they write. It follows, then, that its economic competitiveness is going to be intensely dependent on its abilities to maximize the effectiveness of working parents. Yet, increasingly, the Rodgerses write, business and family are at loggerheads.

During the oversupply of labor that came with the baby boom, businesses could afford to be Draconian adherents to a Norman Rockwell image of the American household at work and play. When the images didn't fit the realities of women going into the workforce, of families divorcing, of workers refusing to relocate, businesses could afford to let these people go. "With the baby boom over and a baby bust upon us, there are now higher costs associated with discouraging entry into the labor force and frustrating talented people who are trying to act responsibly at home as well as at work," they write.

This demographic pressure for change is gaining widespread understanding. The authors argue that employees' perceptions are changing too. "Women and men in two-career and single-parent families are much better able to identify policies that will let them act responsibly toward their families and still satisfy their professional ambitions. Companies that don't act as partners in this process may lose talent to companies that do rise to the challenge."

They emphasize that this affects men as well, and cite two studies they did at Du Pont that found "men's reports of certain family-related problems nearly doubled from 1985 to 1988." They cite other studies showing that inflexibility toward these problems reduces productivity because it causes absenteeism and turnover.

Fueling the need for businesses to modernize, they say, is the growing concern over the welfare of the nation's children as parents try to sort out the competing needs of children, elderly parents and work.

A measure of this pressure is a study the Rodgerses did of two high-tech companies in New England that show that on average, working mothers put in an eighty-four-hour workweek between their homes and their jobs; working fathers put in seventy-two hours; and married people with no children put in fifty. Working mothers on average are working the equivalent of two full-time (forty-two hours) jobs a week.

Their research showed that 35 percent of men and women "with young children have told their bosses they will not take jobs involving shift work, relocation, extensive travel, intense pressure, or lots of overtime." A quarter of the men with young children in another study they did said they would not relocate.

The Rodgerses put forward detailed proposals for companies to implement flexible schedules—and they are mindful of such crises as snow days—for developing part-time work for professionals and managers and for reducing the need for relocation. They make the point that companies must modify their career paths to include the new breed of workers.

Finally, they say, companies must communicate these new policies from the top to the front-line managers—who are the ones, in effect, dictating family policies today.

The media coined the term "mommy track" this year when the business review published the article arguing that the way to respond to work and family pressures was for workers and business to agree on a two-track system, one for fast-trackers and one for mothers. Women with young children say they are still feeling the backlash from that article because it gave their employers license to assume they have a reduced career commitment.

The latest entry into the debate shifts the burden of adjustment to businesses and is aptly titled "Business and the Facts of Family Life." The bottom line is that it's no longer going to be just up to mothers to balance work and family. It's going to be good business for companies to be family-friendly, too.

In Canada, a Grasp on Fairness
DECEMBER 20, 1989

Lynne Revo-Cohen and Karetta Hubbard spent the eighties helping private companies as well as state and local governments adapt to the revolution in the workforce. They say that the good news is that employers are far ahead of where they used to be in adapting to working mothers and dual career couples, but, in Hubbard's words, "people just don't know what to do."

What employers will have to do in the next decade, as in the last, will be governed by the singular exigencies of that demographic explosion known as the baby boom. Thus, the consultants predict that there will be continued interest in catastrophic health plans and a much more concerted effort to sort out work and family issues. They believe that companies will begin to develop frameworks for dealing with the differing intensities of career commitment that come at different stages of workers' lives. Such frameworks will enable people to take time away from their careers for the care of elderly parents as well as for child care. Leaves at different stages of employees' careers create a cradle-to-grave working environment in which all age groups stand to benefit.

Hubbard and Revo-Cohen's firm, which bears their name, is

based in Reston, Virginia. They employ sixteen full- and part-time people who are experts in the fields of benefits, pay equity and compensation, and affirmative action. The firm has been hired by several Canadian newspapers and unions to conduct the pay equity studies at their plants that are required under new Canadian laws designed to eliminate disparities in pay between comparable jobs done by men and women.

The two women knew each other when they were lobbying for pay equity in the federal government. They were both taken with the challenge of turning progressive public policy into reality in the workplace and found there were no private companies doing that. They started with a pay equity study for the state of Ohio, then for New Jersey and for Washington State, which was involved in one of the most extensive and costly pay equity adjustments that have taken place so far. "Now we have moved into county, city and private industry and to do more general work and family issues," says Revo-Cohen. "We set out to do a pay equity study and we realize it is only one of the issues hitting employers in terms of women and minorities."

They find, for example, that when women are paid less, it is often the result of subtleties such as who in a law firm is assigned to litigation and who is assigned to do research. Revo-Cohen tells of doing a training session on sexual harassment for one company whose managers and employees "came kicking and screaming. The session involved role playing. We got called back several more times because it got to the subtleties."

They say that fair play and fair pay for career women are less of a problem for younger men, who are finding that when their wives are being paid equitably, it takes some of the financial pressure off them. "They grew up in a generation where their self-worth wasn't totally related to their paycheck," says Revo-Cohen. "It may be more of a problem for men over forty. Younger men have had working mothers. Older men have more of a conflict, even if they think it is right. That's probably an unfair generalization, but it is what we observe."

"The good news for women is that they now have leverage to shop around," she says. The looming labor shortage is already pushing up women's wages because employers cannot fill jobs. She predicts this shift of power to employees will continue as the trend toward portable benefits makes it possible for people to jump from employer to employer without loss of pension benefits. "It's women and minorities who will benefit because they are 85 percent of the new work force. Of 25 million new workers between now and the year 2000, only 3.5 million will be native white males."

Their experience with Canadian newspapers and with pay equity studies in hospitals has shown them that Canadians are far ahead of us on the work and family issues that will be so important in the next decade. Already the public and private sectors are remedying pay inequities—which they say run around 5 percent of a business's yearly payroll.

"It's quite revolutionary," says Revo-Cohen. "It's so bold compared to what we've done here. It's very refreshing to go there. They are not so afraid of the business community's reaction. They are very concerned about quality-of-life issues. They have a better balance on work and family issues."

Employers and employees trying to sort these things out during the next decade can look north for some answers. It may be cold up there, but the reception Canadians are giving working women is much warmer than it is here.

5

Who's Minding the Children?

The Child Care Tragedy
JULY 17, 1987

On November 6, four detectives from the Miami Police Department went to a low-income housing complex where two children, a three-year-old and a four-year-old, were found dead in a clothes dryer. The children's mother had left them alone. She had already missed one day of work because her child care arrangements had temporarily fallen apart and she was afraid she would lose her job as a cafeteria worker if she did not go to work that day.

Marva Preston, one of the detectives who investigated the deaths, recently told a Senate subcommittee that her supervisors sent her to Washington "to express our concern for the urgent need of child care for working parents. . . . This investigation brought us face to face with a tragic reality, things some of us had only heard of."

The tragic reality is that children are dying because their parents cannot find adequate child care. A month later, in

93

Brooklyn, fire broke out in an unlicensed family day care center. The provider was looking after more children than state standards allowed and could not get them all to safety. A two-year-old and a four-year-old were killed.

We can now add two more names from this area to the list of children who are dead because of inadequate child care.

On July 2, twenty-month-old Antonio Simms of Bowie, Maryland, was found floating in a swimming pool at his baby-sitter's home. Police said the pool had a fence around it, and it wasn't clear how the toddler had gotten into the water.

The baby-sitter, according to police, was not licensed. Both of Antonio's parents were working. The sitter was watching a total of twelve children, ranging from infants to toddlers. A county ordinance requires people who care for five or more children at least twice a week to be licensed.

The child died at Children's Hospital.

In March, a two-year-old boy was killed and a two-year-old girl was injured when their baby-sitter, a New Carrollton, Maryland, woman, allegedly beat them after they had wet their clothing. The baby-sitter has been charged with first-degree murder. The baby-sitter was unlicensed. The parents of both children were working, according to police.

The death of one child was an accident, while the death of the other has resulted in the filing of a criminal charge. What both cases tragically demonstrate is the country's failure to produce a system of good, affordable, monitored day care in which children are flourishing, instead of perishing. In both cases, licensing requirements were not enforced. In the case of Antonio Simms, one person was responsible for caring for twelve children—a task that boggles the mind.

The move of parents, particularly mothers, out of the home and into the workforce has been steadily increasing, and with it, so has the need for child care. Since 1981, however, the limited public funding available for child care has been drastically reduced. Helen Blank, director of child care for the Children's Defense Fund, recently testified about the severity of the situation for low-income parents before the Senate Subcommittee on Children, Family, Drugs and Alcoholism. States with weakened economies, she said, have been hardest hit.

Georgia provides child care for only 8,000 out of 76,000 eligible children. It reduced its child care budget by 37 percent last year by lowering minimal standards for care and reducing the salaries of child care workers. Louisiana is cutting child care funding by 20 percent and already has 9,000 children on waiting lists. States are not enforcing health and safety protections. North Carolina, Blank said, allows one person to care for seven infants. Is there anyone who thinks he or she could give adequate care to seven infants at the same time?

What is happening is a national tragedy. Parents have to work to support their children. Single mothers, particularly, have almost no choice. In 1984, two-thirds of the single mothers and one-fifth of husbands in two-parent families could not earn enough to meet the yearly poverty income level for a family of four, according to Blank. With child care costs averaging $3,000 a year, these families desperately need subsidized care, but most can't get it.

To make matters worse, in 1984, 90 percent of private household child care workers and 58 percent of all other child care workers earned less than poverty-level wages. The children of many of America's working parents are being left alone, or they are being entrusted to a child care system that is subsidized by low wages, overcrowding, understaffing, lack of health and safety standards and nonenforcement of licensing standards.

And they are dying.

Getting Business to Care
JULY 29, 1987

This story begins three years ago when Representative Frank Wolf (R-Va.) sponsored a two-day conference for business leaders in his district to educate them about the various aspects of child care, ranging from tax breaks they could get for on-site day care to the impact of child care problems on the stability of the workforce.

Since then, Wolf and his office have been instrumental in getting businesses involved in opening a child care center in Crystal City and in getting three other centers off the ground.

The next center scheduled to open as a result of these efforts is the Tysons Corner Play and Learn Children's Center, a business- and parent-sponsored operation in Tysons Corner, Virginia, that could well become a model for solving some of the nation's child care problems. Already, it is a model of the business community operating at its very best.

The center is scheduled to open October 15 with the capacity to care for eighty-seven children, ranging from three months old to five years. It will be run by Play and Learn Corporate Child Care, a nonprofit organization founded by Cheri Sheridan, which also runs an office park–based child care center in Landover, Maryland, and the center in Crystal City, Virginia.

The first step in developing the center came when the Tysons Transportation Association (TYTRAN) did a study that established the need for child care in the Tysons Corner area. TYTRAN then raised $100,000 from twenty-one companies in start-up funds for the center. It will be located at Tysons Pond, a development of the Westerra Development Corporation, a California-based firm.

Sheridan says that start-up costs for centers run between $300,000 and $400,000—a prohibitive figure for parents trying to set something up alone. In return for donations, companies get priority in purchasing day care slots for their employes. "A $5,000 donation for a company is a drop in the bucket. Each year they pay an annual fee that allows them to re-up for a year. If they put money into the program, they can write it off as a business expense and they can get something back for it. When you're looking at a $400,000 start-up cost, we need the help from somewhere.

"The biggest obstacle you have to overcome is the image," said Sheridan. "We have to convince the developer that it can be done. When you say eighty-seven preschool-age children, they start to quake. You have to demonstrate that it can work. We took the developer and his wife over to our center in Landover."

In return for setting aside ground-floor space in the building, providing outdoor space for a playground and giving rent concessions to the center, the developer gets a certain number of slots at the center that he then can use as enticements to companies to rent space in his building.

"He can say this space comes with five reservations in the day care center," said Sheridan. "Office parks are changing. They are starting to look for amenities, and day care is a hot amenity right now."

The Tysons Corner slots have been purchased by the twenty-one companies, at a cost of $1,500 each. An advantage of the office park model, Sheridan points out, is that a small company has the same access to on-site care as a large company. Sheridan recalls that a meeting of Tysons Corner business executives after the original TYTRAN study showed the overwhelming need for day care in that area.

"Everyone just sat there and looked at each other," she said. "No one wanted to be the first to try it. Then Earle Williams, the president of BDM, said BDM will buy thirteen slots. A strange kind of muttering went through the room. This had some acceptance. He took the first step and the other companies followed. It was a domino effect."

Companies make the slots available to their employees, who then pay the tuition, which ranges from $81 a week to $110, depending on the age of the child. Infant care is the most expensive, and the hardest to find. Sheridan tells of people using messengers to bring applications for the infant care program to her office. "One woman is engaged. She said, 'We're planning on having a child in two years. Please put me on the 1989 waiting list.'"

"If it can work here, it can work in any other area of the country," said Wolf. "It's purely an educational process."

The people who have to be educated are the people who run companies, and those are the people Wolf was able to reach. He represents a district that has a 2.3 percent unemployment rate, and he could make the pitch that on-site day care is good for recruiting employees and keeping them. It's good for the children and for their parents. But the breakthrough came when business leaders in the county understood that it also is good for business.

Selling Child Care
JULY 31, 1987

Cheri Sheridan, founder and president of Play and Learn Corporate Child Care, has been involved with setting up corporate-sponsored child care for more than three years. Part of the way she makes her living is by persuading people who run companies that their workforce might be better off if the company gave them a hand with child care. And she's figured out a way to do it.

"I use quotes from other CEOs who say it is worth doing," she says. "You really have to be able to demonstrate that other people are doing it. There's a certain sense of wanting to stay current. Very often the conversation starts out with: 'We don't have a child care problem here.' Then you start asking questions about how many men they have, how many women, what's the average age. And slowly the light may dawn that day care may be an issue here."

Then she brings out a summary sheet that tells employers what day care can do for them. There is the 1982 survey of 204 companies asking why employers offered day care. The number-one reason was it helped with recruitment; the second reason was that it improved personnel relations; and, third, it stabilized the workforce.

Sheridan, who has been involved with setting up the corporate-sponsored child care center at Tysons Corner, helped conduct the survey of businesses there to determine what their problems were. "Their number-one problem was recruitment, and morale was second." Day care suddenly looked like a good fit.

Her summary sheet cites a 1984 survey of 178 companies about the impact that provision of child care had on their workforce: 90 percent of the companies said morale was positively affected, 85 percent said it had helped with recruitment, 83 percent said workers' satisfaction was improved, 65 percent said it reduced turnover and 53 percent said it reduced absenteeism.

Then there is the study of seven hundred employees of companies offering some sort of child care: 38 percent said the child care was a factor in their accepting the job, 69 percent said it was the reason they stayed with their employer and 63 percent said it created a more positive attitude toward their employer.

"At a Harvard seminar, they asked the CEOs what their workforce was composed of," says Sheridan. "Seventy percent said it was dad at work and mom at home with the kids at the playground. The reality of it is that less than 25 percent of American families conform to that model. There was a recent Department of Labor study that showed that two-thirds of women in the workforce are working to be self-sufficient: 25 percent are single, 12 percent are divorced, 5 percent are widowed, 4 percent are separated and 17 percent are married to men earning less than $15,000 a year. That sort of bypasses the comment that we wouldn't have this problem if women stayed at home.

"A lot of the decision makers have never had a day care problem in their life," says Sheridan. "One of my goals for PAL is to improve the quality of day care by making the CEOs aware."

PAL is presently operating two centers in large office complexes that offer the benefits of on-site day care without burdening companies with running a center. "Something that's been the most astonishing thing to me has been the impact on the kids," says Sheridan. Instead of having tears in the morning when a child is dropped off at a center, the children know their parents are nearby. "When the kid is hurt and needs stitches and Mom or Dad is there in two minutes it builds a sense of trust."

Sheridan has been working with children in day care for ten years and has seen a shift that disturbs her. "I've seen so many kids that are screwed up. When I first started, I worked with economically disadvantaged children. These kids had seen some pretty brutal things. The kids were withdrawing, they had temper tantrums and problems with aggressiveness. Now I'm working with more upscale children and you're seeing some of the same problems. You have a five-year-old who has had twelve different day care givers," and no consistency in his upbringing.

"It costs an average of $3,500 to put a child in day care and it costs $30,000 a year to put a teenager through court-committed rehabilitation. By the time a child is four years old, 50 percent of what he's going to be as an adult has already been established in things like problem-solving, curiosity, attitudes toward learning. It's a time when we really foul up by putting them in less than optimal care." And this should be of concern to communities and business leaders, as well as to parents, because this is the future workforce.

Money for Care, Not Carriers
NOVEMBER 20, 1987

For the first time in sixteen years, Congress is set to consider a major, comprehensive push to improve the nation's child care system. The initial price tag on this item is $2.5 billion, and you don't have to be a political savant to realize that getting that kind of money out of Congress for any new program is going to be an enormous struggle. That doesn't mean, however, that it can't be done.

The bill introduced yesterday would provide for federal funds to help states expand the variety and availability of child care services, and improve the licensing and training provisions for child care workers as well as help them set up and expand facilities. It also would provide new funding for subsidized child care services for low-income families. So far, the bill has 127 co-sponsors in the House and 23 in the Senate.

And it has the support of ninety-five national organizations, including trade unions, medical associations, women's groups and religious organizations. They have formed the Alliance for Better Childcare in a strategy to combine forces behind one major bill that might get the nation to address the crisis in child care.

Their timing might finally be right.

The last major federal effort to develop a comprehensive child care system was shot down by President Nixon in 1971, amid charges that it was too costly, would weaken families and lead to the "Sovietization" of American children.

Since then, American children of working parents haven't been "Sovietized." They have had to come home to empty houses, they've been left in unlicensed, crowded day care centers and they have simply been left home alone when impoverished parents have had to go to work. Children have been abused and killed in child care and they have died alone at home.

In Dade County, Florida, two preschool children were killed when they climbed into a clothes dryer after their mother left them alone because she could not stay home from work another day. The children had been on a waiting list for subsidized care that had 22,000 names on it. A year later, the list had grown to 26,400.

In the past year in the Washington area alone, seven children have died in child care facilities.

Since 1971, the country has engaged in a lively dialogue about child care at the same time that economic pressures have forced more and more mothers into the workforce. The time for debate about child care is over. America's working parents need help desperately. Whether they are single mothers on welfare, whether they are the working poor, whether they are the working middle class or the working upper-middle class, they are almost sure to be harshly affected at some point by a lack of reliable, affordable, safe child care. No other industrialized nation behaves so foolishly toward its working families and its young.

Part of the blame for this has to be put on the doorstep of working parents who have not used political muscle to improve the child care system. As Robert H. Bork's Supreme Court hearings dramatically illustrated, Congress does listen to the American people. But working parents don't have the time, money or sheer energy to lobby for money and programs that will help their families. They make do on sheer grit, while the defense industry prospers with high-paid lobbyists and gets the most fabulous peacetime accumulation of war toys ever.

Things may be changing. The Alliance for Better Childcare can be the vehicle through which American parents can tell Congress they want help with child care just as the Leadership Conference on Civil Rights provided the leadership in the fight against the Bork nomination.

Let no one in the debates about this bill get away with saying that the money is not there. The defense authorization bill for fiscal 1988 called for $3.9 billion for Star Wars, a defense system of infinitely more dubious value than a good child care system.

Further, the Navy last year asked for a couple of new Nimitz aircraft carriers that go for about $3.5 billion a pop. Add the trimmings—the airplanes that fly off them, the support and escort ships that are necessary to supply and protect them—and you are talking $18.5 billion for each carrier battle group.

Congress has authorized $700 million for the first stage of funding for this project. The commitment got made, in other words, for two carrier battle groups that will cost well over $30 billion.

The money is there, but the essential political question is what it is going to be used for. Now is the time for American working parents to speak out.

Child Care Meets Big Business
DECEMBER 2, 1987

Eileen Hooker was the Washington director of a Chicago-based health company when she had her second child three years ago.

She had been doing a lot of traveling and her life wasn't getting any less complicated. She kept coming across an ad for a child care center on Capitol Hill called Supertots.

Finally, she called the founder of the center, Lenore Riegel, and before long, they went into the child care business together. In October, they made history.

Supertots was acquired by Ogden-Allied Services Corporation, making it the first child care company in the nation to be acquired by a *Fortune* 500 company. Ogden-Allied Services provides building, aviation, leisure, industrial and human services. It has contracts for catering and fueling at airports, for providing housekeeping services at the World Trade Center in Manhattan and for managing stadiums and running such services as stadium maintenance, parking, security and food operations. The Capital Centre is one of its clients, as is the General Services Administration. It has a record of providing business services to both the public and private sectors. Through the acquisition of Supertots, Ogden-Allied has opened a new front.

"They didn't buy a big enterprise," says Hooker. "Basically they bought three people." How this came about is an instructive story about a business success, and it is also a story about how child care is evolving into a sophisticated service industry that is attractive to big business.

Before it was acquired, Supertots had developed its own niche in the child care business. Besides the center on Capitol Hill, it was running a center in Arlington and the center in the Federal Home Loan Bank of Dallas. The centers provide care for infants, younger children and before and after school for elementary school children. The centers emphasize well-trained staffs and parent involvement through parent committees.

Hooker and Riegel initially set up their business as the Center for Child Care Alternatives. It managed the Capitol Hill center and began branching out into other areas. It developed expertise in designing surveys to find out whether a company's employees need a child care center or are better off with another benefit. It also developed expertise in sorting through local zoning, licensing, health, safety and building codes so that any child care facility it helped a company set up would meet local requirements.

"One of the benefits to being small and gutsy is you are creative," says Hooker. The company went after and won the contract to set up and operate a child care center at the Federal Home Loan Bank Board here. "That was the first time that Public Law 99190 was used," says Hooker. That law, sponsored by Representative Frank R. Wolf (R-Va.), allows the federal government to provide start-up costs and to provide space rent-free for child care centers in federal buildings.

The partnership was expanded to three when the women's attorney put them together with Harry Fitzwater, a retired Navy captain who had worked for the National Aeronautics and Space Administration and retired from the CIA in 1985. Fitzwater brought extensive administrative experience to the firm. He also knew someone at Ogden and over lunch one day mentioned that he was involved "in this little company," says Hooker. "The guy said we've been thinking about this for years. At the time we were being courted by an English company. Harry said you've got to meet this guy."

The deal was struck on October 1. Since then, Hooker—who is the senior vice president for sales for the Supertots division—has gotten commitments to set up two more centers. The big difference since the acquisition, she says, is that as an Ogden executive she deals with the top official in a company who wants to know the cost of this new service Ogden is offering. Before, she'd find herself dealing with committees looking into child care. What used to take six months is now getting done in thirty days. Supertots employees, such as the child care workers at the Dallas center, are Ogden employees, and thus eligible for full company benefits. Ogden also takes care of the liability insurance for centers it opens and operates—a factor that has been a big sticking point for companies wanting to help their employees with on-site care.

The acquisition is another step toward child care becoming serious business. The need is certainly there. Think of the possibilities: five years from now, T. Boone Pickens could be engaged in a takeover battle for control of the Supertots division of Ogden-Allied.

Justice for Abused Children
JANUARY 19, 1990

You can't open a newspaper these days without seeing at least one story about a child being accosted, abducted, abused or killed. Some creep is preying on elementary school girls in Arlington. A Reston woman has just pleaded guilty to feeding her two-year-old son mouse poison. In Milwaukee, two men have been arrested in separate incidents and charged with sexually assaulting and killing two children.

All of those stories appeared in one day—Wednesday—of this week.

That same day's newspapers contained stories about the U.S. Supreme Court's decision to review two child abuse cases that were thrown out by lower courts on constitutional grounds that protected adult defendants. The court's decision to take up the cases has been widely hailed by children's advocates as a move that could clarify how far states can go in protecting child witnesses from the trauma of courtroom procedures and having to directly confront adults who are accused of abusing them.

At the very least, it is a move in the direction of reviewing the rules of a criminal justice system and social service system that are not doing nearly enough to protect the nation's children from malevolent adults—who more often than not are people they know and trust.

Experts point to the drug epidemic and to increased awareness and reporting as the two most significant factors for the increase in child abuse reports—and for the increase in the severity of the abuse. The numbers from the nonprofit National Committee for Prevention of Child Abuse in Chicago tell a story of unspeakable social savagery against the young: in 1989, there were 374,000 cases of sexual abuse reported to child protective services. From 1976 to 1980 and from 1981 to 1986, the number of sexual abuse reports increased by 210 percent. Leslie Mitchel, research associate at the committee, points out that these were periods of intense public interest and education about sexual abuse that arose out of several high-profile cases and the television movie *Something About Amelia*.

From 1985 to 1988, the number of children killed increased

36 percent. Last year, more than twelve hundred children died from abuse and neglect, said Mitchel. "There are still many cases that go unreported or misdiagnosed as an accident or as sudden infant death syndrome.

"What is overwhelming now is the drug situation. We are finding many women now who are addicted to crack or cocaine" who are using food money from the Women, Infant and Children program to buy drugs. "If the addiction can't be controlled, you ignore the other parts of your life and the children are suffering," Mitchel said.

Howard Davidson, director of the American Bar Association's Center on Children and the Law, says: "Criminal prosecutors not only see more cases, but they have been increasingly more complex and the abuse significantly more severe. One social reason for that has been drugs. There are innate parenting abilities and protective responses to the child that parents have, and the drugs basically interfere with all of that."

In 1985, the ABA offered guidelines for handling some of the complex legal and evidentiary problems that arise in court with child abuse cases, and it endorsed, in Davidson's words, "the cautious use of these kinds of reforms as long as the constitutional rights of defendants were protected."

Twenty-one states now allow closed-circuit testimony and twenty-seven allow videotaped testimony that lets a child testify without being in the presence of the accused. The court previously had ruled that testimony given behind a screen violates the constitutional clause allowing a person the right to confront an accuser. An additional twenty-two states allow for hearsay testimony—in which a third party can testify as to what a child told him or her about abuse.

"There's nothing new about having to accommodate special needs of witnesses," says Davidson. "We do it with non-English-speaking witnesses and victims that have handicaps that need to be accommodated."

Children, particularly those who are very young, are probably the most helpless, frightened, traumatized and inarticulate group of victims that ever enter a courtroom. Those are the very qualities that make them targets: people think they can get away with abusing children because all too often children can't or won't testify against them. Children aren't the only victims in all too many of these cases. So is the truth.

For the Supreme Court to review the rules is a welcome step in seeking a balance to the scales of justice. The numbers of abused and dead children—the awful stories we hear about daily—are heartbreaking testimony to the fact that those scales are now askew.

6

Schools—The American Kibbutz?

Noel Epstein, friend and colleague, was one of the best education writers in the country before he became publisher of *The Post's National Weekly*. He drew a huge round of applause at a convention of social studies teachers last year when he espoused his pet theory that schools are the new kibbutzes. He believes that we are asking schools to provide so many of the things that families used to do— child care, health care, counseling, drug education, AIDS education, music lessons, sex education, drivers education, you name it—but we insist on grading schools by the old standards of how well the youngsters do on standardized achievement tests. Grade schools, he urges, on all of the things they do and give them the tools and responsibility to do the job. The applause was thunderous. He had hit a nerve.

No institution has been touched more by the forward march of mothers out of the home and into the workforce. Three-quarters of the women with school-age children are now working. Enlightened school districts are grappling with how they can fill the gap between family and school, the two places children spend the

107

majority of their time. In Fairfax County, Virginia, where I live, new elementary schools routinely have two school-age child care rooms built into them. School districts are trying to sort out sex education curricula in the age of AIDS. Some are dispensing birth control information and some school-based clinics are dispensing birth control devices. Some are offering child care so that the teenage mothers in the student body can stay in school and graduate. Still others are offering life skills classes that teach youngsters how to balance checkbooks, a rite of passage parents used to attend to.

Values—what are they, how do you teach them without offending—is a recurring theme in the debates over what schools should be doing. So are questions about educational equity. Are we educating girls to be all they can be or are the schools stunting their growth by programming girls into antiquated, secondary roles? The length of the school year and the school day is emerging as yet another focus of controversy as America looks for ways to regain its competitive edge with countries that do a far better job of educating their future workers. Japanese children, for example, spend a lot more time in school than ours do, more hours a day, more days a year. It follows that they learn more, and this has not been lost in the latest round of educational reforms.

And, finally, nothing in my part of the country causes more consternation than the early-morning announcement on the radio that schools are closed because it is snowing. The Washington metropolitan area has the highest proportion of working women of any area in the country (we also have some of the most expensive housing costs, and most of us see a direct connection), and schools provide child care during the day. When they are closed, we are stranded. On the other hand, none of us want our children carted around icy back roads on school buses, a point made by numerous correspondents who took exception to a column I wrote when Fairfax closed schools for the umpteenth snow day in 1989. Some of us stay home when it snows and some of us take our children to work with us. It is not unusual now to see children inside government office buildings—or newspaper offices—when there is snow outside. There's a bit of a winter holiday spirit in the air when that happens, but it is also a lively reminder of how many of us depend on our schools to do what working mothers used to do.

It's a Boy's World
APRIL 23, 1986

Myra Sadker and David Sadker, professors of education at American University, have been researching the behavior of boys and girls in elementary and secondary schools, as well as universities, for the past six years. They found that in virtually every kind of teaching situation, rural or urban, segregated or integrated, male or female teachers, male students received more attention from their teachers and more helpful classroom instruction.

In the March issue of the *Phi Delta Kappan*, they argue that this unequal treatment of male and female students goes a long way toward explaining what happens to the two groups of students by the end of high school: little girls generally start out testing as well as or better than boys do on standardized tests—in reading, writing and math—but by the end of high school, boys are scoring ahead of girls on Scholastic Aptitude Tests and National Assessment of Educational Progress tests.

The Sadkers' first study, which was funded by the National Institute of Education, observed more than one hundred fourth-, sixth- and eighth-grade classrooms in Maryland, Virginia, Connecticut, Massachusetts and the District of Columbia.

The researchers found that male students were more likely to get "precise feedback." They also were significantly more likely to get praise, criticism and remedial help with an answer than were female students. The less-stimulating responses of "Uh-huh" and "Okay," which they found accounted for more than half of teachers' answers, were more evenly distributed between male and female students.

"Although our research has made the inequities of classroom interaction more apparent," the Sadkers write, "the reasons why males capture more and better teacher attention remain less clear. . . . The majority of classrooms in our study were sex-segregated, and teachers tended to gravitate to the boys' sections, where they spent more of their time and attention.

"Another explanation is that boys demand more attention. Our research shows that boys in elementary and secondary schools are eight times as likely as girls to call out and demand a teacher's attention. . . . When boys call out, teachers tend to accept their answers. When girls call out, teachers remediate their behavior and advise them to raise their hands. Boys are being trained to be assertive; girls are being trained to be passive—spectators relegated to the sidelines of classroom discussion."

The Sadkers subsequently received funding from the Fund for the Improvement of Postsecondary Education to see if the pattern persisted in colleges and, if so, to help college professors get rid of it. Forty-six professors in a wide variety of disciplines at American University volunteered for the project. Field research showed that males got significantly more attention. Subsequently, twenty-three professors volunteered to go through an educational program about inequity and "got rid of it," says David Sadker.

Numerous studies have found these differences in communications patterns persist into the workplace and may affect women's abilities to get ahead. "One of the ways that men dominate professional meetings is through interruptions," the Sadkers write. "When men and women talk with one another, almost all interruptions are by male speakers. Males interrupt females more frequently than they interrupt other males. Men also gain verbal dominance by answering questions that are not addressed to them." When women are interrupted, they write, they typically do not try to regain the floor.

The Sadkers are currently working with teachers and administrators at Groveton Elementary School in Fairfax and Jefferson Intermediate School in Arlington to help them eliminate bias in their interactions with students. Among the devices they use is a film that shows male students getting twice as much interaction with the teachers and four times as many rewards as the female students. It's not a film the Sadkers developed to illustrate their point; it's a model teacher training film.

The bias against female students is unconscious, says Sadker. "It goes undetected because we're living in a sea of bias. We've grown accustomed to hearing people with deeper voices monopolize conversations so it's more difficult to see it."

That doesn't change the effect. Educational reformers who are urging a return to "basics" ought to pay attention to what the Sadkers and others have found. The entire student population might start doing better on test scores and in school in general if the half that started out ahead weren't systematically sidelined.

Stress Among Children
JANUARY 14, 1987

James H. Humphrey is a professor emeritus at the University of Maryland, where he taught health and physical education for twenty-eight years before retiring in 1981. He has written more than forty books, including twenty-eight textbooks that are in wide use in colleges and universities; his last five books have dealt with stress, particularly stress in children. He believes there is a connection between substance abuse in young people and stress—just as there appears to be among adults.

He is the first to say that there is no proof of a connection, but he says that he and others who believe there is a connection are arguing that an effective defense against substance abuse in youngsters must tackle the causes and contributing causes of stress in children. "I have the strong feeling it's the pressure we put on children for grades and other things that provides for a pretty stressful situation for some children," says Humphrey. "Some parents are talking about getting him into college about the kindergarten age."

Compounding the pressure for grades, he says, are pressures to do well on tests and the whole problem of test anxiety that has surfaced in recent years. "Then you have all the family and home stress complications," he says. "It's just a vicious circle for a child. I wonder how they come out as well as they do.

"There's an area now that some people are studying: they call it competitive stress. Not only is it concerned with sports, but you have the Little League syndrome—parental pride in the parent, not parental pride in the child.

"I did a study eight or ten years ago with fifth- and sixth-grade children. One of the questions I asked was what worries you most in school. It came out in general terms that it was the competitive pressure they were put under. These were fifth and sixth graders recognizing this. Then you have an area called school behavior stress. We even have a level of reading called the frustration level. You go into a classroom and you find children trying to do some writing clutching their pencils under tension. This does nothing for their handwriting."

The way math is taught, he believes, often causes the same

reaction—hence the recent area of study known as "math anxiety."
"Mathematics should be as fun a subject as there is, but it's one
that causes great frustration for children with the emphasis being
on the right answer rather than on understanding the right concept.

"We do some negative things in schools that the teachers do.
A kid has ten items on a test and misses three. We put it in a
negative context: you missed three, rather than you got seven right.

"The old-fashioned spelling bee: that's one of the worst things
that was ever foisted on [students]. The kid that gets spelled out
first probably needs the spelling most. He's embarrassed."
Humphrey makes the point that similar competitive situations
show up in class sports activities—who is picked for the baseball
teams first, and who gets picked last.

Compounding the stresses of an overly competitive society, he
believes, are the "changes in female behavior," with both parents
working. "Children are not getting the support they should be
getting in the home. The child comes home and there's no one
there."

He contrasts that with the old-fashioned neighborhoods in
which kids came home from school and went out to play. "It gives
them a chance to let off some of the steam accumulated during the
school day. It's a feeling of camaraderie. They look forward to that.
There's a lot of things in the old neighborhood games that were so
important that we didn't know at the time.

"The theory that I have is that when we start treating for drugs
and so on, it's like the Band-Aid or aspirin approach. The biggest
thing is to spend time with them. Let them know you're there. And
treat them like citizens. To me, those are the most important
things.

"For many years, we talked about children having poor posture. Then we did a study on the causes. One of the most important
things we found was that children with poor posture were the ones
that had emotional problems. They were hunching up to themselves. My whole idea is that when something happens, there's a
reason for it."

If Humphrey's theory is correct, the drive to eradicate drugs
and alcohol abuse in schools will fall far short of the mark unless
the reasons for their appeal to youngsters are addressed. This is
infinitely tougher to do than nailing slogans to the bulletin board or
having assemblies about substance abuse. But what Humphrey is

saying simply makes common sense: it's a lot easier for kids to say no to drugs if there is no reason to say yes.

Something of Value
APRIL 10, 1987

One of the fun things that happen in the life of every working mother—c'mon, it happens at least once to all of us—is arriving home after a long day at the office, topped off by a shopping spree at the food store, to discover that in precisely one half hour back-to-school night is going to begin.

The notice was on the coffee table. It was also on my daughter's face. I said that I was really tired and she said that if all the parents in her class showed up, her class would get to see a movie. I don't know if this was her school principal's idea, or her teacher's idea—both of them are perfectly capable of coming up with this kind of leveraged buy-out. She said the purpose of the event was to meet the third-grade teachers. I asked her older brother who the third-grade teachers were. I figured there was a good chance I already knew them. He said he didn't know. If you have gone to every back-to-school night in the history of your children's lives, you don't skip your youngest one's lightly. In fact, you don't skip it at all.

The parents of the prospective third graders met in the library and we heard the teachers describe the course of study the children would be offered next year. The social studies teacher described how she would be teaching about different countries, and how we are all part of a community of nations.

That, I submit, is teaching a value in the schools.

A few minutes before, I had had a chat with the school's principal on another matter that also had to do with teaching values in the school. I have no idea what her politics or religious beliefs are. I have a pretty good idea what her morals and ethics are. We were in complete accord.

Which, in the whole debate about teaching values in the schools, is the fundamental point. Teaching cannot exist in a vacuum of beliefs, without a clear sense of what is right and wrong. The fundamentalists decry value-free education, but what they are really upset about is education that is not rooted in biblical beliefs. They, however, have drawn attention to a dismaying situation. Instance after instance keeps surfacing in which teachers have abdicated the task of teaching what is right and what is wrong. They raise the hypothetical question, throw it out to the classroom and then go out to lunch.

At the heart of the business of teaching values is "whose values?" Fundamentalist values based on literal interpretations of the Bible aren't going to cut it in public schools, but that doesn't mean that generally accepted values about what is right and wrong should not be taught. Love thy neighbor may be a Commandment, but it is also a rudimentary principle governing civilized communities. It is why we have everything from manners to traffic lights.

A recent *USA Today* editorial on this subject gave a shocking example of value-neutral "teaching." A high school student found a purse containing $1,000. She returned it to its owner. Fifteen of her fellow students decided she had been foolish. They went to their teacher for advice, and according to the editorial, "He demurred: 'If I come from the position of what is right and what is wrong, then I'm not their counselor.'"

This kind of stupefying extreme has driven the political right and left together on the need to return the teaching of values to the schools. A recent conference here sponsored by People for the American Way found a refreshing consensus on this point. People's founder Norman Lear put it one way: "For all our alarm, it is clear that the religious right is responding to a real hunger in our society . . . a deep-seated yearning for stable values."

Floretta D. McKenzie, District of Columbia school superintendent, said she began her career believing schools could not and should not teach values. "I have taken a 180-degree turn on that matter. I don't think we can separate out the teaching of values from public education."

Young people spend eight hours or so a day in school. They spend as much or more time with their teachers as with their parents. Schools are more than a source of knowledge: they are the first exposure that students have to life in a community of people. It is the first formal step they take into the community of nations. To become responsible citizens, they need to be taught and have reinforced in schools such values as honesty, integrity, compassion, responsibility, courtesy, respect for themselves and for others. There is nothing controversial about these values. They are essential to citizenship, and essential to the perpetuation of a civilized society.

Back-to-school night brought that home.

New Vision of Child Care
NOVEMBER 27, 1987

Edward F. Zigler, a Yale University psychologist who was one of the architects of the hugely successful Head Start program, has developed a proposal for a far-reaching new child care system that would be anchored in neighborhood schools.

His ideas are laid out in the December issue of *Psychology Today* in a cover story written by senior editor Robert J. Trotter.

"I want a solution that's going to last for the next 100 years and provide quality day care for everyone," says Zigler. "I think my plan can do that. I've been working on this problem for 30 years, and I can't come up with a better solution. It's simple, it's pragmatic, it's economically viable. These are not new ideas. They've been tried, and they work. I'm just putting it together in one system."

His proposals take into consideration some findings that have gained wide acceptance among child development experts. For example, there has emerged an agreement that an adult care-giver should not be responsible for more than three infants at any time. Educators and child development specialists are taking an increasingly vocal stand against formal schooling for four-year-olds. At that age, they are learning by playing, not by being taught at a school desk, yet the need for child care is so intense in some communities that schools are being pressured into all-day kindergarten for four-year-olds.

Zigler would put three- and four-year-olds in day care programs in the schools, but emphasize play and socialization. At five years of age, a child could proceed into half-day kindergarten—and then home for the rest of the day or into day care at the school, depending on the child's circumstances. Children six to twelve years old who have working parents would have access to before-

and after-school care at the school as well as care during school vacations.

In effect, Zigler is calling for a full-service school that would be the hub for a community's child care services. "I think we have to build a new school in America," he told the magazine. "We have to change the school system. We have to open schools earlier in the morning, keep them open later in the afternoon and during summer."

Many communities that have school-age child care programs already do this, with so much success that many have long waiting lists. Zigler would also give the schools a large role to play in developing infant care, usually the most expensive and difficult care for working parents to find. More than half of the infants of working parents are cared for by family day care providers in their homes or are cared for in centers.

Quality, Zigler points out, is often erratic and uneven, and he cites examples of children being strapped to chairs and being cared for by people so senile they cannot even care for themselves. The children from affluent families have the best shot at getting the more expensive care, while it is the children of impoverished families who are likely to be in undesirable day care situations because that is all their parents can afford. "They are already vulnerable, or at risk, because they come from single-parent homes or from families with little money, a lot of deprivation and poor health care," Zigler says. "And they are being placed at even greater risk by being put into very inadequate child care settings. We are talking about hundreds of thousands, if not millions, of children."

He proposes using the schools as resource centers to help parents find care in their neighborhoods, to provide training for day care workers, and to ensure that the network of family day care homes in the area meets licensing standards.

Zigler worked with Representative John Brademas (D-Ind.) and Senator Walter Mondale (D-Minn.) in making the Child Development Act of 1971, which President Nixon vetoed after a right-wing campaign depicted it as "antifamily."

Zigler proposes financing his current child care proposal by charging fees to those who can pay and by using federal subsidies for those who cannot. He also suggests slight increases in local taxes to support the expanded role of the schools.

For starters, he suggests that the federal government spend $120 million to set up a pilot program of sixty full-service schools, at least one in each state. These models could be replicated once they are working.

Zigler describes his proposal as "a new vision," which it surely is. But he makes the point that between fall 1964 and summer 1965 this country enrolled 560,000 children in Head Start. As he told the magazine: "We can do the same with day care." If the will is there.

Principal as Publisher
MAY 15, 1988

Tensions between high school newspapers and high school principals probably go back to the very first time that a high school editor attempted to suggest that Central High, U.S.A., was not the very best high school ever to exist on the face of the earth.

Unfortunately for high school newspapers, most of them exist at the mercy of the school boards that fund them just as most grown-up newspapers exist at the mercy of the publishers who own them. First Amendment or not, we all live with somebody looking over our shoulders.

There are controls that exist because of privacy and fairness standards, controls that exist because of editors' taste and controls that are exerted by owners who can throw out stories, dictate what they want covered, fire columnists and engage in all manner of equally antisocial behavior without so much as a by-your-leave.

Most tensions that surface during the production of newspapers are resolved without the parties' making a federal case out of it. It is a sign of the times that the tensions between high school principals and the high school press have landed, not in the principal's office with a bunch of parents and kids, but in the Supreme Court with a bunch of lawyers and the First Amendment.

They made a federal case out of it, and they lost. Moreover, the language of Wednesday's ruling is so broad that it can hereinafter be used to justify all manner of censorship actions against high school newspapers that might have previously given the most heavy-handed principal pause.

It is clear from the opinion that this is a case that never should have been brought. It arose out of a series of unusual circumstances, beginning with the fact that the adviser to the Journalism II class at Hazelwood East, in St. Louis County, left shortly before the last edition of that year's newspaper was going to press. Thus, on May 10, 1983, the stand-in adviser delivered page proofs of the May 13 issue to the principal for review—a standard practice—and the principal, Robert Eugene Reynolds, found two articles that, to use the parlance of editors everywhere, he had problems with.

And well he should have.

One of the articles discussed the experiences of three students who had become pregnant. Their names were changed, but Reynolds was concerned they might still be identifiable. He also was concerned that the article contained references to birth control and sex that might be inappropriate for the younger students. These are questions of privacy and taste that are legitimate concerns of anyone in charge of a newspaper.

The second article dealt with the impact of divorce on children and quoted a student as saying her father "wasn't spending enough time with my mom, my sister and I" before the divorce, that he was "always out of town on business or out late playing cards with the guys," and "always argued about everything" with her mother. Reynolds thought the parents ought to have a chance to respond to the comments or to consent to their publication. He probably saved the school board a fortune with that call.

What he did not know was that the stand-in adviser had already deleted the girl's name from the final version of the article.

Reynolds believed that there was not time to make the necessary changes and still do the scheduled press run. He ordered the adviser to drop the two pages that contained the stories. Reynolds's superiors concurred. Three student editors then sued, claiming that their First Amendment rights had been violated.

The Court ruled that the paper was essentially a tool for teaching and that the school authorities were acting as publishers. Not incidentally, the 5-to-3 ruling noted that the two dropped pages contained articles on controversial topics such as teenage marriage and runaways to which the principal had not objected.

The immediate reaction to the Court's ruling has been to focus on a perceived chilling effect on the ability of high school newspapers to tackle controversial topics. Indeed, Justice Byron White, writing for the majority, offered school systems an enormously flexible framework for censorship. "A school," he wrote, "need not tolerate student speech that is inconsistent with its educational mission."

Unfortunately, when you take a case to court, you can come back with a lot less than you walked in with. That's what happened to the student editors and, as a result, to student editors across the country. In this case, however, the students got a lesson in reality, which is that with freedom goes responsibility and that goes for the First Amendment.

Children Send Bush Hard-Hitting Advice
JANUARY 20, 1989

Some of the voters who will be inaugurating a president on January 20, 2001, have already written letters to President-elect George Bush, telling him what they want him to do. Above all, these future voters want him to do something about the homeless.

These young people are in Alma Baylor's fourth-grade class at Kent Gardens School in McLean, Virginia. Baylor, the first black teacher in an all-white Norfolk school in 1965, says she believes in teaching her students about values and to care about the realities of the world around them.

"I would like it if you tried to get rid of drugs and help people who have taken them," wrote Dean Elliott. "I would like it if you would try to give more care to the homeless so there wouldn't be any more people on the street."

"Put all homeless children in schools and homes," wrote Lauren Reigle, who also wants Bush to get rid "of all nuclear weapons," and to stop pollution.

"I want you to protect our country," wrote Suzanne Eisner. "I want people to have freedom for different religions. A few months ago, my temple got vandalized. I am mad that people still do these things in America. I heard that some crazy people burned a cross on someone's lawn. Please help us feel safe."

Yu-Chan Moon also asked Bush this week to stop drug dealing and to give homes to the homeless. "I think we should also save lives, stop crimes, stop pollution, give jobs to the people and give advice to people. . . . I hope everybody will like you."

"I think that the space program is very interesting," wrote Matt Rorie, but he wants that money used for the homeless. "Space can wait, the homeless can't."

"To help stop pollution, we could stop producing cars and use horses," suggested Sally Votaw. "As for housing the homeless, we could let them sleep in subway stations and places such as that until we can build more shelters."

Kristina Lomperis listed the most important problems to be drug smuggling, sheltering the homeless and "child/teen-ager/ adult abuse."

Eleanor B. Pearson cited the greenhouse effect and explained its causes. "May I recommend that we reduce the cutting down of trees and that we reduce the burning of petroleum."

"Will you stop the drug sellers and cigarette sellers?" wrote Eric Hamilton. "Will you help us make peace? Will you help the black Americans?"

Ali Mostafavi wants police officers to be paid better "because they are risking their lives so our country won't have a lot of crimes."

"I would like you to protect the endangered species," wrote Kathleen Deso. "I would like it very much if you tried to make better laws for black people."

"You should be concerned about cleaning up the environment, taking care of the homeless, providing more jobs for people who aren't working, stopping crimes against people and animals and getting rid of drugs," wrote Yoo Jeong Lee.

"I think that something more should be done about blacks' rights, women's rights and nuclear weapons," wrote Jennifer Michael, who signed her letter "Your friend so far."

Rohini Singh put "being more fair to blacks" on her list of concerns, and Nicholas Gil wants to "give more black people jobs."

"We could give them [the homeless] jobs," David Ragsdale suggested. "Nothing too hard, and then give them different, higher-paying jobs as they get better at their jobs and learn more."

"I want you to do a lot of stuff that will make America perfect" was Jimmy Triplett's opening.

"Another thing I would like is for guns to be banned so that a lot of people may not get hurt and shot," wrote Alejandra Delgado.

Julie Smith agreed. "I think there should be more gun control," she wrote. "Today five children were shot and killed and many others were wounded in an elementary school in California. This would never have happened if the man who had killed them had not had a gun. Please work for gun control."

"I'm Katherine Mann. I'm nine years old," wrote my favorite correspondent. She wants Bush to "help stop drugs, stop crimes, help people get along better, house the homeless, and get jobs for unemployed people. There has been a lot of violence going on and a lot of people don't like it. Schools (mostly elementary) are beginning to be dangerous places because there have been shootings and bombings in some schools. I'm worried and scared about all of these things and I want it to stop."

Bush, who wants to be known as the education president, has some wonderful young people coming along who are looking to him with high expectations. These future voters care about the environment, the homeless in our midst and civil rights. Thanks to teachers like Alma Baylor, they are learning about values.

Dusting of Snow Sends Chills Up Spines of School
FEBRUARY 8, 1989

My children attend Fairfax County schools in Virginia, which means that they have every reason to hope that the moment a snowflake appears on the satellite weather map, their schools will either open late or not at all. Fairfax County has firmly established itself as a leader in school closings.

Several weeks ago, the first snow of the new year blanketed the area, which is to say there was a light dusting of snow. By dawn's early light, Fairfax had delayed the opening of school for two hours. So had many other jurisdictions. This brought great joy to my home, where the resident thirteen-year-old heard the news on the radio and went through the house like the town crier. He then went back to bed for a couple of hours of extra sleep— something that can do wonders for any adolescent's attitude toward life.

My daughter the nine-year-old, who can sleep in with considerable enthusiasm, looked at the snow outside and promptly returned to sleep as well. She was to leave the house at 10:10 a.m. By the time her brother left at 9:25, some serious snow was falling, which is to say the weather forecast was calling for an inch or two of accumulation. My daughter started predicting that the schools would soon close. When you live in Fairfax and look out the window and can actually see some serious snowflakes falling, that's a good bet.

I, however, explained that that was highly unlikely because the high school and intermediate students were already in school and the county would not keep some schools in session while others were canceled. Five minutes later, the radio announcer came on with the news that Fairfax County had canceled all school and high school and junior high school students were en route home. This was 10:00 a.m. As it turned out, my son never even got off his bus, which simply turned around at the school and brought the children home.

I was still home because I had an elementary school child who was still home. How many working parents, however, had not had the foresight to arrange their family that way and were already at work when their youngsters were being returned home from school? How many parents had to leave work and go home? How many had to take vacation time to stay home, and how many children ended up staying home alone that day?

It's unfair, of course, to expect school officials to know exactly how much snow is going to accumulate. They've proved time and again they are not divine. Suffice it to say, however, that when the snow stopped in early afternoon, National Airport reported one inch of accumulation and Dulles three inches. We're not even talking a mini-blizzard here, yet school officials in most jurisdictions sent children home by bus in the snow in the middle of the morning when they could have waited a few hours and sent them home in the sunshine in midafternoon. And the kids would have had a day in school, instead of a day at the mall.

Yesterday dawned gray and icy, and I delivered a 6:30 wakeup call to my son. A few minutes later, the resident town crier went through the house heralding the fact that schools would open two hours late. At 8:30, he went through the house again, heralding the news that schools were closed.

This provoked considerable dismay in the resident adult, who, like most adults paying outrageous taxes and mortgages for the privilege of living in Fairfax County, has to work. Fortunately, my children are old enough to make plans to get together with friends who have older siblings staying home with them. But what happened yesterday to all the other working parents who had their child care routine fall apart on them at 8:30 a.m. because some roads might still be a little icy?

Fairfax and Fauquier were the only jurisdictions to close yesterday. If the roads were icy in Fairfax in the very early morning, they weren't icy for long. By midday, the sun was out. The children got an unexpected day off and the county's working parents got yet another kick in their child care arrangements from a school system that is utterly terrified by a little bit of bad weather. When conditions get a little rough—when getting to school or work might require a little discomfort, grit and determination—the school system's response is to close the schools.

This area has the highest percentage of working mothers of any metropolitan area in the country. When officials close the schools because of a little bad weather, and that includes hot spells, it causes enormous inconvenience to working parents and their employers—something the local school systems have yet to grasp. Quite apart from that, however, the hasty retreat from a little adversity is a dreadful example to set for the children.

Saving America's Future
FEBRUARY 17, 1989

The National Governors Association, under its chairman, Virginia governor Gerald L. Baliles, has issued the first of six task force reports on how America can compete successfully in the new global economy. Appropriately, this first report is on the sorry state of the country's children—and what states can do to improve their health and productivity.

"These children are our principal asset," writes Baliles in his overview of the report. "If we are to develop a new agenda for America and its role in the world, we must begin by investing in America's children—to ensure their future and our own. For we cannot compete beyond our borders unless we become competitive within our borders."

Arkansas governor Bill Clinton, chairman of the association's task force on children, put our present situation bluntly: "Our children are behind in important educational skills, and too many are affected by the related problems of poverty and insufficient health care." States, he argues, are particularly well positioned to develop a comprehensive approach to child development that is rooted in prevention—such as the prenatal care programs that give babies born to low-income mothers a healthier start in life.

The report paints a grim picture of wasted resources and the abysmal failure of our educational system to retain students through high school and to graduate students who can compete with the youth of our trading partners. Our teenage pregnancy rate is higher than that of twenty-nine out of thirty developed countries—and about three times as high as Japan's. Our white infant mortality rate is nearly twice that of Finland, Japan and Sweden, and our black infant mortality rate is nearly twice that, and on par with the infant mortality rate in Costa Rica, Poland and Portugal. We have a greater percentage of children living in poverty than Australia, Canada, West Germany, Norway, Sweden, Switzerland and the United Kingdom.

The report cites results of international science tests administered to children of thirteen industrialized countries by the International Association for Evaluation of Educational Achievement. American twelfth graders scored last in biology, eleventh in chemistry and ninth in physics. They scored tenth in geometry, twelfth in algebra and last in calculus. And the report cites a study done in a major American city that found that 45 percent of the high school seniors could not identify the United States on an unlabeled world map.

One clue about why American students fare so poorly compared with students in other countries lies in an arresting graph developed by the Illinois governor's Office of Planning. It shows the number of school days per year in selected countries. In Japan, students attend school 243 days a year. In the United States, they attend an average of 180 days a year. Japanese youngsters attend school two months more each year than their American counterparts.

While the governors' report does not address specifically the striking difference in school attendance, this is one area that ought to be examined. Adults who have gone through public high schools know full well that history courses barely have time to get into the twentieth century, for example. With the explosion of knowledge in the sciences, these courses must be similarly short-circuited. What is the case for the short school year? America is no longer an agrarian nation in which youngsters are needed for planting and harvesting of crops. What is the point of long summer vacations for schoolchildren in a society in which a parent is frequently not even home to care for them? Why not lengthen the school year by a month or so? Over the course of twelve years of school, that would give a child the equivalent of one full additional year of education.

About 25 percent of young people currently drop out of school before completing their senior year. The governors' association report makes several recommendations for improving the middle schools so that they address "the special needs of young teen-agers." These include certification and training requirements for middle school teachers, "a requirement that does not generally exist." It also recommends adopting middle school structures that will make it easier for the youngsters to make the transition from childhood and elementary school to the confusions of adolescence and high school.

America's youth is very much in the news these days, and there is a growing understanding that too many children are being consigned to the unproductive, hopeless fringes of society. The governors' association report charts a course of action that governors and states can take to invest in the nation's children and to reverse the trend in which far too many young people's futures have been squandered.

Running the Schools with the People in Mind
JUNE 7, 1989

My vote for school superintendent of the year goes to Robert R. Spillane, the head of the Fairfax County schools, who has made a bold—and long overdue—move toward recognizing that nearly three-quarters of the women who live in Fairfax County work outside the home.

At a four-day retreat with School Board members last week, Spillane proposed that the county abandon its outdated practice of closing elementary schools two hours early on Monday afternoons. That promptly provoked the comment from Walter J. Mika, Jr., president of the Fairfax Education Association, that Spillane was "off the deep end." The FEA represents the majority of the county's 4,500 elementary school teachers and you can tell from the opening bell that its discussion of Spillane's proposal is going to be on a high plane.

What's at stake here is time. The elementary school teachers argue that they need the two hours a week for planning and conferences. Parents, particularly those in single-parent households and in two-income households, argue that the short school day on Monday creates yet another child care problem for them. Parents who work early shifts at a number of government agencies can manage to get home around 3:30 p.m., the time when buses deposit most elementary school children at their homes. It is another matter to get home at 1:00 or 1:30.

The history of America's modern child care crisis is riddled with incidents in which latchkey children have seriously injured themselves. Research on latchkey children has repeatedly found them to be more fearful and insecure, as well as more vulnerable to sibling abuse, than children who come home to an adult.

Against this dismaying backdrop, parents who must leave children alone after school try, at the very least, to minimize the number of hours that they do so. Over the years, they have repeatedly complained about the early Monday closings in Fairfax, which were implemented in the early 1970s when 43 percent of women in Fairfax held jobs outside the home. Janice Hamilton Outtz, a specialist on demographics of working women in Washington, estimates that more than 70 percent of women in Fairfax now work outside the home.

Sam Sava, executive director of the National Association of Elementary School Principals, is all in favor of Spillane's move to do away with short Mondays. "The trend is not only to have school systems serve full days but many of our school systems are beginning to establish after-school study centers," he says. "So rather than have students go home to an empty house, they attend after-school study centers and someone is there to help them with reading and math and so on."

Sava said his association surveyed elementary school principals recently to find out what they are doing to "meet the major social changes that have been taking place in our society and how best to organize the schools to help the children who really are the victims when changes aren't made." He said that 73 percent of the principals who responded to the survey felt that schools should take on extra responsibilities such as providing care for school-age children and enrolling children at an earlier age. "If they had appropriate financial resources, they would move in this direction," says Sava.

He says that schools must respond not only to the changing academic needs of children, but also in some instances to their changing custodial needs. As an example, he says that many principals have begun extending the school year and have added summer school and summer camp programs. All of this takes money, says Sava, and communities need to recognize what has happened and to provide the necessary resources.

Sava does not underestimate the importance of planning periods, but he points out that other school systems use "substitutes or aides that provide teachers free time for planning purposes rather than closing school." Most area school systems do not routinely close for this.

Rather than pitting parents against teachers, as the FEA appears poised to do, Spillane would do well to frame this move in a context all too often lost in educational debates: namely, that school systems exist to meet the needs of children, and not, as Sava puts it, "to maintain bureaucracies."

"In turn," says Sava, "by recognizing the needs of parents, you will not only provide better educational services to children, but the parents will recognize you are trying to help them and they in turn will support the schools. By providing alternative methods of staff planning, you'll have an educational community system that's best for all."

Spillane is trying to provide just that, and he deserves parents' and teachers' support.

To Barnard and Beyond
NOVEMBER 8, 1989

This is a time of year when many young women are making a decision about where to go to college, and a good many of them will at least give a thought to attending a women's college. What follows is an unabashed endorsement of such schools.

I am well aware of the fact that many students choose their college after taking the measure of various academic departments, food plans and dormitories, and then making the final decision on the basis of some fetching student seen crossing the quad—whom they will never set eyes on again.

I never even saw the college I attended before I went there. It was the college my mother had gone to and the college my sister had gone to. And when I endorse women's colleges, it is the college I think of first. Unlike some other women's colleges, Barnard has struggled hard to maintain its autonomy from Columbia University. It still has its own faculty and degree requirements. It is an environment where women come first.

This year it celebrates its centennial with a series of events, including a dinner last week in Washington, which has one of the largest alumnae groups outside of New York. Ellen V. Futter, the forty-year-old alumna who is president of the college, was in town for the dinner and in an interview she talked about what a women's college offers.

"I don't think we so much nurture," she said. "We don't coddle. We take people seriously and we respect them. And in that way we empower them.

"The classroom climate is still a chilly one for women in an awful lot of places in American higher education. In subtle and not so subtle ways, it makes a difference—like not calling on them in class, not spending as much office time with women students, not encouraging them to go into nontraditional fields. The investments made in women at a lot of institutions are modest. The result is women don't go on in the same way the Barnard graduate does. The full force of Barnard as an institution is to encourage women to go on and be what they can. We start with women who are among the brightest in the country and you put those two things together and you get these hugely impressive outcomes."

The outcomes come in stars and in numbers: graduates include Margaret Mead; Jeane Kirkpatrick; Joan Rivers; Twyla Tharp; Suzanne Vega; Mary Gordon; Francine du Plessix Gray; Erica Jong; Susan Stamberg; Judge Judith S. Kaye, the highest-ranking woman in the New York courts; and Jacqueline K. Barton, the first woman to win the National Science Foundation's Alan T.

Waterman award for the most promising scientist under the age of thirty-five.

A recent survey by Franklin and Marshall College found that Barnard ranked second in the country among small, private four-year colleges in the raw numbers of graduates who went on to get Ph.D.'s. Oberlin, which is coeducational, was first. Barnard was followed by Smith, Wellesley and Swarthmore. "It's not just Ph.D.'s who are stars," Futter said. "It's women in fields that often are not receptive to them. International relations, economics. Women in science typically will come from a place like Barnard. Our faculty is roughly 50 percent women. When taking chemistry, the student is likely to have a woman chemistry professor. That role model remains important to them."

Barnard has responded to the increasing importance of math for professional women by initiating a requirement in quantitative reasoning. "They develop a basic numerical competence," Futter said. "It's empowering and ultimately that's what Barnard is all about."

Futter, a lawyer and mother of two young children, said students are still worried about the issues that so profoundly troubled their predecessors. "They know they can go on if they work hard in any field of their choosing. But there are also some realities. They do very well at the entry level and are mired in the middle. They sort of know that their mothers, aunts, friends of their mothers have gone on professionally. But they can see it is daunting. I talk a lot with them, and it is still my most disappointing answer. They say, what's the formula? I tell them there is no formula.

"If we can be as women and as men and women more generous of spirit in understanding that there are different routes from here to there, and if our institutions could respond to that, we'd be more flexible. There'd be more opportunity for leave, not just for child care, but leave to care for aged parents, for divorce, for intellectual refreshment. If we could get to a point where there's not a right or wrong, and you even get to change your mind about what's right for you, this will be very liberating for all of us, especially men. Women are already thinking this way."

7

Women and Politics

Two-thirds of the fathers in a study done in the early eighties were ordered to pay less in child support than they spent on their monthly car payments. By the time Congress tackled the disgraceful state of child support enforcement in 1983, 65 percent of the women with children with an absent father were raising the children without any money from the fathers. Only 59 percent of these women even had court-ordered awards. Worse, within a few months after these awards were ordered, most fathers had fallen behind. One study found that fewer than 10 percent were fulfilling their total obligations voluntarily.

Barbara Kennelly, a Democratic congresswoman from Connecticut, manipulated the seniority-obsessed House to get an assignment to the all-powerful Ways and Means Committee early in her first term. She was the first woman ever appointed to that committee, which is one of the most pivotal in determining how tax dollars are raised and spent. She used her position to push for legislation that would overhaul the nation's child support enforcement. She made that her issue, and it is safe to say that it never would have gotten the priority handling she gave it from a man on Ways and Means. After all, it never had before she got on the committee. As a result of her rock-solid commitment, other women and men in Congress got behind the move to force absent fathers to obey court orders and start supporting their children. Since the landmark child support enforcement amendments of 1984, billions have been collected and turned over to female-headed households, helping them escape welfare rolls in some cases and significantly improving the standards of living of thousands of others. It was the Republican women in Congress who joined forces with Margaret Heckler, Ronald Reagan's first secretary of health and human services, to persuade the administration to make the new child support collection mechanisms available to all single parents, not just to those who were on welfare. Thus single working mothers finally got some help from the courts and social service agencies for doing something they had been unable to do by themselves, namely, collect child support so that their families were not driven into poverty by divorce. Women in Congress, and the men who became their allies, along with leaders of women's organizations, were able to use the political process to vastly improve the child support system that had previously allowed millions of men to walk out of their families without ever looking, or paying, back.

But reform in child support enforcement was one of all too few victories that women and families wrung out of Congress. Federal legislation to develop safe, affordable child care has languished. So have bills to set a minimum federal standard for parental and medical leave. "There just aren't enough of us," Kennelly said one night at a dinner to raise money for the Women's Campaign Fund.

Less than 5 percent of the members of Congress are women. The incumbency rate for members of Congress is higher than it was for the Politburo. Conservatives are starting a drive to limit the number of terms that members can serve, and this is something that women's organizations should support. It may be the only way to break the iron grip that the special interests have on Congress and to end the lifetime tenures that men who control most of the seats have as well.

Sarah Harder, the former president of the American Association of University Women, calls these family issues "kitchen table issues." These are the kinds of things women try to sort out while they are at the table, more often than not with the telephone in hand talking to a sibling or mate. Who is going to take what shift caring for Grandma? Who is going to pick up the heir apparent at the day care center? Who can take time off from work to care for the elderly relative who has been discharged—all too soon—from the hospital?

Advocates of family assistance programs inevitably face the question of how the country could pay for them. Harder tartly observes that this question isn't asked about putting up $150 billion to $300 billion to bail out the savings and loan industry. At a press conference last year, she put the problem in terms of our international competitiveness. "The very countries that are whipping us are the countries that have had the policies we are talking about for forty years. It is very clear that it pays off."

Neither the Republican nor Democratic parties have covered themselves with glory in responding to the changing needs and work patterns of American families. Marge Roukema, the feisty probusiness Republican congresswoman from New Jersey, has become one of the most outspoken supporters of progressive family policies on Capitol Hill. "Child care has become fashionable to discuss," she told me in an interview, "but there are other issues not being firmly addressed, particularly by my party. We Republicans have talked loud and long about family values, but when it means going beyond lip service, we are very slow to promote issues that are fundamental to families, particularly to two-worker families today.

"Two workers are the norm today. They are not getting rich, they're getting by. Who takes care of the children or Grandpa, who gets out of the hospital sicker and quicker? Women and men should not be losing their jobs because of a seriously ill child or seriously ill parent. They need a short leave time to take care of a critical situation.

"I had initially been very skeptical on this matter until I began to look at it and realized it was a fundamental, bedrock issue. It is not depriving business of their right to bargain. It is a minimum labor standard, just as we have set a whole host of minimum standards as society has changed."

As women in Congress have gained seniority, they have made their marks. Patricia Schroeder, a Democrat from Colorado and dean of the women legislators, made a serious run at the presidency in 1988. As a member of the House Armed Services Committee, she was able to make her points trenchantly when she accused the American military establishment of having a serious case of "missile envy." It was she who coined the term "Teflon presidency," which turned out to be the only derogatory term the Democrats were ever able to stick Ronald Reagan with. She and the other women on the Hill have taken the lead in trying to promote family policies, and in trying to preserve the gains that women made over the last two decades.

It is women elected officials in the statehouses who are protective of women's rights to reproductive freedom. Women in Congress are leading the fight for reproductive rights there. They are leading the fight to preserve the civil rights gains women have made in education and in the workforce. They are holding the line against a Supreme Court that is systematically pulling apart the fabric of civil rights protections for women and minorities that has been erected over the past twenty-five years.

These women are living proof that women voters must exercise their own enlightened self-interest by electing more and more women to public office. Women politicians will work to help women, just as male politicians have worked to help men. But the women elected officials are the first to say that there aren't enough of them to do the job. They need help. They need more women in the House, the Senate and in the state legislatures. Women have had the vote for nearly seventy years. They are just beginning to use it.

On Forgetting to Remember
MAY 27, 1987

Remember the Ladies, Abigail Adams wrote her husband, John, on the eve of the Declaration of Independence. He was serving in the Continental Congress meeting in Philadelphia and she was managing the farm and household back in Massachusetts. "Remember," she wrote, "all Men would be tyrants if they could. If particular care and attention is not paid to the Ladies we are determined to foment a Rebellion, and will not hold ourselves bound by any Laws in which we have no voice, or Representation."

And she urged the men who wished to be happy to willingly "give up the harsh title of Master for the more tender and endearing one of Friend."

John Adams was not exactly what today we would call supportive. He wrote back that her ideas made him laugh. "Depend upon it, we know better than to repeal our Masculine system. Altho they are in full Force, you know they are little more than Theory. We dare not exert our Power in its full Latitude. We are obliged to go fair, and softly, and in Practice you know We are the subjects. We have only the Name of Masters, and rather than give up this, which would completely subject Us to the Despotism of the Petticoat, I hope General Washington, and all our brave Heroes would fight."

This now famous exchange tells the story of the political, legal and economic dependency of women at the time of the founding of the Republic. The founders, seeking freedom from those very bonds themselves, could not and did not extend those freedoms to women or slaves.

As part of the nation's celebration of the two hundredth anniversary of the Constitution, the Smithsonian Institution recently sponsored an international symposium on "Constitutional Roots, Rights and Responsibilities." Among the papers delivered was one by Sylvia Law, a professor of law at New York University, in which she looked at "The Founders on Families."

Lawyers, public policy makers and judges attempt to resolve modern legal controversies by looking back to the intent of the founders, she said. But when these matters involve conflicting visions of family and the role of women, looking at the original intent does not provide us with modern answers. The founders' "dominant conceptions of families denied the liberty, equality and even personhood of women," Law argues. "Today there is broad consensus, across a moral and political spectrum, that women are full human beings, entitled to the panoply of classic liberal rights that our Revolution and Constitution sought to secure to white men. The challenge today is to envision constitutional and cultural arrangements that read the words, 'We the People,' quite literally, even though that was not originally intended."

One of her most stunning findings is that there was no mention of women and families in the formal debates, the *Federalist Papers* and various recorded discussions leading to the ratification of the Constitution. Women were assistants and had no place—legal, political or economic—in their own right. Even though the right to vote was attached to owning property, it did not extend to unmarried women who owned property.

During the Revolution, women assumed the responsibilities for homes and families and found it difficult to return to their wholly subservient role after the men came marching home. Women had run boycotts of British goods and had attacked merchants who stocked them. Women had raised funds for the army. Many continued to be politicized after the war was over. Courts began to recognize their property interests and the rights some women had obtained through prenuptial contracts. Marriage came to be thought of as a means to happiness, not merely a means to procreate.

And then an interesting twist occurred that continues with us to this day. Writes Law: "Women's function was redirected to the vital Republican enterprise of inculcating qualities of virtue in the young. Our Founders assumed that the democracy could work only if citizens were 'virtuous' in their public and private lives." They founded, she writes, "the Republican Mother," redirecting women's roles to educating the future citizenry—giving women a momentous role in the future of the young Republic—and neatly avoiding their political participation.

As we honor the two hundredth birthday of the Constitution, it is well worth remembering its history and who was left out. Women, writes Law, "have always played a vital role in constructing our Nation. A challenge for the coming century is to reconstruct the family, and the society of which it is an integral part, to promote the liberty and equality of all people."

Including the Ladies.

Thatcher's Toils of Success
JUNE 17, 1987

A woman I know called on Monday, quite furious. It seems that she'd watched the weekend talk shows and had the misfortune of hearing three male commentators describe Margaret Thatcher as "lucky" in winning her third election. They said she'd had weak opposition. Which, of course, is about as insightful as saying that President Reagan was lucky in winning reelection because he had weak opposition.

Margaret Thatcher is, quite simply, the most successful woman in the world today. She is the first prime minister in modern British history to win three consecutive terms, and she did so in a landslide. She will soon pass Winston Churchill and H. H. Asquith as this century's longest-serving prime minister. She is the senior leader of the Western Alliance. Thatcher proves that women can govern nations as effectively as anybody. She has been criticized for having an autocratic management style and for dominating her cabinet, but it is a leadership style that, for her, seems to work—her government is not crippled by Iran-contra scandals. Her integrity is beyond question: no dear friends of the opposite sex have been caught spending the night at No. 10 Downing Street.

Last November, while visiting Reagan, Thatcher was inducted into the hall of fame of the International Women's Forum, which was founded in 1982 to create opportunities among women of achievement. At a ceremony at the British Embassy, she revealed a side of her that is seldom seen—the part that is female, pioneering and desirous of helping other women.

In her acceptance speech, she said she is often asked: "How did you do it?"

"It wasn't suddenly done," she said. "It was done by quite a lot of work and by steadily taking advantage of each opportunity as it came." She recited a quatrain that she said applies to women, too: " 'Heights by great men reached and kept were not attained by sudden flight. But they, while their companions slept, were toiling upwards in the night.'

"One only gets to the top rung on the ladder by steadily climbing up one at a time and suddenly all sorts of things which you thought at first—all sorts of powers, all sorts of abilities which you thought never belonged to you—suddenly come within your own possibility and you think, well, I'll have a go, too.

"For me," she said, "I wish we had more women using the enormous potential that they have. You know we've had years and years and years of able, talented women, very few of them coming into public life and I think most of our women politicians would agree with me today when I say it would be a lot easier for us if there were more of us so that each one of us is less conspicuous and each one is no longer viewed as something of a peculiarity.

"It seems to me very strange when one's male colleagues say, 'My goodness, you're the best man we've got.' And you don't always take that as a compliment, you know. If there were more of us coming into public life, it would help."

She spoke of the traditional relationship between the United States and Great Britain and our common heritage of freedom under the rule of law. "I've been so proud to be able to talk to President Reagan today to see how we can be certain, how we can always maintain that freedom for ourselves, for future generations, for the United States and for Europe and that in securing it and in maintaining it we give a little sign of hope to others who do not yet have it.

"Women have a tremendous part to play in the life of the country, in the life of the community, and in almost every particular business and profession. May I say that I did meet Sally Ride. . . . She had been so thrilled to be the first woman astronaut, and I was so thrilled to meet her. I don't know whether she thought the same when she met me as I thought when I met her. Well, you really are what I would call an ordinary woman of extraordinary qualities. And that, I think so often when I meet so many women who made it to the top. They seem so ordinary when you meet them, and yet everything they've done has been of such extraordinary quality.

"I hope that what you are doing will bring inspiration, ambition, to many young women so that they are not satisfied with anything less than giving of their best and achieving their highest ambition and of going to the very top, which I'm sure so many of them will."

Thatcher closed with the promise to do "my level best" to maintain the "special link" between the United States and Britain and said she would "do everything I can do to help other women get to the top as I was helped in the past."

She never said a word about being lucky.

Enlightened Self-interest
OCTOBER 18, 1989

Feminist leader Eleanor Smeal remembers well: it was 1982 and she was in Tallahassee, Florida, sitting in restaurants near the state capitol drinking cup after cup of coffee with Elaine Gordon, one of thirteen women in the state House of Representatives. The two tacticians were tasting defeat.

Gordon was a sponsor of the Equal Rights Amendment. Smeal was president of the National Organization for Women, which had raised millions to try to get the amendment ratified in thirty-eight states. They needed three more states and Florida had been one of their last hopes, but the male-dominated legislature had repeatedly betrayed them. Male legislators would tell them they were for the ERA and then they would vote against it. On June 21 of that year, the Senate defeated the amendment, effectively killing the ERA.

Last week, seven years after the defeat that many thought would neutralize the women's movement, the Florida Senate dealt the antiabortion movement as staggering a blow as it dealt to the women's movement in the summer of '82. The Senate Committee on Health and Rehabilitative Services defeated three proposals advanced by Republican governor Bob Martinez to restrict abortions. The next day, the Senate Health Care Committee defeated three bills that would have regulated abortion clinics. The special session, the first to meet since the Supreme Court ruled that states could limit abortion, was a resounding victory for the women's movement.

What made the difference was not just the groundswell of abortion-rights public opinion. It was also the number of women in the Florida legislature.

The contrast between the way women vote and men vote on the issues of women's rights could not be more vividly demonstrated than by the numbers that came out of that Florida Senate last week. Ninety percent of the women senators were for women's rights and freedom of choice, as were 80 percent of the women in the House.

The body that killed the ERA had only four women in it—three of whom were ERA supporters. Six years later, the forty-

member Senate has ten women in it, nine of whom are supporters of a woman's right to have an abortion. There are 120
members in the House, sixteen of whom are women. Smeal said
thirteen of them favor abortion rights. The support in both houses
was bipartisan.

There was a full vote of the Senate on a motion to discharge
the clinic regulation bills out of committee. The discharge motion,
which needed a two-thirds majority, failed in a 22-to-18 vote. In
that vote, two-thirds of the male senators voted against the abortion-rights position.

After the ERA died in the graveyard of the Florida Senate,
leaders of women's organizations vowed to bring more women into
elective office and into state legislatures. Florida, very appropriately, was their first target. "That fall we said we'd double the
numbers and we did," said Smeal. "We went from four in the
Senate to nine and now we have ten. The women have worked their
way up the seniority system so they hold chairs and power."

Elaine Gordon isn't on the sidelines anymore. She is head of
the House Health Care Committee, which killed all of the Martinez proposals. The Senate Health Care Committee, which killed
the clinic regulations, is headed by Jeanne Malchon, a Democrat
who was elected in the fall of 1982, defeating an opponent of the
ERA. The Senate Health and Rehabilitative Services Committee,
which defeated the abortion restrictions, is headed by Eleanor
Weinstock, who was elected in 1986 after serving eight years in the
House.

"We knew going in that we were going to win," said Smeal,
"but not by how much. The anti-votes switched in our direction.
One of the sad things about the ERA campaign is we would go in
winning only to lose narrowly because the votes were switching
away from us magically. This time, they were switching to us
magically.

"The naysayers say women will vote like men. And they
didn't. They stuck with us and the Republican women bucked
their party.

"All of these women said they wouldn't have been there if it
hadn't been for the ERA campaign," she said. "It's the state with
the most women in the legislature in the South and it's way above
average for the nation, too. If we had equal numbers, we would be
talking about passing positive legislation like child care, but at
least we are able to stop the negative."

Feminists have been urging women to elect women for years. The lessons of Florida are that it can be done even in a conservative, Southern state and that elected women will vote differently from men on issues affecting women. It's simply a matter of enlightened self-interest. "You see something like this," said Smeal, "and you know it makes a difference."

Women Voters Pass Some Tests
NOVEMBER 10, 1989

Think of it: the first black governor ever has been elected in the cradle of the Confederacy because he backed a woman's right to legalized abortion. Someone should tell Lee Atwater, the guitar-picking chairman of the Republican National Committee, that it wasn't Beethoven rolling over in Virginia Tuesday night, it was Harry Flood Byrd.

Much was made of the race in the gubernatorial contest between Lieutenant Governor L. Douglas Wilder, the black Democrat, and J. Marshall Coleman, the white Republican. In the end, that race turned on women's rights and Wilder was elected because women were not about to give up rights that they had been guaranteed since the 1973 Supreme Court decision legalizing abortions. Is George Bush listening?

A veteran Democratic Party worker tells of handing out sample ballots for Wilder in the overwhelmingly Republican Chesterbrook precinct of Fairfax on Tuesday afternoon. Woman after woman took the Democratic ballot and announced that she was a Republican for abortion rights and was voting for Wilder. He won the precinct by three votes. Democratic candidate for lieutenant governor Don Beyer won it by eight and Attorney General Mary Sue Terry swept it by 120 votes.

The impact of the abortion vote was most clear in the race for lieutenant governor, where both candidates were white. Beyer, a Volvo dealer who has never held political office, campaigned as an outspoken defender of abortion rights. He came from far behind to blow away his antiabortion opponent, state senator Edwina Dalton, the golden girl of the state's GOP. The result in New Jersey, where both gubernatorial candidates were white, was even more devastating: Democrat James Florio, the abortion-rights candidate, won 62 percent of the vote over his antiabortion Republican opponent. Democrats also won control of the New Jersey Assembly, which means that it will be a Democratic legislature that redraws the legislative and congressional districts in that state after the 1990 census.

Mary Crisp, the former co-chairman of the Republican National Committee, is among a group of party moderates who have formed the National Republican Coalition for Choice in an effort to persuade the party to return to its pre-1980 support of abortion rights. The group, which includes a number of congressional staff members, was formed after the Supreme Court's *Webster* decision giving states the right to regulate abortions. One of its goals is to elect abortion-rights candidates in Republican primaries.

"If we can identify and mobilize the pro-choice majority within the party, we can help the party move to where it belongs traditionally," says Crisp. She believes the looming redistricting process will create pressure on the party leadership to moderate itself or face the loss of statehouses and state legislatures, which would affect its representation in Congress. State races, she points out, are where the abortion-rights effort is going to be focused in the foreseeable future.

The Coalition for Choice will be represented at Sunday's abortion-rights rally here. "The pro-choice people in my party felt they had a constitutional right, that women were protected," says Crisp. "It was only when *Webster* came down that this outrage surfaced.

"I've seen over the years how the radical right took over precinct after precinct. The moderates never seemed to have the intensity and the political will, but we are capable of doing exactly what the right wing has done, now that we've seen the urgency and the concern.

"There is no moral ground for the administration on the issue. What they know is winning and losing," she says. "When they start losing the elections, there is no doubt they will moderate their position."

There is precedent for such presidential reversals: Woodrow Wilson was an opponent of women's suffrage. He got religion when the Republican party won the majority in Congress in 1918.

"The party has a real dilemma," says Crisp. "They're going to try to find a way, but it's hard when the president vetoes [federal abortion] funding bills and then says at a press conference that the party is broad enough to contain more than one point of view. That last veto that was so harsh for poor women was just more than moderate Republican women could accept." She says two women in her own family who had never voted for a Democrat voted for Wilder.

The elections in New Jersey and Virginia are watersheds in the modern women's movement. They mark the first time since women got the vote in 1920 that men and women have crossed party lines in large numbers to vote to preserve women's rights. It marks a new day in American politics as well: women emerged at long last as a voting bloc ready to vote its self-interest. They aren't rolling over and playing dead anymore.

U.S. Taking Baby Steps
AUGUST 3, 1988

"Day care got more air time last week on ABC, CBS and NBC news shows than any other campaign topic," *USA Today* reported on Monday. The newspaper's conclusion was based on findings by the Conference on Issues & Media, which analyzes coverage for content and air time, and it led to the obvious further conclusion that day care will be one of the hot topics for the fall campaign.

One of the people responsible for turning day care into a hot political topic is Representative George Miller (D-Calif.), chairman of the Select Committee on Children, Youth and Families. He has devoted much of his public life to the job of making America safer for children and families. Miller's committee recently pulled together some facts comparing the United States and its family policies with other industrialized nations.

The unenviable conclusion any American must reach is that we are far, far behind. We have presidential candidates talking about day care—and that's progress—but we are almost nowhere on any number of other public policy initiatives that might give some support to working families.

Testimony provided to the select committee shows some stark contrasts between the United States and its trading partners around the globe:

The United States and South Africa are the only major industrialized nations that do not have some form of job-protected
maternity leave.

Sixty-seven industrialized nations provide a weekly or
monthly cash benefit to families for every child, regardless of the
family's income or the employment status of parents. Several
European nations, including Spain, France and West Germany,
provide maternity grants at the time of childbirth to help families
with the costs of a new baby. France, Austria and West Germany
give supplemental family allowances for single mothers. Norway
gives them extra pay for living expenses, education and child care,
priority in day care centers and one year's leave from work. Norway
also reimburses women who live in remote areas for all necessary
expenses when they move closer to a hospital ten days before their
babies are due.

Congress is still considering a family and medical leave bill
that would mandate that employers give unpaid, job-protected
leave to employees for family illness and the birth or adoption of a
child. The bill would require employers to continue paying health
insurance for the absent employee. This legislation has met with
adamant opposition from the business community, led by the U.S.
Chamber of Commerce, which claims the government is trying to
mandate benefits.

By contrast, 135 other countries have family policies, and
125 of them mandate that employees get paid leave. Some sample
leave policies: Japanese women get twelve weeks of leave, at 60
percent of their regular pay. French mothers get sixteen weeks of
leave at full pay, and unpaid leave for up to two years is available
for mothers and fathers. Spanish mothers get fourteen weeks' paid
maternity leave, and those who are breast-feeding are released
from work twice during the day for thirty minutes for nine months,
with no reduction in salary. While American mothers struggle to
get employers to allow them to work part-time, Spanish parents
who are taking care of a disabled child or a child under the age of
six are allowed to cut their workdays by a third to a half, with a
proportionate cut in salary.

Most European children are in a free, public system of
preschool. West Germany, for example, has a program that serves
75 percent of its three- to six-year-olds. In the United States, 60
percent of the three- to five-year-olds are in preschool, but most
are in private programs. Head Start, this country's hugely suc-

cessful program for low-income children, served only 453,000 youngsters in 1987, fewer than one out of five who are eligible.

Nearly a quarter of America's pregnant women get late or no prenatal health care. By contrast, German women get a mother's pass on their first obstetrical visit that entitles them to ten such visits during the pregnancy and one visit six weeks after the birth. The result: 98 percent of the women have a mother's pass at the time of delivery. The proportion of low-birthweight babies born in European countries is about 4 percent, compared with 6.8 percent in the United States.

Day care is not only a hot political topic, it is an important one for the welfare of working families and the nation's future. Day care, however, is only one of a number of programs that most other countries have developed to strengthen their families and nurture their future workforce. Day care is at the top of the agenda of what working families need, but it is only a start.

European Gender Gap
OCTOBER 26, 1988

Eleanor Smeal, former president of the National Organization for Women, went to Europe this summer to find out why European women have made so much more progress than American women in winning representation in their countries' parliaments. The answer, very simply, is they changed the rules.

The European Parliament, which represents the twelve countries in the Common Market, passed a resolution in September endorsing a quota and affirmative action system calling for equal numbers of men and women in the representative bodies of member countries. This resolution is the end result of a drive that began in Norway in the early 1980s, when the Social Democrats instituted a rule requiring that neither sex account for less than 40 percent of the party's candidates.

Ironically, the Social Democrats adopted the rule because the party was experiencing a gender gap and was looking for ways to attract female voters who might be lured to splinter parties that had adopted such rules. The idea rapidly caught on with the Social Democrats, who have major-party status in most of the Common

Market countries. Norway, which is not a Common Market country, has a female prime minister; eight of eighteen cabinet ministers are women, and 34 percent of its parliament members are women.

"Norway's been having an economic crisis," said Smeal. "They took child care and made it nonnegotiable" in looking for ways to cut the budget.

In the United States, by contrast, only 5 percent of the members of Congress are women, and just this past session, Congress was unable to pass a $2.5 billion child care bill or a very modest bill providing for unpaid leave when workers have family or medical emergencies.

Smeal said ten of the twelve Common Market countries have adopted rules or quotas and timetables for increasing the representation of women in parliaments. After the September election in Sweden, which has an affirmative action plan rather than a minimum gender rule, 38 percent of the people elected to its parliament were women. In the Netherlands, 30 percent of the people in parliament are women, and in Denmark, it is 29 percent. West Germany has 15.4 percent women in its parliament and the other countries are between that and 6.4 percent. Only Greece, with a mere 4.3 percentage of women in its parliament, is behind us.

Smeal, who is now president of the Fund for the Feminist Majority, traveled with three other women leaders to five of the countries and attended the European Parliament debate on increasing the number of women in decision-making centers. In their talks with 110 women leaders, they came away with the conclusion that European women have succeeded because they have made equal representation a major goal and have secured support within and without the party structures for it, as well as support from their governments.

Smeal said that in some of these countries, party rules were changed late in the day, when opponents were out of the room. It became obvious, she said, that women had secret meetings across party lines. Women in these countries warned that the goal has to be equal representation of seats, not merely of candidates, because the parties will contrive to have men run for the safe seats and women run in the closer races. Also, women in Norway and Sweden warned that as the number of women increases in parliaments, power shifts to the parliamentary committees. Thus, in Norway, women constituted 34.4 percent of the parliament and only 17 percent of the committees. The Social Democrats recently

passed a rule requiring that neither sex hold less than 40 percent of the seats on any committee, or on any public board or
commission.

Smeal believes the gender gap can be used to spur one of the
major American parties into rules changes that will open up the
political system to blacks, women and Hispanics, who have
nothing close to equal representation.

Both party platforms have language committing them to electing more women to public office. The Democrats adopted rules in
1976 requiring equal representation of women at the party's conventions. In congressional elections, however, 95 percent of the
incumbents win because of what Smeal calls "incumbent protection rules. The system just constantly reintrenches them. It's
cutting out blacks, it's cutting out Hispanics and women and it's
cutting out the force for keeping the country modern and up to date
and able to change. Something has to change or we'll be content
with being spectators to an all-male sport at the top. Our friends
abroad said they're not going to take that. They're going to change
the rules."

And it worked.

Vox Populi Sovietskaya
MARCH 22, 1989

Woman's Day magazine entered into an extraordinary joint venture
last summer with *Krestyanka,* the largest women's magazine in the
Soviet Union: the two would do a survey of their readers' attitudes
about the state of their families and publish the results.

They got an earful.

While American women are surveyed routinely on everything
from their work lives to their sex lives, this was a relatively new
experience for Soviet women, particularly those living in rural
areas who were able to participate in such a survey by mailing in
their questionnaires. Thirty thousand American women and
200,000 Soviet women participated in the survey.

Several results stood out: women in both societies are feeling
stressed and overburdened, and women in both societies believe
that alcoholism is a huge problem and a major cause of marital

breakup. Seventy-seven percent of American women cited poor communication as the leading cause of divorce, but a whopping 43 percent of American women cited alcoholism as a leading cause.

"It was the number-two problem for us," said Ellen Levine, editor of *Woman's Day.* "I was stunned. I thought as an editor I'd better pay more attention to it. We get carried away by the drug problem and begin to ignore the old problems that aren't as sexy."

Levine and a group of American women met early last summer with a group of Soviet women to develop the questionnaire. Among the American women were Ethel Klein, an associate professor at Columbia University and a leading expert on political polling of American women. After her return from that trip, Klein said the Soviets are just beginning to experiment with counseling and therapy. The political system, however, makes it difficult for them to use the Alcoholics Anonymous model, in which addicts turn to a higher power—which doesn't mean the state. Marital therapy differs also, she said, because in the Soviet Union, "there is only one role for therapy, which is to keep the couple together. Therefore, you don't create the space for exploration, which is what you need to make therapy work."

Half of all marriages in the Soviet Union end in divorce, and 79 percent of the women surveyed blamed alcoholism for marital collapse. Because of severe housing shortages, many young married couples live with their in-laws. Thirty-nine percent of the Soviet women surveyed blamed parental interference for marriage failure, making that the second leading cause.

More than half of the Soviet women surveyed and 88 percent of the American women surveyed felt their work in the home was undervalued, and women in both countries felt the stress of family and jobs. Twenty-eight percent of the Soviet women wanted more appliances and consumer goods to help them out while 24 percent of American women wanted more child care to help them cope. Women in both countries wanted men to help more with the housework.

American and Soviet women have very different views of what they want in marriage: more than half of the Soviet women said love is the most important ingredient in a happy marriage; more than half of American women said friendship. American women, by a margin of 73 percent, want their husbands to be communicative. Only 9 percent of the Soviet women thought that important.

"We did not sense anger at men," said Levine. "Around here, there's a great deal of anger at men."

The most striking barometer of intense dissatisfaction with their own lives, however, showed up when the women were asked whether they wanted their daughters to repeat their life experiences: almost 65 percent of American and Soviet women said no. Both said they want their daughters to be better educated than they were and both said they want their daughters to have husbands who give them more help at home.

"There's this universal language for the future," says Levine. "Get educated and get help."

Women in both countries, Levine found, are worried about upcoming generations. A *Krestyanka* editor who visited the United States in connection with the survey told Levine that the Soviets have raised a generation they consider spoiled, infantile and unwilling to work.

"And we have raised a generation we think of as very materialistic and very indulged," said Levine. "I think the survey marks the beginning of exploring things together. At the same time we are holding all these talks on disarmament and nuclear issues it would be interesting to hold mini-summits on some of these personal issues like the future of the family."

Not a bad idea. If the survey shows anything, it's that women in both countries have a lot they want to say.

Eastern Bloc Women's Time Has Come
FEBRUARY 9, 1990

A prediction: After the Communist parties of Eastern Europe finish dismantling their totalitarian control of the electoral processes, there may well be more genuine democratic government in Europe than there is here. In country after country, there appear to be multiparty systems of governance emerging, and it is within this framework that people feel that they can have a real impact on their government and that they will vote.

France, with five parties, has a voter participation rate of over 80 percent in presidential elections. Here, with two parties, only 51.1 percent of the eligible voters voted in the 1988 presidential election. We may live in a democracy, but only half of us participate in it. Meanwhile, in other parts of the world, people are dying to exercise a right we take for granted—and don't use.

Women political activists in Eastern Europe have an opportunity to be founding members of these new political parties and movements and if they take advantage of what is happening, they will end up having much more power and influence in the governing of their countries than women do here. Women politicians in America are doing relatively well in local politics, but in state and national affairs they constantly run up against a system that overwhelmingly favors incumbents, and the incumbents are almost always men. Ninety-eight percent of the incumbents in the House of Representatives who stand for reelection win. Only 5 percent of the House members are women. The most recently elected woman ran and won in a special election to fill an empty seat.

Political parties in Western Europe have been much more responsive to women politicians in recent years than have those in the United States. Eleanor Smeal, head of the Fund for the Feminist Majority, has studied the emergence of women in European politics for ideas about what might work to the advantage of women here. She believes that current developments in Eastern European countries will be heavily influenced by the leftist parties in Western Europe, where these parties have set positive action quotas for getting women elected to parliaments. She says the movement started with the Green Party in West Germany, which set a goal of electing women to 50 percent of its party's seats.

"They were taking votes from other parties and the other parties started putting in these positive goals," she says. "The competitors to the Communist parties will be these other small leftist parties." She says the European Parliament has a women's committee that has suggested that the parliamentary parties adopt rules that affirmatively include women. "The parliament is already 17 percent women and the committee says it should be more. That is being pushed by the Democratic Socialist fronts." The West German Social Democrats have a goal of 30 percent female representation.

"In Norway and Sweden, it is 40 percent. In Spain, it is 25 percent. It has gone all through the social democratic system and I'm sure the new parties will adopt a positive quota system," says Smeal, who believes that the Western European countries and their parties will be the most closely emulated examples for the Soviet Union and the Eastern European countries.

"There's a great opportunity for the advancement of women. If you notice all these pictures, the Communists did not have us very high or very represented. Some of us do want to go there and see if we can be a positive influence and hope that it gets contagious and comes back here."

Political consultant Joanne Howes, head of the Women's Vote Project, also believes that the absence of non-Communist political parties and power centers offers women unprecedented opportunities in Eastern Europe compared with what they have run into here. "There is this vacuum," she says. "I think the question is, is the way women have been socialized in Eastern Europe such that they won't assert themselves into this vacuum? Will they wait and defer to men or will they move the way we saw them in Finland? Those women were able to seize the moment. What you'd love to be able to do is go over to Eastern Europe now and share our experiences of how we have gotten shut out from power. I fear the women will be working at their jobs and taking care of their kids and therefore won't have the time and energy to assert themselves into this political process, and perhaps defer to men. This is a wonderful moment to change that."

If it happens, Smeal believes that it will force the political parties in the United States to take aggressive measures to put women into comparable positions of political power. "It's going to make us look pretty backward if we don't do something and the rest of the world does," she says.

An Outrageous Experience
DECEMBER 16, 1988

It would be a perfect ending for the Decade of Greed: Congress, in a complete collapse of leadership, closes the books on the $155 billion deficit it helped accumulate in fiscal year 1988 by giving itself a 50 percent pay raise. Without ever having to vote on it.

The pay raise was unanimously recommended Tuesday by a presidential advisory commission, and President Reagan can either change it or accept it. Unless both houses vote him down, his recommendations will go into effect thirty days after he submits them with his budget on January 9. The advisory commission also recommended 50 percent pay raises for the president and vice president, the federal judiciary and thousands of other top government officials. You don't need a tarot card to read how this is going to come out.

Various arguments and rationalizations are bubbling up for why the taxpayers should give those public servants such munificent pay raises. One is that members of the House and Senate will henceforth and forevermore (at least until they need money again) forgo honoraria from speaking engagements in return for having their salaries boosted from $89,500 to $135,000 a year. A Common Cause study showed that senators averaged $23,138 and House members averaged $12,203 in such fees last year. For most, the pay raise would more than doubly compensate for their honoraria loss.

Another argument coming from the Greek chorus that accompanied the recommendations is that people are leaving public service. "Judges are leaving in droves to return to far more lucrative law practices," commission chairman Lloyd Cutler said. He said that more than five hundred major league baseball players are paid more than members of Congress, federal judges and top State Department officials. The point he misses is that major league baseball players generate huge amounts of revenue for owners, television networks and local stations, and the tens of thousands of people who earn a living working in baseball stadiums. Most of the people the commission wants to recompense so handsomely have been generating huge amounts of debt for the nation and the average American taxpayer, who is already staggering under a ghastly Social Security and income tax burden.

And the awful truth of the matter is that a lot of that tax money is then wasted. Cutler, saying the federal pay extravaganza would cost taxpayers a mere $128 million next year, justified it by saying it was "probably no more than what gets spilled at the Pentagon every day." If you think about that, you might start getting really mad at (1) Cutler's cavalier attitude and (2) the whole idea of paying a dime to people who are letting taxpayers' hard-earned money be wasted at that rate.

If people ran a business with the outrageous extravagance that members of Congress and various federal bureaucrats engage in, they'd have been fired years ago.

Representative Tony Coelho (D-Calif.) made the heartbreaking pitch for the salary raises on the grounds that "people with college-age kids can no longer be involved in public service."

I got news for him: people in private service can't afford to be involved with college-age kids. The mean family income in the United States in 1987 was $30,853. Does he think parents who are sending kids to college on that income are going to want to pay a penny more in taxes to ease the lot of congressmen who are earning $90,000?

Members of Congress, like the president and the military, all get free, socialized medical care, while more than 37 million Americans have none at all. Members of Congress elected before 1980 will be able to convert all unused campaign contributions to their own use when they retire. At the end of 1987, sixty House members had nest eggs from this source of more than $300,000.

Finally, members of Congress, who bear considerable responsibility for inflation, have insulated themselves against it by indexing a fabulous pension system. Margaret Chase Smith, the Maine Republican who retired in 1973, has received more than $1 million in pension benefits. She gets $88,715 a year, more than twice what she ever made in Congress. Former representative Ben Reifel (R-S.D.) and former senator Albert Gore (D-Tenn.) have also received more than $1 million in pension benefits since they retired.

The federal deficit is threatening the nation's future and is the most important single problem the incoming Congress and administration have to face. To propose this huge pay increase for those at the very top levels of government now is nothing less than an absolute outrage. At a time we should all be tightening our belts, our leaders are trying to line their pockets.

Bailing Out the S&Ls
JANUARY 4, 1989

For the better part of the past decade, a multitude of well-meaning organizations have tried to get Congress and the Reagan administration to help bail out families and children who are sinking in the nation's child care crisis. The answer from Washington has been: No dice. Or: You had the kids, you solve your child care problems.

For years, the answer was that it would cost too much. In the last days of the last Congress, the Senate ended up torpedoing a $2 billion child care package after a fight over who would set child care standards. After a decade in which dozens of children have perished because they have been poorly supervised, the nation's political establishment has done nothing of real consequence to help the nation's working families provide care for our future workforce.

That same political establishment, however, is about to pour billions into bailing out the savings and loan industry, proving once again that folks who run things have a way of protecting their own. When the free market fails, the free marketers are the first to turn to the federal government for a handout. Representative Patricia Schroeder (D-Colo.) has often called the defense contractors the welfare queens of the eighties. The bankrupt S&Ls and the greedy rogues who ran them into the ground are making a run for that title.

The only accurate thing one can say about the cost of cleaning up the S&L industry is that estimates start at $50 billion and have gone as high as $100 billion. More than five hundred of these thrift institutions are insolvent.

Deregulation, that biblical commandment of the free marketers who came to Washington in 1981, allowed the conservative thrift industry to become the personal playground of entrepreneurs who used depositors' savings for high-risk loans, often to pals and business associates. A couple wanting to get a loan for their first two-bedroom home were a lot more likely to get turned down by one of these Johnny-come-lately S&Ls than a guy wanting a $5 million loan to start a porno/candy store franchise.

Texas S&Ls and those who did business in that state were particularly hard hit when the state's economy went into a slump. James O'Shea, chief economic correspondent for the *Chicago Tribune*, in a six-part series on the S&L crisis, summarized its roots as a "story of corruption, government misdirection, political manipulation and just plain bad luck. There is plenty of blame to go around."

There were also plenty of bad business operators and a lot of corrupt ones. The industry's tangible capital, wrote O'Shea, is only 0.5 of 1 percent, compared with the 5 to 6 percent tangible capital that federally insured banks have. S&Ls, in other words, are operating on air.

They are also operating with awesome political clout, going all the way up to House Speaker Jim Wright of Texas, who personally intervened to block legislation that would have expanded the power of regulators to close down insolvent thrifts.

O'Shea's series also describes events aboard a yacht named *High Spirits*, the *Monkey Business* of the S&L scandals. The yacht, which sailed into the Washington Marina in May 1986, was owned by a San Antonio shopping center that had borrowed $10.3 million in February from Vernon S&L. The yacht was used extensively by members of both political parties. Representative Tony Coelho of California, then head of the Democratic Congressional Campaign Committee, hosted eight parties on the yacht from May through September, and that romance yielded $60,000 in donations to committee members from Vernon officials, borrowers and Texans with ties to Vernon. Three weeks after Coelho's last party, according to the *Tribune* series, Speaker Wright pulled the reform bill from the calendar. Federal regulators have subsequently found that 95 percent of Vernon's loans went bad.

Just after Christmas, federal regulators announced an $8 billion plan to attract new owners and to refinance nine S&Ls. Texas will get a $5.1 billion bailout. McLean Federal S&L, which chose to do its lending business in Texas rather than the gold-plated suburbs of Fairfax County, will be acquired by NV Ryan with $66 million in federal assistance.

No regulations have been changed to prevent the same rotten business practices, outright corruption and political back scratching that have characterized this unparalleled financial disaster. And there is absolutely no guarantee that federal assistance will keep this from happening all over again.

But nobody's saying no dice. Helping families is an infinitely better investment than bailing out rogues. Child care pays dividends—but children don't pay off politicians.

The Fortress of Incumbency
MAY 24, 1989

Members of the House of Representatives, who are engaged more in soul searching than in legislating, have the kind of job security that union members can only dream of. Once elected, the only thing that seems able to beat them is scandal, and that has to be of the four-star variety.

Ronald Reagan, in a speech in Chicago over the weekend, made the point that incumbents are so good at staying in office that there is less turnover in Congress than in the Supreme Soviet. David A. Stewart, an Arkansas Democrat who was co-chairman of a weekend conference in Kansas City, Missouri, on congressional incumbency, put it slightly differently: "You have a better chance to get elected to the Politburo of the Soviet Union than you do of unseating a member of Congress."

Incumbents are returned to office historically at a rate of 99 percent. Richard Kopke, a former political action committee director who was at the conference, said that challengers in the last two elections won 14 races and lost 795, a reelection rate of 98 percent.

If Congress has remained an overwhelmingly white male institution—there are twenty-four blacks and twenty-six women in the House—that's because it has figured out ways of perpetuating its hold on power.

Unlike the presidency or some governorships, there is no limit on the number of terms members can serve. Once elected, they become the objects of affection of the innumerable political action committees in town that start spreading money around for the members' reelection campaigns before they've been assigned office space. Incumbents have publicly financed staffs to tend to their every need and, more important, to their constituents' needs. The goodwill that builds, of course, is priceless.

Franking privileges allow members to send free mailings to their constituents informing them of all the worthwhile activities they are undertaking in Washington. Those constituent communications routinely pick up in volume as the election cycle gets under way. In 1988, the total cost to taxpayers of the franking privilege was $113.4 million.

As for fund-raising, reports released at the end of February by the Federal Election Commission for the 1988 election showed that it cost $458 million to elect the 101st Congress, with incumbents enjoying a tremendous advantage.

Incumbents in the House outspent their challengers by three and one-half times. The Democrats raised $145 million while their challengers raised $29.5 million, and the Republicans raised $110 million while their challengers raised about $22.2 million.

Incumbents enjoyed a huge advantage in contributions from political action committees. Democrats in the Senate raised about

$16 million from PACs while their challengers raised less than $5 million. Republicans raised about $15 million while their challengers raised $3.6 million.

PACs gave House Democrats a stunning $55.5 million, compared with $8.1 million received by challengers. House Republicans got $30 million while their challengers received $2.2 million.

Even the fifty-eight House members who faced no primary or general election opposition raised more than $7 million from PACs. Mike McCauley, field organizer on campaign finance issues at Public Citizen, makes the point that twenty-seven of the unopposed incumbents were elected prior to 1980, which means they can convert their campaign money to their private use when they retire. An analysis by the congressional watchdog group found that 190 members were elected before 1980 and their campaign nest eggs average $206,382. Public Citizen also found that of all the members elected in the 1988 campaign, the average cash on hand was $154,334, which gives them a considerable jump in fundraising over any opponent.

Most PACs continue financing members with safe seats or who are unopposed because they want continued access to them, McCauley says. They are more concerned with gaining acess than with good government.

Members of the House and Senate are squirming over the honoraria question—the list of who got paid what came out this week—while avoiding the more threatening issues of campaign finance revision. They should not be surprised to see the same citizenry that became aroused over the pay raise turn to take a hard look at the 99 percent success rate of incumbents.

Curtailing PAC activities or limiting the number of years of service to, say, twelve are obvious ways of breaking the stranglehold the incumbents have on Congress. They've stacked the deck in their favor, so they should not be surprised if voters decide to change the rules.

Family Matters, People Say
JUNE 23, 1989

A clue that something new and different was going on appeared last February when magazines like *People* and *Money* and *Soap Opera Digest* published a survey entitled "Tell the President: Your Family Matters." They were among twenty-four national magazines that donated more than $5 million in advertising space to determine public opinion about work and family issues.

More than 200,000 readers filled out the one-page survey and thousands sent in letters as well. Perhaps the biggest surprise in their answers came in the overwhelming numbers by which they want more government and business initiatives to help men and women balance the demands of their families and their work.

The idea for the survey originated with Kathy Bonk, a veteran strategist in the women's movement, who helped coordinate it with the Child Care Action Campaign, the Great American Family Tour and Lifetime cable television network. "The real shift," she says, "is that ten years ago and five years ago, child care and sick kids were always private problems with private solutions. Right now, the public is saying it's not just my problem to solve. Government and private sector employers have a responsibility to help families cope."

Ethel Klein of Columbia University, a leading specialist on the gender gap in American politics who helped analyze the survey findings, spotted a sea change in attitudes from the early 1980s. At that time, she pointed out in her analysis, "only four out of 10 working women said companies should share in the responsibility of providing day care, and the public did not want the federal government to spend more money on day care. Today, almost everyone (87 percent) agrees that there must be a joint effort between private employers and government on care-giving needs."

Among the survey's findings: 74 percent of the respondents think family issues should be a top priority for Congress and the administration. While 78 percent of the women who work outside the home feel that way, 70 percent of the women who do not work outside the home agreed. Women felt that way no matter what part of the country they lived in. Fifty-three percent of the men who responded put those issues as a priority.

Eighty-one percent of those who answered the survey said that the federal government does not pay enough attention to child care and other family issues. Ninety-three percent of the respondents believe that workers should have the right to take leave from their jobs to take care of a new child or a seriously ill family member without losing their jobs.

Congress is considering a parental and medical leave bill that would give employees up to ten weeks of unpaid leave for family emergencies. One of the most striking findings of the survey is that among the 93 percent of the people who favor such leaves, 69 percent of them think employees should receive some pay during their absence. A substantial majority of women at all income levels, and in every region, supported paid leave.

"People want paid leave," says Bonk. "The proposal that's in Congress is so far behind where people are today that it's quite remarkable."

Business lobbies have bitterly fought any parental leave legislation on the ground that it would open the door to federally mandated benefits such as health insurance programs. A propitious sign for more sensible family policies emerged yesterday when the American Medical Association endorsed, for the first time, federal efforts to require employers to provide health insurance for full-time employees. The AMA's support for efforts to insure the 37 million people in the country who have no health coverage is yet another strong signal of deepening support for a whole range of policies that will protect and promote the health and welfare of families.

Vince Breglio, who was the pollster for the Bush presidential campaign, told a panel after release of the survey that he did not believe serious political candidates in 1990 "can avoid discussing the issue of child care. I don't believe they can avoid discussing the issue of long-term health care."

Up until now, says Bonk, there has not been an extensive voting record on family issues in Congress. "We'd be hard-pressed to say family issues will defeat or elect candidates in the next election," she says, "but the way it is standard to say economic issues are going to affect the voter, more and more it is acceptable to say that family issues are likely to play a role in the elections. In this Congress there will be votes on child care, the minimum wage and parental leave. In those races where a candidate voted against all three, he's going to be hard-pressed to say he's for the family."

Lessons for Lobbyists
AUGUST 16, 1989

Given the gravity of the problem and the staggering cost of fixing it, the bailout of the savings and loan industry got done in record time. Once again, the taxpayers are going to be picking up the tab for public officials who were out to lunch when crooks and incompetents were romping through a deregulated financial system in search of spoils.

The final cost varies with every news account: one day it's $166 billion, another day it's $300 billion. So many S&Ls are in danger of going under or may be unable to meet the new federal requirements that no one really has any idea yet of the extent of the disaster and how much it is going to cost to fix. The bottom line—that wonderful jargon that crept out of the accountants' offices during the avaricious eighties—is: a lot.

But the bottom line is also the fact that when the thrift industry needed a hand from Uncle Sam, it got it. Sure, there was the usual hand-wringing and finger-pointing that gets done when some corrupt or decaying segment of American industry gets in trouble, but help eventually came, just as it did when Chrysler needed a bailout. And it came quickly.

Congress—and a finger does need to be pointed at the House Banking Committee—passed regulations that allowed the thrift crisis to occur, and Congress was anxious to avoid getting blamed. It was Congress, for example, that boosted the federal insurance level from $40,000 to $100,000 per account—more than doubling taxpayer liability for protecting depositors from the crooks and bad businessmen who flocked to the S&L industry during the early eighties in search of a fast buck. And it was Congress that allowed the thrift industry to diversify from its traditional niche of home mortgage loans into the treacherous terrain of office and apartment building ventures in the oil-dependent economy of the Southwest.

The faster the bailout, the less scrutiny Congress would get for its role in this debacle. Aside from requiring thrifts eventually to maintain tangible capital assets worth 3 percent of their loans, versus 1.5 percent and less, and aside from steering them back into the home loan mortgage business, the bailout law contains little to prevent a recurrence of the crisis. And the taxpayers are still insuring the depositors.

The moral of this story is that when the boys need money, it's there. In the hundreds of billions.

Whatever happened to those sad stories we used to hear from Congress and the White House about the deficit? About how we can't afford any new programs because the coffers are empty? About how we'd love to expand the universe of the poor who are covered by federal health programs, but sorry, folks, we can't afford it?

The federal deficit has been the excuse given by Congress and the Reagan administration for a decade of neglect of social programs, new and old. During that time, even the most obtuse members of Congress came to realize there was a desperate need for federal intervention in the country's child care crisis, but so far it's been all talk and no money.

This summer, the Senate finally passed a child care bill, but the House isn't scheduled to act on its bill until this fall and there's no guarantee that the Bush administration will act favorably on that child care legislation. There is no guarantee, in other words, that the generation of children who need care now will get it before they have children of their own.

The tab for the Senate child care bill is under $2 billion, a mere drop in the bucket by S&L bailout standards. Yet child advocacy groups have spent years lobbying—and they have documented dozens of cases of children dying because of poor care—and they still haven't obtained money to build an infrastructure of safe, affordable care for the millions of children who need it.

The cost of the so-called war on drugs is a mere skirmish, by S&L bailout standards. The commitment from the federal government this fiscal year was about $5 billion and the Bush administration is proposing $6 billion for the 1990 fiscal year, with drug war director William Bennett wanting another billion. At most, the commitment would be about $7 billion to go after a scourge that is threatening the very fabric of our social order.

No one is better wired into Congress than the financial community. The thrifts officials who made all those political contributions in the eighties got their payoff.

The S&L bailout sets new standards for federal largess at the taxpayers' expense. But it's given the folks lobbying for a real war on drugs and a real effort on child care some high-powered ammunition. The next time members of Congress start acting like tightwads and saying there's no money, they can say: Baloney.

8

Who Decides?

Bush's Clouded View on Abortion
JANUARY 27, 1989

President Bush has wasted no time in restating his opposition to abortion and his desire to see the Supreme Court overturn *Roe v. Wade,* the 1973 decision that made abortions legal throughout the United States. Bush's position may be politically sound, but it is logically, ethically and morally reprehensible.

On Monday, White House spokesman Marlin Fitzwater read a statement enunciating Bush's present position: "He is opposed to abortion except when the life of the mother is threatened or when there is rape or incest. The president supports a constitutional amendment that would reverse the Supreme Court's *Roe v. Wade* decision. . . .

"He supports a human life amendment with exceptions to save the life of the mother or for victims of rape and incest. And he opposes the use of federal funds to pay for abortion except when the life of the mother is threatened."

161

Opponents of abortion argue that a fetus is a human being from the moment of conception and deserves all the protections of the Constitution from that moment. The amendment that Bush supports would extend this protection to the unborn and make most abortions illegal.

During the first presidential debate, Bush said that he hadn't "sorted out the penalties" that ought to be imposed on women who obtain illegal abortions and the physicians who perform them. In that same debate, he said: "Abortion is sometimes used as a birth-control device, for heaven's sake. See the millions of killings accumulate. . . ."

If Bush believes abortion is killing, then women who obtain abortions are guilty of premeditated murder. There is no middle ground in this. So, too, is the person who performs the operation. And if abortion is, indeed, the premeditated murder of a fetus, it is the premeditated murder of all fetuses. A fetus conceived during rape or during an act of incest is no less entitled to protection than a fetus conceived during an act of love. The fetus cannot be held responsible for the violence and evil that accompanied its conception. We do not condone murdering the born children of rapists.

The Roman Catholic Church, which has been leading the drive to make abortions illegal, at least has the virtue of consistency. "The opposition to direct abortion is absolute," says Richard Doerflinger, of the pro-life section of the National Conference of Catholic Bishops. He describes pregnancy that results from rape or incest as "a tragic circumstance where great harm has already been done to the woman, but that doesn't empower anyone with the right to attack the life of the child."

Pregnancies that endanger the life of the mother, he says, have "become vanishingly rare. . . . Situations like diabetes and hypertension, all of these are treatable now." The church draws a distinction, however, between direct and indirect abortions in which chemotherapy for a cancer patient might endanger a fetus, for example. "That's not considered as the equivalent of an abortion," he says. "The intent is to cure the mother's cancer and not to end the life of the child."

The latest study by the Alan Guttmacher Institute found that only 1 percent of the women who obtained abortions in 1987 were rape or incest victims, and only 3 percent cited health as the major reason for terminating the pregnancy. Most were concerned about how the baby would change their lives, about not being able to afford a child, not being ready for the responsibility of a child and not being in a stable relationship in which to raise a child.

These are the same reasons that drove women to seek illegal abortions before 1973 and will continue to drive women to seek them if they are made illegal again. The difference between now and then is that an average of eighteen women were admitted each day in 1969 to New York City municipal hospitals for treatment of incomplete abortions, according to the institute. In 1970, more than twenty-five women in 100,000 who had abortions died—more than the number of women who died in childbirth. Today, death and surgical complications from legal abortion are rare.

The Supreme Court has agreed to review a Missouri case that could lead to a reversal of *Roe v. Wade* this term. What's at stake here is not George Bush pandering to the right wing fundamentalists or the Roman Catholic Church in order to win an election. That's a done deal. What's at stake is the health and safety of more than 1 million American women who each year decide that they are going to terminate a pregnancy. Bush swore to uphold a Constitution that guarantees the separation of church and state. He ought to be doing his utmost to guarantee that women are able to make this most personal decision free of government-imposed religious dogma.

Cruel Meddling
FEBRUARY 10, 1989

A Long Island family's private agony has become the latest cruel chapter in the abortion controversy. Nancy Klein, who is about seventeen weeks pregnant, has been comatose since she was injured in an auto accident December 13. Her husband, Martin, has asked to be named her legal guardian so he can authorize an abortion that might enhance her chances of recovery. Antiabortion activists have gone to court to oppose him.

Klein's request is the first time a husband has sought guardianship to give consent to his wife's abortion. Thus the case was bound to generate considerable attention and the antiabortionists couldn't let it alone.

Klein, a thirty-four-year-old accountant, has the backing of his wife's mother and father. "She deserves every opportunity to live and do as well as she can in her recovery," Klein told *Newsday*. "How could she not be entitled to that? I could never live with myself knowing I didn't give her every opportunity."

But the ordeal, he said, has left him physically and mentally exhausted. "I'm sure I'm not the only one who's been through a tragedy. It's just been exaggerated through this issue, which has attracted so much attention." Further, he said, "it was not our intention to have any sort of public attention. We are basically private people, like most people. We're all uncomfortable with it. I know Nancy would be."

Nancy Klein, thirty-two, suffered extensive brain damage in the car accident. North Shore University Hospital, where she is hospitalized, refused to perform the abortion unless her husband is named her legal guardian and can give consent. In late January, he filed legal papers in State Supreme Court in Mineola asking the court to give him the right to consent to the abortion because his wife is unable to do so. Dr. J. J. Smith, a professor of obstetrics and gynecology at Albert Einstein College of Medicine, filed an affidavit saying the pregnancy could threaten Nancy Klein's life and that he believed an abortion was indicated.

Hospital officials, however, have contended that an abortion is not medically indicated.

Enter John Short, founder of a Long Island antiabortion group, who promptly went to court, asking it to declare him legal guardian of Nancy Klein so he could prevent the abortion. He told *Newsday:* "I would think the mother would want her life extended through the child and I think the father, after all this is over, once he sees the child, he'll realize he was saved from making a tragic mistake."

Zealots who think they are in direct communication with the Almighty on the abortion issue have no hesitation in speaking on behalf of people they've never even met. Thus, Martin Klein, who is trying to deal with the devastating situation with his wife, and who is trying also to take care of the couple's three-year-old daughter who is suddenly without a mother, has to endure having someone he never heard of bursting into his life and going into court with some sanctimonious hogwash Klein clearly doesn't buy.

Does the court tell Short to mind his own business and get lost?

Not right away. A hearing was set for February 1 in which the hospital, the district attorney—who is an antiabortion activist—and the state attorney general were asked to show cause why Klein should not be appointed guardian. The courtroom was packed by antiabortion and pro-choice advocates who heard medical experts testify in explicit detail as to the condition of Nancy Klein's body. *Newsday* columnist Paul Vitello subsequently wrote that her privacy "was the most obvious victim" of the proceedings.

And that day, Lawrence A. Washburn, an antiabortion lawyer, filed an order on behalf of John J. Broderick, of Syosset, Long Island, saying he wanted to become the legal guardian of the fetus. The Klein family was being thoroughly invaded by outside agitators.

On February 3, State Supreme Court justice Bernard McCaffrey ruled against both Short—saying he had no legal standing—and Broderick, saying his petition was premature because a fetus is not considered viable until it reaches twenty-four weeks of gestation.

On Tuesday, McCaffrey appointed Klein his wife's guardian. Hours later, an appellate judge stayed the ruling, pending an appeal by Short and Broderick. A decision on the appeal is expected today.

What have these so-called "pro-life" zealots done? They have delayed an abortion—which makes it more dangerous. They have turned a family's private tragedy into a public circus. They have put a man who is doing everything he can to save his wife's life through absolute hell. And the courts, by giving them any standing whatsoever, have contributed to this travesty against the Klein family. This isn't "pro-life." It is vicious.

Sickening Display
JULY 7, 1989

Liberals and abortion-rights advocates can now empathize with conservatives who have spent the last twenty-five years railing against the judicial activism of the Supreme Court. The lesson out of this session is that what the Court gives, the Court can take away—and a radical Court can savage in three weeks more than two decades of decisions bolstering the civil liberties and rights of Americans.

It is as sickening a display to liberals as the liberal Court of yesteryear must have been to conservatives. There is a lesson here for both sides: nine people with lifetime tenure and who answer to no one have stupefying powers to change the fabric of individual lives.

Anyone who still cleaves to the myth that the justices follow the law of the land and not the winds of political change ought to be forever disabused of that notion after this session. The three justices appointed by President Reagan did more to further the backlash that was the Reagan Revolution than the Reagan Justice Department did in eight years.

The Supreme Courts of the past have anchored their decisions in the Constitution and in precedents. This Court repeatedly departed from precedent when it threw out twenty-five years of civil rights legislation designed to protect blacks, women, older Americans and people with disabilities from discrimination in the workplace. Then, on the final day of its term, it eviscerated the protection given by the court in 1973 to women who sought safe, legal abortions without interference by their local politicians, parish priests or fundamentalist ministers.

That decision, *Roe v. Wade*, gave women a constitutional right to an abortion in the first trimester of pregnancy under all circumstances. It gave states the right to limit abortions after the first trimester and the possibility of fetal viability set in. On Monday, the Court gave states the right to limit abortions and set conditions under which they may be performed at any stage, beginning from the moment of conception. While the Court stopped short of overturning the right to an abortion enunciated in *Roe*, it opened the door for extensive state meddling—it has already started in Florida, Louisiana and Massachusetts—in the most intimate aspects of a woman's life.

By allowing state legislatures to pass laws restricting a woman's access to abortion, the court has plunged the country into bitter, divisive political war that will be waged in campaigns for years to come. Women, no longer safeguarded by the Court, will be subjected to the tyranny of packs of self-anointed zealots in benighted state legislatures across the country.

They are not going to stop abortions. They will only make them deadly. One has only to remember the carnage that existed before 1973 when women showed up in emergency rooms across the country bleeding to death from botched illegal abortions to know what will happen if those sanctimonious bullies are not stopped.

Abortion-rights advocates will be looking toward all branches of government for protection, predicted Marcia Greenberger of the National Women's Law Center. They will seek federal legislation protecting abortion rights. "The other thing that's very clear is that not only abortion but contraception is at stake here," she warned. The Court let stand a preamble to the Missouri law that states that life begins at conception. Justice John Paul Stevens, in his dissent, wrote that this violates the establishment clause of the First Amendment as well as previous court decisions allowing the use of contraceptives, some of which work after the sperm has fertilized an egg.

In a blistering dissent, Justice Harry A. Blackmun made no attempt to conceal his contempt for the politics being played by the plurality and his fear that the constitutional protections of *Roe* are doomed. "Never in my memory has a plurality announced a judgment of this court that so foments disregard for the law and for our standing decisions," he wrote.

"Of the aspirations and settled understandings of American women," he wrote, "of the inevitable and brutal consequences of what it is doing, the tough-approach plurality utters not a word. This silence is callous. It is also profoundly destructive of this Court as an institution. To overturn a constitutional decision is a rare and grave undertaking. To overturn a constitutional decision that secured a fundamental personal liberty to millions of persons would be unprecedent in our 200 years of constitutional history."

The packed Court that is one of the most costly legacies of the Reagan epoch is headed in that direction. It is now up to the men and women of this country who value privacy and individual liberty to protect their rights with their votes. They cannot look to this Supreme Court anymore.

A Matter of Conscience, Not Religion
OCTOBER 27, 1989

If women thought that they had achieved the right to decide their own reproductive destinies without interference from the state, federal government or Catholic Church, this week's events should prove a jolting revelation. Two votes and one veto have drawn battle lines in the abortion fight that will be hard to escape in the next elections.

In the House vote to override President Bush's veto of the $157 billion labor, health and education bill, the majority of the Republican members stood by the president and refused to let federal funds be used to pay for abortions for poor women who become pregnant as a result of rape or incest. A majority of the Republican women members have favored extending Medicaid abortions to these women since the fight broke out two weeks ago. All told, eighteen of the women members of Congress voted to override and eight voted not to, including Maryland Democrat Beverly Byron. Roy Dyson, a bachelor, was the only other Maryland Democrat who voted against the override.

The influence of the Catholic Church was felt by legislators on both sides of the vote. Four of the women who voted against the override are Catholics. At least four of those who voted to override are Catholics, including Republican Connie Morella, who represents Montgomery County. Morella, who has brought up nine children, has her credentials in order on matters of motherhood.

"I feel the church offers guidelines and theology," she said yesterday. "I feel as a legislator the right of privacy of a woman is critically important," particularly in cases involving "rape or incest, where others are allowed to have an abortion if they can afford it. We have discriminated against the poor who are victims of rape or incest. We do not allow them to make a choice. What I have always felt about abortion is the woman makes the choice and government offers alternatives—counseling, adoption, funding to carry to term. I don't see it as being incongruous with church teaching.

"What I thought was really rather heartwarming is when this issue came up on the floor a couple of weeks ago, without doing any orchestrating in advance, a majority of Republican women got up and spoke in favor of it." She said they also wrote President Bush asking for his support on the measure, but he never answered.

Representative Nancy Pelosi (D-Calif.), another Catholic, voted for the override. "I am a Roman Catholic," she said on the floor. "I have five children, and I have received thirteen years of Roman Catholic education." It taught her, she said, that she "should respect the intelligence of the women of America, that we should respect their ability to take responsibility for their actions." She, too, deplored the hypocrisy of allowing abortions for pregnant rape victims who can pay and not for those who cannot.

Representative Barbara B. Kennelly (D-Conn.), also a Catholic, spoke of "liberty, justice, rule of law for all" and "separation of church and state, words that go to the very fabric of our democracy.

"The right vote today is a vote to override so the basic tenets of our government can continue to be our basis of democracy," she said.

But to Representative Henry J. Hyde (R-Ill.), a Catholic and longtime leader of the antiabortion faction in the House, it comes down to the doctrine of when life begins: "Do we hate the criminal [rapist] so much that we impose capital punishment on the child of that criminal?"

Representative Robert K. Dornan (R-Calif.) consistently invoked the pope, the Catholic Church's 352 active American bishops and Mother Teresa in his remarks against the override. In a one-hour postmortem at the conclusion of the session, and in one-minute remarks yesterday morning, he decried the abortion-rights votes of the Catholic members of the House and blamed them for the continued legalization of abortion. He said the "self-proclaimed Catholics" in the House provided the margin for abortion-rights victories and called upon the bishops meeting in Baltimore early next month to "address" this.

While the House was putting its members on the line with their abortion votes, the Pennsylvania legislature was voting in restrictions that, among other things, force a woman to notify her husband before having an abortion and forbid abortions for sex selections. How they intend to enforce the latter is a mystery. As for the former, a woman will have to bring a note to her doctor, saying she had told her husband she was going to an abortion clinic. Patriarchy is alive and well in Pennsylvania.

The abortion-rights forces took losses this week in the Pennsylvania legislature and in the House of Representatives. In the end, however, those losses will serve to politicize women and to produce a record with which they can turn out of office legislators who allow governments and churches to meddle in the most private, intimate aspects of women's lives.

Innocent Victims in the Abortion Wars
DECEMBER 1, 1989

The parental consent and notification laws that are the latest battleground in the abortion war have nothing to do with the health and welfare of pregnant teenagers, as the laws' defenders would have us believe. What they are really about is reducing the number of abortions, parental control and punishing girls who get in trouble.

Those laws are all the more ugly and vicious because abortion foes use them to inflict their views on teenage girls who cannot vote and thus cannot defend themselves against this assault on their bodies, dignity and their right to decide whether or not to continue a pregnancy. The zealots who have secured passage of laws in twenty-four states making it harder for teenagers to get abortions are doing to kids what they can't do to adult women.

What is tragic is that grownups are letting them get away with it. A poll just released by the National Abortion Rights Action League shows that 60 percent of adults favor the laws, which come in a variety of permutations. Some require notification of one parent, some both, some require consent of one parent, some of both parents, and some throw in waiting periods so a kid can sweat it out a couple of more days before terminating a pregnancy. Most of them allow a teenager to go before a judge to get permission for an abortion if she can establish that her own welfare would be endangered if she told her parents. She can also go to a judge to establish that she is mature enough to make the decision without her parents' consent. Ohio and Minnesota are trying to weaken even this bypass, and the Bush administration has gone so far as to support parental veto of a minor's abortion.

Have we all forgotten so quickly what it was like to be a

teenager? Have we forgotten what it was like to be terrified of even the most well-meaning parents, let alone a judge we've never met? The judicial process is daunting to the most sophisticated adults. Think what it does to a pregnant teenage girl. And think of the plight of a teenage girl who finds herself pregnant and does not want to humiliate her parents. Or the teenager who is subsisting on the margins of emotional chaos because she lives in a family where the parents are abusive, or alcoholic, or drug addicts. How about the teenager who can tell her mother but whose father ran away from home ten or fifteen years ago, never paid any child support and has by all rights and reason forfeited any say at all in this child's life. She should need his consent? Why?

The argument that abortion foes trot out to support that unspeakable meddling is that they want to promote family unity and the child's welfare by involving the parents in her decision. They say that schools can't even give a child an aspirin without the written consent of the parents.

Supporters of reproductive freedom argue that in healthy families, the daughters will talk to their parents. It is in the dysfunctional families, they argue, that girls cannot go to their parents and that they must be able to terminate a pregnancy without harassment from the state. The cruel irony, of course, is that it is girls from the dysfunctional families—loveless ones that are plagued by addictions, wife-beating, incest and other forms of destructive behavior—that are the most likely to end up pregnant at a very young age.

"These laws are more about parents' rights," says pollster Harrison Hickman, whose firm polls for the abortion-rights group. "This has to do with punishment and control. We ask them in focus groups what good would this law do. And they say, well, parents should be involved. Not a small part of this is the recognition that this person who is developing sexually is about to leave their control and it's a holding on."

The public has made it clear in polls and, more important, at the polls that it doesn't want states abridging abortion rights of adult women. Hickman says that voters haven't really started thinking through the ramifications of these consent and notification laws. The tragic fact for both adult women and teenagers is that when abortion is made difficult, women die.

Indiana requires parental consent. Rebecca Bell, a seventeen-year-old from Indianapolis who by all accounts was close to her parents, did not go to a doctor when she found out she was pregnant. She did not want her parents to know. She died on September 16, 1988, from an infection that occurred after she tried to self-abort. Her parents are actively opposing those laws that would cost other teenage girls their lives. For that is the toll those laws exact, and those of us who remember friends who died or were rendered sterile from illegal abortions have an obligation not to allow today's teenagers to be sacrificed on the altar of the antiabortion zealots.

Politics of the Anti-Saloon League
DECEMBER 6, 1989

If the Grand Old Party keeps playing its cards right in Virginia, it will soon go the way of the Anti-Saloon League. The what? Precisely. This weekend's vote by its hidebound conservatives to throttle future candidates with an antediluvian posture on abortion is the kind of self-destructive move that spreads pure glee in the ranks of the opposition.

The Republicans haven't elected a governor in Virginia since 1977, when John Dalton beat populist Henry Howell. This fall they took a direct hit when J. Marshall Coleman, a former attorney general with a financial line of credit that wouldn't quit, still managed to lose to Democrat Lieutenant Governor L. Douglas Wilder. Wilder was for abortion rights and adamantly so. Coleman was in the dark ages, and unreconstructibly so.

Thus the GOP managed to do the unthinkable: it got a white Republican candidate beaten in the cradle of the Confederacy by a black Democrat on the abortion issue. Any person who tries to kid himself or herself into thinking that wasn't the preeminent voting button for women in Virginia is woolgathering.

Fairfax County, for example, is living in gridlock, and Coleman, a McLean resident, had a far more sophisticated understanding of the region's transportation nightmare. By all rights, he should have taken the county. Fairfax sends Republicans to Congress and it votes Republican in presidential contests. In the 1981 gubernatorial race, which had a 59 percent voter turnout in Fairfax, Coleman got 48.2 percent of the vote and Democrat Charles S.

Robb got 51.9. This year, with a 56.9 percent turnout, Democrat Wilder won Fairfax with 56 percent compared with only 43.9 percent for Coleman.

There are roughly 200,000 more women than men registered to vote in Virginia, and in the last three statewide elections, the votes of women and minorities have given the Democrats a sweep of the top three state offices. You'd think by now that the folks running the state's Republican party would be getting the message. Or, more to the point, you'd think that the Republicans in the state would be getting new leaders to run the party.

Moderate Republican activists went to the party's Central Committee meeting this weekend with a resolution allowing the party to back candidates regardless of their position on abortion and stating that the party believes both abortion-rights and anti-abortion positions can be "honorably held." The resolution was tabled by a 40-to-27 vote.

"If this is the way the party is going to react, it doesn't bode well at all for Republican victories in elections," says Mary Crisp, the former co-chairwoman of the Republican National Committee who is a prominent member of the National Republican Coalition for Choice. "It seems to me when they lost with Coleman on this issue primarily that they would have seen the light. There's a lesson here for the moderates, for pro-choice Republicans in Virginia to begin to take back the precincts and to take over the party organization by becoming deeply involved and holding those positions that give them power.

"What strikes me is that it is almost like they'd rather lose. Their sense of power is more important than a bigger vision of possibly winning on the broader issues and governing. That's where the real power is. It isn't in party organization," says Crisp.

Anne B. Kincaid, Coleman's liaison to the Christian right, wrote in a memo that the lessons to be learned from his defeat were that the candidate should never waffle on abortion. In a later interview, she claimed that "the majority of Americans favor a ban on the majority of abortions." This has got to be news to every reputable pollster. The fact is that more than 90 percent of abortions take place in the first trimester and an overwhelming percentage of Americans believe that women should be able to terminate those early pregnancies. And they voted that way with both feet in northern Virginia, which carried the state for Wilder.

That was not lost on Ohio attorney general Anthony J. Celebrezze, Jr., who is expected to run for governor, and who changed his political position on abortion this week. While he opposes it personally, he said women should have the right to choose, that he would support public funding of abortions for poor women and would veto any legislation banning abortions.

That's not waffling; that's a 180-degree turn.

What has happened is that people who took a right for granted now fear that it will be taken away. That goes counter to the currents of American history which have always worked toward securing greater freedoms. The one exception to that occurred when Prohibition was enacted. But it didn't last, and the Anti-Saloon League didn't either.

If "Them" Becomes "Us"
MARCH 28, 1990

The most horrifying stories to come out of Romania after the destruction of the Ceausescu regime were the revelations about the "population policies" of the dictator and his wife. Contraceptives were banned. Women were forced to bear children they couldn't even feed. Babies were abandoned or they starved. Romania's death rate from illegal abortions was among the highest in the world.

Womb police inspected pregnant women in factories to make sure that they had not terminated their pregnancies. Economic sanctions were leveled against couples who did not produce children after two years of marriage. Women who had not married by the age of twenty-five had to pay penalty taxes. Women who did not have proof of monthly examinations to determine whether they were pregnant lost their free medical care and driver's licenses. These policies, which forced women to bear children they did not want and could not care for, resulted in death and destruction of untold numbers of women and infants. The carnage was so awful that the first thing the new government did after executing the Ceausescus was to legalize abortion.

What happened in Romania has not been lost on American women who understand that their own reproductive freedom is threatened by the state, and that they, too, may be forced to bear children they do not want. Legislation passed last week in Idaho and Guam is essentially the same as the abortion ban of Ceausescu.

In Romania, abortions were permitted only when the pregnancy was the result of incest, if the fetus was deformed, if the mother's life was in danger, if she had already produced five children, or if she was over forty. Guam, a territory, has just passed the most repressive antiabortion legislation in the United States. It makes it a crime to advocate abortion. In Romania, it was a crime to advocate birth control. Guam permits abortion only when the woman's life is threatened. It does not even permit the exceptions the Ceausescus allowed. Guam is 90 percent Catholic.

The Idaho legislation bans abortion as a means of birth control, although what it means by that is so vague as to be meaningless. It allows abortions in roughly the same categories as the Ceausescus did: when the pregnancy is the result of rape or incest (if the victim is under eighteen), when there is profound fetal abnormality or if the woman's health is severely threatened. Civil penalties starting at $10,000 could be levied against physicians performing abortions.

Ceausescu's madness began in 1966 because he wanted to increase the size of the workforce. The suffering he caused Romanian women has only just begun to get attention in the West—and in the western press. What the Ceausescus were doing, which could not have been entirely unknown to western governments, was a small price to pay for keeping happy one of the "good guys" in the Communist bloc who would stand up to Moscow. President Carter even entertained those two great humanitarians in April 1978. If he spoke to the Ceausescus about their human rights violations against Romanian women, it wasn't reported.

Margaret Atwood, the Canadian author of *The Handmaid's Tale*, says that a common motif in totalitarian regimes is reproductive control of the population. She says that what was going on in Romania was known in alternative feminist circles. "The same thing happened in the thirties with the Jews and Hitler. It was known and not given play. There was a lot of the disbelief reaction." Also, she says, there is the common reaction of "that's them," a common way of responding to the horrors that occurred in the Soviet Union under Stalin. "We in North America live very sheltered lives," she says.

That could be changing very swiftly.

Legislation enacted in Idaho was designed to give the U.S. Supreme Court an opportunity to overthrow *Roe v. Wade*, the 1973 decision that legalized abortions. The Guam legislation is already in court. In Maryland, an entire state legislative session was brought to a grinding standstill when sixteen zealots filibustered in the Senate in an attempt to inflict their own population policies on that state. During the twenty-five years that Romanian women were victims of the harshest and most invasive population policies, American women were taking for granted their right to make these decisions without interference from the state.

As the rest of the world is embracing democracy and freedom and looking to the United States as its beacon light, the United States is starting to take away the most basic freedom that American women have. The tolerance this government showed toward the policies of Romania ought to chill the soul of every person who thought that these were private concerns, and not the business of the state. It's not happening to "them." It's happening to us.

9

Motherhood in the Marketplace

The Baby M Case
APRIL 1, 1987

The Baby M case, decided yesterday in favor of the biological father and his wife, has presented in agonizing detail all of the reasons that surrogate motherhood contracts ought to be tightly regulated by law or banned altogether. These arrangements may work out sometimes. But when they go wrong, they are a disaster. As these regulations are currently constructed, they exploit low-income women and turn babies and human relationships into commodities to be brokered by lawyers and purchased by the well-to-do. Motherhood is put on the marketplace.

The Baby M case started out wrong and went downhill from there. The surrogate contract, which Bergen County judge Harvey R. Sorkow upheld, contained possible elements of fraud. Dr. Elizabeth Stern claimed she was infertile. She was not. She had a mild case of self-diagnosed multiple sclerosis, which she did not have confirmed by a specialist until October 1986. She did not consult a specialist about the risk of MS in pregnancy before deciding not to bear a baby, nor did the couple consult with adoption agencies before deciding they would not be able to adopt. William Stern wanted a genetic link.

Signs that Whitehead would have trouble giving up the baby were evident before the contract was signed. These signs were not fully explored by the clinic that drew up the contract and collected $7,500—which was not refundable under any circumstances. Whitehead did not have an independent lawyer protecting her interests when signing the contract nor did she have any in-depth counseling about the potentially devastating loss she might feel in relinquishing the baby. The social system that ought to govern such arrangements, as it does adoption procedures, utterly failed both couples.

After Whitehead refused to give up the baby, the Sterns—armed with New Jersey's preeminent family law expert—went into Sorkow's court and got a temporary order giving them custody. Here is where the legal system failed both couples and the baby.

There was a mighty legal issue at hand. The validity of these contracts has never been upheld in an American court. Indeed, English courts have ruled them unenforceable, with an English appellate court describing them as "a totally inhuman proceeding," and "a sordid commercial bargain." The English Parliament subsequently outlawed commercial surrogate parenting. Yet, Judge Sorkow—without Whitehead's being in court or having a lawyer to represent her—ruled that the baby could be taken away from her biological mother and given temporarily to the Sterns. At that point, Sorkow—with no legal precedent—gave more weight to a contract than to the deep, emotional organic bond that exists between a mother and her baby.

Whitehead by then had fled to Florida with the baby, where detectives hired by the Sterns tracked her down. She had had the baby four months. The baby was returned to the Sterns, where she remained, and for all intents and purposes the case was closed. For the Sterns, possession was nine-tenths of the law. For Whitehead, a tenth-grade dropout married to garbage collector, it didn't matter.

Judge Sorkow, having issued the temporary custody order, then turned the case into a custody case. And the Sterns went into court with the best legal and psychiatric weapons money could buy. Whitehead couldn't even get a lawyer to take her case until three weeks before the trial started—and he, with background in working with mothers who had given up their babies, was consistently barred from bringing up testimony about the psychological impact of a baby on adults and the legality of surrogate parenting. Judge Sorkow called the case "a routine custody case," and that turned on "the best interests of the child."

From that point on, the case hinged on the relative fitness of the two couples, which was heavily influenced by psychiatrists. But a critical reading of the psychiatric reports is enough to make one wonder about the profession. Whitehead's powerful desire to have her baby was interpreted as narcissism; Dr. Stern's unwillingness to become pregnant was not. Whitehead's coloring of her prematurely white hair was taken as further proof of narcissism, while William Stern's desire for a genetic link was not. Whitehead's ability to play patty-cake was questioned; Dr. Stern's self-diagnosis of MS was not.

Sorkow terminated all Whitehead's parental rights. In his decision, Sorkow wrote that he felt the Sterns would be better able to explain to the baby in the future the extraordinary origins of her birth. What they may never be able to explain to her is what they did to her mother and what she did to them. The solution to infertility—alleged or real—should never be commerce, and it should never risk such pain.

The Wisdom of Solomon
FEBRUARY 5, 1988

New Jersey Supreme Court chief justice Robert N. Wilentz has delivered a decision worthy of Solomon in the Baby M surrogate motherhood case. The ninety-five-page ruling provides a framework for resolving the emotionally charged case in the best interests of the child without brutally destroying the child's mother, as the lower court had done.

The 7-to-0 opinion gave custody of Melissa Stern, who is now twenty-two months old, to her biological father, William Stern, and his wife, Elizabeth, with whom the child has lived since she was four months old. The court found that, taking everything into consideration, the Sterns could provide a more stable home life for a little girl who will desperately need it.

That was the only point on which the Supreme Court upheld Superior Court judge Harvey Sorkow. Most significantly, the Supreme Court ruled that commercial surrogate contracts were nothing more than thinly disguised baby-selling schemes—"designed to circumvent our statutes." It found that Sorkow was wrong when he awarded temporary custody to the Sterns after Mary Beth Whitehead-Gould changed her mind about giving up her baby and again last March, when he ruled that surrogate contracts were valid and awarded permanent custody to the Sterns.

Sorkow terminated Whitehead-Gould's parental rights on the spot and allowed Elizabeth Stern to adopt the child within hours of his ruling. The Supreme Court ruled that he was wrong there, too, and threw out the adoption.

This means that Whitehead-Gould, who has since remarried, is entitled to visit her daughter. The court ordered that the issue of visitation be decided by another judge, who should bear in mind that Whitehead-Gould is "not only the natural mother, but also the legal mother, and is not to be penalized one iota because of the surrogacy contract. Mrs. Whitehead, as the mother . . . is entitled to have her own interest in visitation considered."

The ruling is not binding on other states, but it does establish principles of decency and the public interest that any judicial or legislative body would do well to incorporate in evaluating these arrangements. It reaffirms the sanctions against baby-selling, the paramount importance of parental rights and the very narrow rules under which they can be terminated. The ruling reaffirms the state's overriding interest in regulating adoptions and requiring that they be done through approved agencies. Third parties—such as lawyers fixing up surrogate schemes for profit—won't do, nor will their in-house counseling services, which the court found protected no one involved, least of all the child.

For the first time since Whitehead-Gould began her legal struggle, she found a court that put more value on motherhood and the relationship between a mother and her baby than on a piece of paper. "It seems to us that given her predicament, Mrs. Whitehead was rather harshly judged—both by the trial court and by some of the experts," Wilentz wrote. "She was guilty of a breach of contract, and indeed she did break a very important promise, but we think it is expecting something well beyond normal human capabilities to suggest that this mother should have parted with her newly born infant without a struggle. Other than survival, what stronger force is there? We do not know of, and cannot conceive of, any other case where a perfectly fit mother was expected to surrender her newly born infant, perhaps forever, and was then told she was a bad mother because she did not."

The court ruled that in custody questions involving newborns "only in the most unusual case should the child be taken from its mother before the dispute is finally determined by the courts on its merits. The probable bond between mother and child, and the child's need, not just the mother's, to strengthen that bond, along with the likelihood, in most cases, of a significantly lesser, if any, bond with the father—all counsel against temporary custody in the father."

The court concluded with the hope that the Sterns and White-head-Gould can work out visitation themselves, in "the best interests of the child." It has given all of the parents involved a chance to do this, by recognizing the legitimacy of all of their rights and by granting the full force of the law's protection to all of the parties involved.

And by outlawing commercial surrogacy, it took motherhood out of the marketplace, where it was subject to the totally inappropriate laws of commerce. "There are," Wilentz wrote, "values that society deems more important than granting to wealth whatever it can buy, be it labor, love, or life."

The Sterns and Whitehead-Gould will not appeal the court ruling—a sign of what a very wise man Chief Justice Wilentz must be.

Nature Too Chancy for Contracts
APRIL 22, 1988

We can now add another sad story to the growing list of reasons that surrogate motherhood is a bad answer to infertility problems. In this story, the woman who volunteered to carry a child for another couple had the poor judgment to give birth to twins. She was willing to give them up. The couple, however, wanted only the girl. It's not clear whether they made this decision by going eeny, meeny, miney, mo, or whether there was a deeper philosophical or practical reason behind their selection.

And it doesn't much matter: what does matter is that the male infant who was conceived under the contract was left without parents.

According to *USA Today,* Patty Nowakowski, twenty-seven, of Iona, Michigan, gave birth nearly a month ago to twins. She and her husband, Aaron, already have three children. The infertile couple told her they did not want a boy and picked up the female baby, whom they will adopt. Nowakowski and her husband subsequently put the male baby in foster care.

This week, however, they changed their minds and decided to keep him and adopt him. According to the newspaper article, the Nowakowskis decided it was unfair for him not to have parents and quoted Patty Nowakowski as saying: "We're willing to love him and accept him just like our other children." She also said: "We were trying to provide a baby for someone that couldn't have one, and this happens." Her conclusion: If surrogacy for money can't be regulated, "eliminate it."

The baby broker involved in this situation was Noel Keane, the Dearborn, Michigan, lawyer who arranged the "Baby M" case that backfired when the birth mother decided she could not give up the baby. The mother, Marybeth Whitehead-Gould, had been paid $10,000 to be artificially inseminated with the sperm of William Stern and to carry the baby for him and his wife, Elizabeth. The legal battle that followed in New Jersey lasted two years, and finally wound up in the state's Supreme Court. A lower court judge had upheld the surrogate arrangements as legal and ruled that the baby belonged to the Sterns. The Supreme Court eventually overturned the lower court on all legal points, but gave the Sterns custody on the grounds that the baby's best interests would be met by them. Whitehead-Gould recently won more visiting privileges with the baby.

The New Jersey Supreme Court became the first to declare surrogate agreements unenforceable and little more than thinly disguised baby-selling schemes designed, in the words of the court, "to circumvent our statutes." In the ruling's aftermath, a number of states began looking at legislation that would regulate or ban surrogate motherhood. Nowakowski told her story to a Michigan legislative committee that is considering a bill that would regulate surrogate arrangements for money and another bill that would ban the practice entirely.

Another surrogacy case gone awry surfaced recently in Maryland when a woman carrying a baby for an unidentified couple tried to find out more about them so she would know what kind of home the baby would be going to. The agency that arranged the contract required that the couple and the mother remain unknown to each other. The mother canceled her contract and planned to give the baby up for adoption if the couple did not come forward after the birth.

In January, a Michigan mother who gave birth to twins decided she wanted to keep them and refused to give them up to an Arkansas farmer who is their biological father. Laurie Yates, the mother, won a court ruling that the surrogacy contract was unenforceable. Judge Timothy Green of Gratiot County Circuit Court wrote: "I think it goes without saying that surrogacy denigrates human dignity. Contracts of surrogacy are void as contrary to public policy."

Yates subsequently relinquished her rights to the twins, thus avoiding a custody fight, and they now live with their father.

The Nowakowski case is yet one more example of why these contracts are contrary to sound public policy. The twins will now grow up apart, which creates a whole new set of problems for them and their parents. The Nowakowskis have done a very decent thing, and they now have the cost of raising a fourth child. What are the biological father's obligations in situations like this? What happens when a child is born handicapped, or when the child has a genetic defect transmitted by the mother? What happens when the little boy gets older and wants to know where he came from and finds out he wasn't "picked"? There are reasons why we have laws against baby-selling, which is essentially what surrogacy is, and Patty Nowakowski has become another witness in the case against it.

10

Modern Times

"Some women have taken the law into their own hands. Several years ago, at the end of a sold-out basketball game at the Capital Centre, the traffic jam in the ladies' room was worse than in the parking lots. Finally, a group of women noticed that no one was waiting to get into the men's room. They promptly turned it into a multiuse facility and cut the line for the ladies' room in half. Beer drinkers in the line were eternally grateful for their brave act."
　　　　　　　　　　　　　　　—"POTTY PARITY"

"The least that people who insist on having business breakfasts could do is have late ones. Starting, say, around noontime."
　　　　　　　—"BREAKFAST: NOBODY'S BUSINESS"

"Historically, politicians have been on par with foreign correspondents when it comes to being family

*men. Now, all of a sudden, we are getting an earful
about families from politicians who are in tough
races. I, for one, would like to see the next person
who bows out say something neat, simple and accurate, such as: 'I'm getting out of this race because I
know I can't win.' That's the kind of person I'd like
to vote for."*
                                       —"THE POLITICIAN AS FAMILY MAN"

*Jimmy the Greek: "He was part of a whole phony,
glitzy world where nothing is real, not even work,
where fame and notoriety count more than brains
and talent, where ignorance is no handicap, where
ratings are a measure of value and superficiality is a
single layer of facial foundation. Jimmy the Greek
was a media creation and CBS was by no means the
only media that played a role in this symbiotic
relationship. Now everyone is horrified to discover
that he isn't very bright, after all."*
                                       —"CBS's $750,000 GAMBLE"

*"There seem to be several morals coming out of the
televangelical scandals. One of them is that anyone
who thinks, or thought, that Jim and Tammy were
going to go quietly into that good night, or otherwise vanish into disgrace, is going to be dead
wrong. They have a knack for publicity and maintaining high visibility that's got to have presidential
candidates writhing with envy. Of course, if any of
them could persuade his wife to get tarted up like
Tammy Faye, he'd get a bundle of publicity, too."*
                                       —"BUT DISGRACE DOES PAY"

Breakfast: Nobody's Business
APRIL 18, 1986

Not very long after I returned to work after the birth of my
daughter, an editor (who was fairly new) suggested that we ought to
get together for breakfast. At first, I thought he was joking. Then I

realized he wasn't. I told him he was welcome to come out to my house and join the family for breakfast—he looked horrified at that thought—but that I didn't do breakfasts downtown.

I still don't, but if the invitations I've been getting are any reflection of reality (a dubious proposition, perhaps, but the only one that comes to mind), I'm the lone holdout against this dangerous trend called the business breakfast. It's perhaps the most uncivilized thing to come along since putting metal screwtops on wine bottles.

The business lunch is bad enough. In my business, you're either writing notes during a luncheon interview, which means your food gets cold, or you're doing fancy footwork on behalf of your career, which means your digestive tract may shut down, or you're having a delightful lunch and really not working at all, which means you're cheating.

In my business, we call this "cultivating sources." Other businesses call it "making useful contacts." It's a nice way of getting to go to nice restaurants and not having to pay the tab yourself, so it has its compensations. And by lunchtime (unlike breakfasttime), most people are awake and within some geographic proximity of the location where this ritual is to take place.

As best I can tell, the business breakfast is taking hold in two forms, both equally pernicious. The first is the business breakfast with your boss (a peer, a fellow human, would never suggest such a thing) or some other individual you have business with who suggests that the two or three of you, as the case may be, get together for breakfast. These meetings are held at private tables in downtown hotel restaurants (these being the only eateries usually open at 7:30 or 8:00 in the morning).

An exception to this has been made in Washington by at least one famous business lunch restaurant—Joe & Mo's—which opened nearly two years ago for business breakfasts. Mo Sussman reports that "we're doing well with it," with breakfast fares ranging from normal breakfasts to toast and a pot of hot water. "It's a small-ticket item and quicker, but you get a lot of things done. It's a very effective use of time."

The other kind of business breakfast that is taking hold is the "special breakfast" (a type of event that, when held at lunchtime, is called a "special luncheon"), where a crowd of people gather to hear panelists debate weighty issues or speakers hold forth on worldly topics.

My most recent invitation, for example, was to hear an important judge make a speech at a downtown hotel—at 8:00 a.m. This would have required me to arise around 6:00 a.m. in order to get dressed (showing up at business breakfasts in your nightie is considered too casual) and battle the commuter traffic downtown.

Since my children do not leave for elementary school until 8:45 a.m. I would have had to leave them home alone for an hour and a half in the morning, time enough for them to commit all manner of crimes against property and humanity. While some people may function very well at 6:00 a.m., I find the best function I perform at that hour is deep sleeping.

So do a number of my friends and associates. One who has been particularly appalled at the business breakfast phenomenon figures he would have to leave his home at 6:30 a.m. in order to make the typical business breakfast, which means getting up at 5:30 a.m. "I can't function at that time of the morning," he said, which was easy to believe, since he had trouble saying "five-thirty ayem."

He says he would miss seeing his wife and sons and that business breakfasts are antifamily and antipeople. "Furthermore," he says, "what about the Letterman factor?"

It turns out he is one of a growing number of addicts to "Late Night with David Letterman," which airs at 12:30 a.m. Letterman addicts don't get to sleep until after 1:30 a.m. unless they tape the show on their videocassette recorders, which they seem to be reluctant to do because that isn't really having the whole David Letterman experience, which includes being sleepy the next day.

Perhaps people do get a head start on the day with the business breakfast. But I submit it adds anywhere from an hour to two hours to the workday, which is an hour or two taken away from the family or aerobics or other worthwhile activities. The least that people who insist on having business breakfasts could do is have late ones.

Starting, say, around noontime.

The Politician as Family Man
SEPTEMBER 25, 1987

Senator Paul S. Trible (R-Va.) has been taking a lot of flak the last few days for announcing that he would not run for reelection because he wanted to spend more time with his family. I, however, am behind him 1,000 percent. In fact, he's going to be my role model for the remainder of the month. I, too, would dearly love to quit my present job so that I can devote more time to my family. (This happens after every vacation.)

Of course, our circumstances are a little different. Trible is still interested in politics and has made it clear that he has not ruled out the idea of running for governor of Virginia. What appeals to him about that job is the fact that the governor's residence is right next door to the governor's office, and he seems to think that would let him spend more time with his family. It's a new angle on working at home.

The present tenant, Democratic governor Gerald L. Baliles, had some words of caution for Trible, however. At a news conference this week, he said that Trible had the wrong idea if he thought being governor was "a nine-to-five job." Baliles's press secretary, Chris Bridge, who has two children, says that Baliles had been in his office until one or two o'clock in the morning "on four separate occasions in the last week and a half." So have people on his staff, she says. "We couldn't even count the times we've been here until one or two in the morning because he is here."

To hear her tell it, being governor of Virginia may not be the ideal job for someone who is trying to juggle family and career. First, there is a lot of traveling around the state. Baliles also has been on two-week trade missions to China and Europe this year and heads out shortly for another two-week trade mission to Japan. Second, there are the personal appearances and speeches. "One day we counted 135 requests for appearances, speeches and attendance at events."

Bridge says she doesn't question Trible's sincerity about wanting to spend more time with his family. "While his intention may be to free up more time for his family, the schedule this governor has will not reflect that intention."

No discussion of Trible's attempts to juggle family and career would be complete without mentioning the fact that the first-term senator was facing the possibility of a very tough race against former governor Charles S. Robb, who managed to get the state Democratic party back on the map. Robb, who has been playing hard to get and hasn't made a move to campaign for the job, had a fifteen-point lead over Trible in a late July poll conducted by Mason-Dixon Opinion Research.

This prompted some political analysts and observers to suggest that Trible, who had been actively campaigning and fundraising, was pulling out because of Robb, not because of his family.

The only person who really knows the truth of the matter is Trible himself. What is incontrovertible, however, is the fact that Trible has now joined a growing list of people who are citing family considerations as a reason for bowing out of political races. Gary Hart quit his presidential race, saying, in part, that he refused to submit his family to further gossip. Senator Dale Bumpers (D-Ark.) said he wouldn't run for president because it means "a total disruption of one's life and the life of his family," and, if victorious, family closeness is "necessarily lost forever." Governor Bill Clinton of Arkansas bowed out saying he did not want to be away from his daughter for the long periods a presidential campaign requires. New York governor Mario Cuomo also cited what was "best for my family" in announcing that he was sitting out this dance. San Antonio mayor Henry Cisneros has taken himself out of consideration for any statewide races in 1990, including the governorship of Texas, citing the health of his infant son, who was born with severe birth defects. No one on earth would quarrel with the legitimacy of Cisneros's position, but there are people who might start wondering about some of the others.

Historically, politicians have been on par with foreign correspondents when it comes to being family men. Now, all of a sudden, we are getting an earful about families from politicians who are in tough races. Have we come upon a generation of born-again family men? Are present-day politics too tough on families? Or, perish the thought, are they simply using their families as a politically fashionable excuse?

I, for one, would like to see the next person who bows out say something neat, simple and accurate, such as: "I'm getting out of this race because I know I can't win." That's the kind of person I'd like to vote for.

Growing Older with a New Grace
AUGUST 5, 1987

Gloria Steinem turned fifty and said being fifty now is like forty used to be. The quote was widely publicized and everyone I know this side of fifty took a lot of comfort in it. Steinem, it turns out, wasn't the only one who felt that aging isn't nearly as horrid for women as it is cracked up to be.

Woman's Day magazine and the Avon Corporation teamed up to do a poll on how women feel about aging, and the result from the 499 women over twenty-one, in a nutshell, was that the vast majority feel just fine. On a Bo Derek scale of 1 to 10, women of all ages in the survey gave themselves a 6.5 on average. Women under thirty-five gave themselves a 6.8, women thirty-five to forty-nine gave themselves a 6.6, and women fifty and older gave themselves a 6. Only 12 percent of the women polled said they had ever worried about losing a boyfriend or husband to a younger woman, and only 17 percent said that growing older was something they worried about a lot. A mere 12 percent said that being attractive to men was something that they worried about a lot, and only 20 percent believed that looking younger was an important factor in being attractive to men.

Topping the women's list of worries was their health, followed by their weight, physical appearance, having a job they liked, having a job that pays better and being too old to accomplish what they would like to accomplish in life.

The women seemed unconcerned about their own aging and about the ages of other people. For example, 76 percent said they would not be bothered if they saw a woman dating or married to a much younger man, and a resounding 83 percent said they would not be bothered seeing a man dating or married to a much younger woman.

Ellen Levine, editor of *Woman's Day,* said the survey grew out of a phenomenon at the magazine. "We were sitting in the office and somebody was turning thirty and somebody was turning forty and somebody was turning fifty and nobody was crying. And we said, 'Let's find out what other women are thinking.'

"Women are feeling a lot better about aging. It is really a part of the fabric of everything that's happening. Women have more choices now, and they don't have to rely on their face and their body because they are valued by themselves and by others for qualities other than their youth and their physical beauty."

Eighty-eight percent of the women say they never lie about their age. Yet 85 percent say they like it when someone says they look younger than they really are, and more than half say that they work hard at looking attractive. About three-quarters are watching their weight and the way they dress, 59 percent are exercising, 32 percent are coloring their hair, 64 percent are using skin creams and 18 percent are using antiaging products.

Gail Blanke, vice president of communications at Avon, said the results did not surprise the company. "We've had the feeling for some time that women are feeling better about themselves. The fact they don't lie about their age [is] because they feel so good about themselves. They feel good about how they look. The reason they feel good about how they look is that they are taking such good care of themselves. They are exercising, they are eating the right food and taking care of their skin. In the cosmetics industry, the skin care category is the fastest-growing category. Women think of skin creams not as a luxury but a necessity and they are using them. So who cares how old you are if you look wonderful?

"Women are more interested in what they are doing and what they are accomplishing than they have been in the past. They are taking risks. They are judging themselves according to their own priorities, and they have the courage to set those priorities for themselves. Among those priorities is taking control of their lives and making the decisions as to how they are going to be happy."

The attitudes in the survey reflect the profound changes in the way women look at life. "Women are just not afraid anymore" is the way Blanke puts it. "They are not afraid of making mistakes. They are not afraid of what other people think. The most important judge in their lives is themselves.

"Over the last ten years the number of self-employed women has increased at twice the rate of men. Women are feeling good enough about themselves to take the risks and learn new skills they want to learn. You don't have to hang on to a particular age, a particular look. You can keep on moving, keep on changing, keep on growing. It's possible that age could become, even for a woman, irrelevant."

That's my kind of survey.

Soccer Parent
NOVEMBER 25, 1987

It occurred to me last Saturday, when I was standing in arctic winds on the soccer field at a local high school, that my career as a soccer parent was more than half over. By the end of the weekend, it occurred to me that this may not be an entirely bad thing. I didn't bargain for Little League.

This season opened ominously. The first game was an away game that got rained out. The second game was an away game that also got rained out, only nobody bothered to tell us. But the parents, at least, took that in good stride since no one was terribly keen on the idea of standing in the rain watching our twelve-year-old sons play soccer. We had done that already. A number of times.

The third game of the season was also an away game, and by then the parents of the team were as eager as the kids to see a game actually get played. That day, the referees didn't show up. Perfectly nice parents whom I have known for years were making perfectly dreadful suggestions about what to do to the coordinators responsible for referees. We knew years ago what we were getting into with a traveling soccer team, but so far this fall all we'd done was travel.

The following weekend, the season actually got under way and we played a game, chalking up the first victory of the season. Normally, I take a dim view of nonparticipants in a game using the term "we." For example: it strikes me as totally absurd for somebody who is sitting on a barstool in Washington to use the term "we" in discussing a Redskins game. With soccer parents, however, there is a logic to the term "we." We produced the players. We feed them. We drive them around the Beltway for games, which is what happened a couple of weeks later when we ended up on a Sunday afternoon near the Capital Centre.

This time, the referees did show up and one of them was in a terrible mood. Or else he was on a power trip, which is not unheard-of in adults who are involved in children's sports. In any event, our coach—a mild-mannered former college soccer star who has been known on occasion to raise his eyebrows at officiating (never his voice, of course)—protested a call in such a fashion as to attract a referee's attention and he received a yellow card warning. His attempts at explaining what he had done were immediately met by a red card and he had to leave the field. This was a moment of high drama in the history of our soccer team, which went on to win.

(Unfortunately, there was more to come. I had locked my keys in the car. If you want to feel like a real dummy sometime, try telling a woman behind a locked door about how you were in her neighborhood for a soccer game and locked your car keys in your car and could you borrow a coat hanger that you will bring right back. "Don't bother," she said, handing out a coat hanger.)

The season dragged on longer than usual this year because snow caused a lot of makeup games to be canceled. On Saturday, teams all around the area were playing in the kind of cold that turns people blue. The highlight of our game came when it ended.

Real drama, however, occurred the following day on a field in Annandale.

Before the game started, the woman referee warned the coaches that if they started yelling at her, she would red-card them. The game began well enough, but our team scored on an unusual circumstance. The opposing coach argued that it wasn't a goal, and there was much consulting of rule books and so forth, and while the goal stood, so did the ugly mood. Our team scored again, and the next thing you know adults from the other team—including the linesman—were yelling at the referee and she yellow-carded the coach. The yelling continued, however, and within a few minutes the referee stopped the game and gave a red card to the coach.

Whereupon he withdrew his team from the field, forfeiting the game, minutes before the end of the first half.

None of our kids had ever seen such a display and neither had any of the parents. The teams were not able to play the last game of the season. Moreover, the kids on both teams were witnessing a display of unsportsmanlike conduct more appropriate to "The Bad News Bears" than to local youth soccer.

Soccer took off in this area partly in a reaction to the overly competitive and overmanaging adults who thought Little League was a farm system for the Yankees. Unfortunately, some of those competitive pressures are now affecting soccer. Each season, the local leagues have had to issue warnings to parents and to coaches about their behavior on the sidelines. And that's too bad.

It's supposed to be a sport for kids and not a power trip for adults.

CBS's $750,000 Gamble
JANUARY 20, 1988

The most astonishing part of the whole Jimmy the Greek Snyder episode was not what he said, but what he got paid for what he did. His is an inspiring story of our time, in which somebody, somewhere in the dim past, decided to put an oddsmaker on television and make him a star. And being a star is what Snyder did for a living.

And what a living it turned out to be. According to news reports at the time of his firing, Snyder was being paid $750,000 on a one-year contract from CBS to talk about football. Snyder did not do particularly demanding work for that money, nor did he bring any transcending talent—or knowledge—to the airwaves. He showed up in press boxes, but he was by no means a journalist. He had parlayed a remarkably limited shtick into mega media bucks.

He was what is known as a media personality.

Media personalities have not been around all that long. In fact, it is a relatively new occupation and is still searching for a good definition. The Labor Department's list of occupations doesn't even include this category, which not only makes it difficult to define exactly what media personalities do, it also makes it impossible to determine their average annual incomes. It's a safe bet, however, that Snyder's annual income of $750,000 was right up there for a media personality.

Snyder played his role well. He was large, and loud, and wore bright clothes. You could not miss him if you tried. He had opinions on everything and delivered them with an energetic self-assuredness that was the envy of every con man (or would-be con man) who had nothing better to do with his weekend afternoons than watch sports on television.

Snyder at the race track was a spectacle unto himself. He would arrive and depart with fanfare befitting someone who had just trained a Triple Crown winner. He would give the odds on a race and tout his favorite with the supreme confidence of a man who had never, ever been wrong. Whether he had any idea of what he was talking about was irrelevant. He was a showman. He exuded self-importance and thrived upon it. You could actually say he made a living off it. You can bet your next mortgage payment that CBS never would have dropped $750,000 a year on a self-effacing oddsmaker who would sit quietly in a race track press box feeding speed figures into a computer and come up with accurate predictions for a horse race. That guy could have picked ten winners in a row and he'd have been labeled a researcher—and paid accordingly.

Media personalities must have style. One of the early media personalities in the sports world was Casey Stengel, who was a much-revered figure among sportswriters. He was a world-class raconteur, albeit at times an incomprehensible one by reliable accounts. But he was much more than a media creation. He was also a first-rate baseball manager.

Snyder was a media creation who started off in Las Vegas, according to his own account, by doing public relations for Howard Hughes' hotels. He, again by his own account, dabbled in odds-making to help out his friends. By the early seventies, columnist Jack Anderson was quoting his odds on presidential elections and dubbing him the nation's number-one oddsmaker. (Who's number two?) Snyder wrote a syndicated newspaper column giving odds on football games and fights. Never mind that bookmaking is illegal, we all know these kinds of columns are just to give the guys at the office a little assist in their friendly bets. The fact that Snyder was a convicted gambler who had been pardoned by President Ford merely added a little authenticity to the creation. Sportswriters quoted his odds, and on dull days in dull towns, they wrote about him. Over the years, he went from being a Vegas hustler to a full-fledged media personality.

He was part of a whole phony, glitzy world where nothing is real, not even work, where fame and notoriety count more than brains and talent, where ignorance is no handicap, where ratings are a measure of value and superficiality is a single layer of facial foundation. Jimmy the Greek was a media creation and CBS was by no means the only media that played a role in this symbiotic relationship. Now everyone is horrified to discover that he isn't very bright, after all.

CBS, however, was the only one paying him $750,000 a year at a time when it is savaging its payroll. No doubt the network fired him because of his unseemly racial remarks. But what a nice excuse he gave them to act on such a heady matter of principle. For a brief moment, the folks who operate in that world could do something real.

And save three-quarters of a million bucks a year.

Putting Racism to Rest
FEBRUARY 3, 1988

Every professional gambler dreams of a chance to fix a professional football game, and this Sunday it finally happened. Jimmy the Greek put the fix in two weeks ago. And what we watched, all 105 million of us, was the Jimmy the Greek Memorial Superbowl. There was a lot that still needed to be put to rest.

It must be impossible for a white person, male or female, to know what it is like to grow up black in this society. White middle-class women have gotten a taste of discrimination, and the effect is devastating. Blacks get it from the day they are born. They live in a society where the norm, the standard of excellence, is white and everything else is different. And they know that no matter how well things might be going for them, somebody could jump up out of nowhere and call them boy.

Which is exactly what Jimmy (the Greek) Snyder did on January 15, that fateful day at Duke Zeibert's, when, without benefit of formal education in these matters, he held forth on a mixture of American history and anthropology—or was it biology?—and started 1988 off with headline-making nouveau racism.

According to Snyder, blacks are superior athletes because they work harder than white athletes do. And: "The black is a better athlete to begin with, because he's been bred that way. . . . This all goes back to the Civil War, when, during the slave trading, the slave owner would breed his big black to his big woman so that they would have a big black kid. That's where it all started."

And that's where it all ended for CBS's resident oddsmaker, but the damage had been done. In a single sickening mouthful,

Snyder had once again asserted the white man's divine right to generalize and stereotype, to divide the races, to denigrate the black athlete and to stomp all over the most precious thing a person has: his dignity.

Blacks playing in the NFL know perfectly well why so few blacks have played quarterback in that league, and why no black quarterback had ever started on a Super Bowl team before Doug Williams started on Sunday. The prevailing wisdom in the league has always been that blacks aren't smart enough to play quarterback in the NFL. Simple as that.

Too, there have always been questions about blacks "quitting" when they are hurt. Also, there's the matter of leadership. Quarterbacks have to lead the team, you see. Can a black provide the kind of leadership an NFL team needs to get to the Super Bowl? Or, put in less spiritual terms, what NFL coach was willing to take the risk of handing over his owner's multi-million-dollar NFL franchise to a black quarterback?

Not very many. Williams didn't start a game for five years in the NFL—the equivalent of a lot of players' entire careers—before replacing the injured Jay Schroeder last September. By then, Williams was thirty-two and hoping to be traded, looking for a final shot at starting for an NFL team.

In an interview with *Washington Post* staff writer Jane Leavey, Williams spoke bluntly about what it was like in the NFL. He described it as the "brawn over brain thing, it's why we don't have a black president and secretary of state and all that good stuff. . . . Not because we can't but because they don't think so." The knock on him—that he threw too hard—was a code for "we weren't smart enough. We didn't have touch."

"I am an invisible man," wrote Ralph Ellison. "No, I am not a spook like those who haunted Edgar Allan Poe; nor am I one of your Hollywood-movie ectoplasms. I am a man of substance, of flesh and bone, fiber and liquids—and I might even be said to possess a mind. I am invisible, understand, simply because people refuse to see me. . . .

"You wonder whether you aren't simply a phantom in other people's minds. Say, a figure in a nightmare which the sleeper tries with all his strength to destroy. It's when you feel like this that, out of resentment, you begin to bump people back. And, let me confess, you feel that way most of the time."

During the third quarter of Sunday's game, the animated scoreboard in the stadium featured a film on the top quarterbacks of 1987. Williams, leading a team to a Super Bowl victory, didn't even get a call. After two years in the U.S. Football League, he had gotten only one call, and that was from the Redskins, the only team in the NFL that was interested in his services.

"The bottom line is opportunity," he told Leavey last September. "If you get the opportunity everything else will take care of itself no matter what it is."

Which is what happened in the Jimmy the Greek Memorial Super Bowl. Williams was a very visible man who had the opportunity to take care of a lot of stuff. And he did.

But Disgrace Does Pay
FEBRUARY 26, 1988

It's getting to be too much. Now comes the news that NBC television has hired Jim and Tammy Bakker to be consultants for its Movie of the Week, *Fall from Grace*, which is one of the most famous tumbles to have occurred in the 1980s. CBS is also doing a movie about the Bakkers, *God and Greed: The Jim and Tammy Faye Bakker Story*. There's a moral to this story: scandal sells.

Actually, there seem to be several morals coming out of the televangelical scandals. One of them is that anyone who thinks, or thought, that Jim and Tammy were going to go quietly into that good night, or otherwise vanish into disgrace, is going to be dead wrong. Those two are going to be making news and comebacks, and most assuredly money, for a very long time. They have a knack for publicity and maintaining high visibility that's got to have presidential candidates writhing with envy. Of course, if any of them could persuade his wife to get tarted up like Tammy Faye, he'd get a bundle of publicity, too.

What Jim and Tammy could tell NBC movie producers that they would believe isn't clear, but perhaps NBC thinks that getting the Bakkers in as consultants will lend some authenticity to the project. Tammy wants Sally Field to play her part, and perhaps she can coach her on how to cry on cue. Tammy's got that down pat. She can do it on the air and off the air. The press tried to get some

reaction from the Bakkers after the Rev. Jimmy Swaggart publicly
confessed to his flock that he failed in his battle with Satan.
Bakker said he was "deeply saddened" and that Tammy had cried
when she'd heard the news. Bet me.

The sordid details of Swaggart's secret life are just beginning
to emerge. If the early photos of his inamorata are on the mark, he
stands a good chance of being spared the *Penthouse* and *Playboy*
photo spreads and interviews that helped keep the Bakker saga
going. Deborah Murphree is not a church secretary and she
doesn't look like Jessica Hahn.

One thing that seems strikingly clear about both Swaggart
and Bakker is that both of those Bible-thumping churchmen have
serious problems with women and sex. Jessica Hahn's account of
her encounter with Bakker—if it is true—leaves the reader with
the distinct impression that this is a man who is probably incapa-
ble of a loving, sexual relationship.

Sources close to the Assemblies of God inquiry into Swaggart's downfall have said that he has been battling a fascination
with pornography and pornographic literature that goes back to his
boyhood. What actually transpired when he met with prostitutes is
still not clear. Nor is it clear what is meant in this situation by
pornography. Assemblies of God fundamentalists, and others, have
made the war against pornography a centerpiece of their movement. Fundamentalists were behind the campaigns to force stores
to stop selling *Playboy* and *Penthouse*. Those are not the folks
known for drawing fine lines of distinction when they are on the
attack. So, who knows? Swaggart's battle with the devil may have
been over his reading of *Playboy*.

Christian fundamentalists have been the heart and soul behind efforts to keep sex education out of the schools, and, failing
that, to force schools to preach abstinence. Adultery and promis-
cuity are right up there alongside communism and godlessness on
the list of deadly sins. Those are people who have more than a
quaint, old-fashioned idea about fidelity in marriage. Swaggart
made a living preaching against lust. He wrote in his autobiography that the Lord gave him his calling when he was a mere nine
years old, right about the time he apparently began his battle with
the forces of evil. A psychiatrist could have a field day with that.

So another moral to come out of the religious scandals may be
that it is wise to wonder about people who become obsessed with
the evils of sex. What are they afraid of, and why? Or, put another

way, people who try to repress normal patterns of human behavior are going to find it emerging in abnormal ways. For Swaggart, his obsession took him into some of the seediest sections of New Orleans in quests that threatened to expose him and topple him from the most powerful—not to mention profitable—teleministry going in America.

He's now scheduled to undergo a period of counseling and rehabilitation. That's a natural sequel to his autobiography. ABC can grab his story for a piece of the action on the televangelical scandals. And in a year or two, Swaggart can be back preaching again and passing the collection plate. The final moral of the story is that there is no such thing as disgrace anymore.

An Abstract Issue Turns to Concrete
APRIL 20, 1988

One of the nice things about writing a newspaper column is that you get paid to have opinions about things that very often won't have much direct effect on you. This is particularly true if you are successful at it and make lots of money. You can take the high road on some of the great social issues of our time with the knowledge that you can probably insulate yourself and your loved ones from the fallout of your high-mindedness.

Columnists—and politicians, too, for that matter—have gotten caught on any number of occasions preaching one thing and practicing another. Busing proved to be one of the great ethical donnybrooks, for example, as moneyed liberals took the high road in favor of busing and then took the back roads to send their children to private schools by car pool.

Over the years, I have written about the efforts of women to level the playing field of life. That metaphor didn't just come out of nowhere. One of the aspects of this leveling process has been the efforts of women to get an equal shot in athletics. This has included columns about young girls seeking the more challenging level of play that exists on boys' teams. Girls who have wanted to be on all-male soccer teams have had an ally in this space. So have teams that have been banned from tournaments or organized play because they had a girl on them. What difference does it make? If she's good enough to make the team, she should be able to play.

This Sunday, the abstract came home to roost.

My son the twelve-year-old's soccer team—hereinafter known as Green—was scheduled to play a Maryland team—hereinafter known as Red. We all arrived a half hour before game time, as required, so the boys could warm up. Parents visited with one another until the game started. I watched the final stages of the warm-up and noticed that one of the Red players had very long hair. We're not talking below the shirt collar. We're talking below the shoulders.

My son walked by on the sidelines. "Is that a girl on that team?" I said. It had been at least three years since the boys had played soccer on or against an integrated team.

He said: "Nah. It's just some guy with long hair."

I watched the guy with long hair for a few minutes, and there was something not quite right. The game began with the player assigned to the middle of the forward line. I walked up to our team's manager. He works for the Central Intelligence Agency, so I figured he ought to know. He was making notes on his clipboard.

"Is that a girl on their team?" I asked.

"We don't know," he said tersely.

I wandered over to where his wife was sitting. She also works for the CIA. She was talking with several other mothers. I asked her the same question. She said: "That's what we're trying to figure out."

We all turned practiced eyes toward the field. The mysterious Red player was fast and aggressive, but was also fairly far away. "It's a girl," I declared after a few minutes.

"She touches her hair like a girl," announced another mother.

We continued watching for clues as the Red team mounted a series of attacks. At one point, there was speculation that the Green boys had figured out she was girl. "They're laying off her," one parent ventured, without much evidence other than the fact that the mystery player hadn't been sacked, which, looking back, might have been worth a penalty.

The Red team scored. As the dust cleared, it became clear that the mystery player had scored the goal. Play began again at the line of scrimmage, and before long, the mystery player was taking the ball downfield and the question of gender was cleared up once and for all when an enthusiastic parent on the other side of the field hollered for all the world to hear: "DO IT AGAIN, NICOLE!"

At which point approximately twenty-five parents on the Green side of the field said: "NICOLE?!"

The score was tied 1–1 at the half, and never in the history of sports has one half-time huddle been so thoroughly dominated by a member of the opposite sex. The Green coach tried to clear up any confusion by telling the boys they had to treat her like any other player. The parents—no sexists in our midst—backed him up.

At one point in the second half she had the ball and was headed toward our goal and several mothers on our side lost it. They hollered: "GET THE BALL AWAY FROM THAT GIRL!"

She didn't score again, but Red won the game 2–1. Nicole was a wild card, no question about that. But when the abstract came home to roost, one thing was absolutely clear: For a girl to make a team playing at that level, she has to be one terrific player.

And she was.

Home on the Range
JUNE 17, 1988

My vote for Couple of the Season—and maybe for the whole year— goes to Walter and Nancy Stewart, the Potomac, Maryland, home- owners who are engaging in the practice of "meadow gardening" and driving their neighbors bonkers. Individualism isn't dead after all.

According to the story in yesterday's *Washington Post* by reporter Jo-Ann Armao, the Stewarts bought their home in Poto- mac three years ago for $440,000. Walter Stewart is a research scientist at the National Institutes of Health who has made news in the past for his efforts to fight misconduct in science. Nancy Stewart is a lawyer with the U.S. Justice Department. One of the delightful aspects of this story was the discovery that you don't have to be a starving college student anymore to be a nonconform- ist. Here are two people who haven't been co-opted entirely and who've made a decent living. It's nice to know that's possible.

You'd think that an NIH scientist and a government lawyer would fit perfectly into a swank Potomac subdivision, but under- neath their yuppie credentials beat the hearts of rebels. And the Stewarts have committed the one act of rebellion that residents of the suburbs cannot stand: they don't cut their lawn.

Folks in the suburbs will forgive a lot in their neighbors—loutish behavior toward children, unleashed dogs, motorcycles, loud disputes in driveways and terrible taste in landscaping schemes—but lawns are an entirely different matter. Lawns simply must be mowed. And there is a very good reason for this: lawns show. And therefore, unlike bloody indoor battles between spouses, the state of neighbors' lawns affects everyone else's visual pleasure.

To put it more bluntly, they affect everyone else's fortunes, because lawns affect property values. When property values are at stake, neighbors think nothing of trying to impose their upscale notions of suburban standards on those few folks out there who are brave enough to try to liberate themselves from the tyranny of suburban chores. And as property values continue to go through the roof around here, we are going to be hearing more and more stories about property values vs. property rights.

The Stewarts traded in lawn mowing for the more natural approach of land management called meadow gardening. That's a nice way of saying that they turned their lawn into a meadow, full of wildflowers and tall grasses and weeds and everything else that can take root in nature's landscaping plans. And, of course, meadows make wonderful hiding and nesting places for snakes and field mice and lots of other small animals that have been driven into ecological exile by the construction boom that has ravaged the countryside.

Meadow gardening is nothing new. Thalassa Cruso, an Englishwoman who has become one of America's most celebrated gardeners, wrote glowingly of one of her own country lawns that she converted into a meadow. "I let this grass grow high and tall and full of the wildflowers of the hedgerows, and it looks like a fine sweep of herbaceous wild plants. . . . The seeded grasses and the tall ox-eye daisies nodding in the wind are restful and a pleasure to the eye."

In Potomac, however, a meadow is not considered a pleasure to the eye, it is considered an eyesore. The Stewarts got their first taste of Suburban Standards two years ago when they arrived home with their children and found a snooty note in their mailbox that said: "Please, cut your lawn. It's a disgrace to the entire neighborhood." Whoever wrote it didn't have the guts to sign it or to approach the couple in a neighborly manner to discuss the problem. This is the way guerrilla warfare is conducted in the suburbs: stuffing anonymous notes in mailboxes.

The Stewarts responded with a five-page environmental-impact statement to their neighbors that said, in effect, their meadow was a lot healthier way to go than the chemically soaked lawns all around them. Somebody apparently complained to the county, which ordered the Stewarts to mow the lawn and cited a weed law of dubious legal standing, which the Stewarts have vowed to challenge. They say the weeds pose no danger to anyone and that Montgomery County can't tell them what their property ought to look like.

Thus, the classic battle lines have been drawn between government and the individual, and so far, the individuals are winning. In a display of real statesmanship, the county has delayed taking the case to trial, and the County Council is going to look at some amendments that might allow alternative lifestyles in suburban laws.

The Stewarts are standing up for the meadow garden, and in so doing they are protecting a lot more than their right to enjoy wildflowers growing in the wind.

Fight Is Monument to a Decade of Greed
JUNE 29, 1988

Twenty years from now, historians will very likely single out the Tyson-Spinks fight as one of the telling cultural excesses that characterized the 1980s. At $33 million for ninety-one seconds of work, this was no metaphor. This was truly the fight for the decade of greed.

It brought out the worst in nearly everyone connected with it, or who tried to get connected with it, and nearly every sordid disease of the body, mind or character that got big play in this decade showed up in one or more of the parties to this event. Never have so many tacky people gotten so rich, so quickly. Michael Spinks and the people around him emerged as the class act, and he lost. This is not a decade in which the good guys have come out winners.

If you were writing an amorality play about the fight—morality plays don't sell in the present climate—you'd have trouble finding a publisher. Editors would find your characters too flawed. They want at least one hero, and they prefer him not to get flattened in the first round. Even Jackie Collins, who has made millions turning bad taste into best-sellers, would have trouble making those folks appealing.

Tyson won the fight, but greed and decadence won the day. The decline of the Roman empire is becoming less and less of a far-fetched analogy. Ivana Trump, wife of the fight's billionaire promoter and a pretty good self-promoter in her own right, had the perfect quote for the night: "This is just phenomenal. I think it is a little bit like a car race. There is a smell of blood in the air." Happily for Spinks, we don't feed the losing gladiator to the lions.

Her husband, Donald Trump, paid $11 million to play host to the fight, which was held in the Atlantic City Convention Center, adjacent to his Trump Plaza hotel—and, more importantly, his casino. It took a half hour to announce the celebrities in the crowd before the fight, many of whom were flown in on Trump's personal fleet of helicopters. For the very rich, helicopters are really the only way to get around these days.

Close friends of the couple were treated to ringside seats— which were going to the socially unconnected for a mere $1,500 a pop—and to a prefight gala that featured twelve hundred pounds of lobster tail and sliced filet in pink peppercorn sauce. One of the reasons the rich stay rich is that after a certain point, they get a lot of stuff for free.

The live gate alone figured to generate a record $12.3 million, and with various closed circuit and TV deals, the whole package was supposed to gross $70 million. Tyson will get about $20 million and Spinks was guaranteed $13.5 million, win or lose. Just to add a little perspective here, Tyson got $500 for his first professional fight, three and a half years ago.

Tyson is twenty-one years old, a high school dropout who got his start as a mugger and thief in Brooklyn and was doing time in reform school by the time he was eleven. There, he was discovered by the legendary boxing trainer, Cus D'Amato, who became his guardian. D'Amato died in 1985, his partner, Jimmy Jacobs, died in March and while his other partner, Bill Cayton, still holds a management contract with Tyson, he clearly doesn't hold his heart and soul.

Those belong to Robin Givens, twenty-three, an actress whom Tyson wed in February and who has been at the center of controversy ever since. So has her mother, Ruth Roper, forty-four, who filed a court suit against New York Yankee Dave Winfield, claiming he gave her an unspecified venereal disease. The suit was recently settled out of court. News reports about Roper and Givens have not been flattering: Givens, who attended Sarah Lawrence, was the only person booed at graduation. She has subsequently claimed to have attended Harvard Medical School, which has no record of her presence. She married Tyson without signing a prenuptial agreement, and you can bet your next paycheck that both she and her mother would have shopped around a good bit longer for a suitable mate had Tyson been a sparring partner for Joe Palooka. She was loudly booed when she was introduced to the fight crowd.

She sat next to Don King, the sleazy promoter who looks like he does his hair by sticking his finger in an electric socket. King is doing everything he can to cut himself in on the action and to cut Cayton out. HBO reported Monday night that Givens has filed suit against Cayton so King, for now, looks like he's got the inside track.

Tyson has been called a human money-making machine. He's going to need it. The bet here is that greed will play as big a role in the final chapter of this amorality play as it has at the beginning: the champ's going to get plucked like a chicken.

Public's Right Not to Care
AUGUST 5, 1988

This is probably heresy for anyone in the news business, but I'm hoping that Governor Michael S. Dukakis and Vice President Bush will resist demands that they release their medical records to the public. I've had it up to here with presidential colons and graphic illustrations of surgical incisions and learned accounts of various clinical procedures being practiced on the leaders of the free world. Enough, already.

Some of this debate about candidates' private lives and the public's right to know—and here you can fill in the blank about the topic du jour—ought to be rephrased in terms of the public's need to know. Sure, the public has a right to know if the candidate for president is a raving drunk, lunatic, womanizer, thief, liar or if he's just plain stupid. Unfortunately, it doesn't always work that way.

The voting public has been badly burned on at least a couple of occasions with its presidents and vice presidents, so it should come as no surprise that voters want to know as much as possible about who is running for the highest offices in the land. It is in this climate that all sorts of questions about candidates' personal, professional and fiduciary lives are being asked by the media and by the candidates' opposing camps. Legitimate inquiry—what the public needs to know—has been replaced, however, by an unhealthy climate of suspicion. A candidate who doesn't tell all about his finances, health, love life or whatever is immediately vulnerable to charges that he is covering up some dreadful flaw.

This is precisely what we are seeing in the rumor-mongering going on about whether Dukakis sought psychiatric care after the death of his brother in 1973 and his reelection defeat in 1978.

So what if he did? He suffered two of the losses that show up on all the lists of life's greatest traumas: the loss of a family member and the loss of a job. Both of these are devastating episodes, and if a person gets some professional help to work through them, more power to him. That's a sign of someone who values his mental health and is willing to take steps to protect it. That's a sign of stability, not instability.

Turns out, however, that the Dukakis campaign adamantly is denying that he sought psychiatric help at any time in his life. And it turns out that, as best anyone can figure, he is the victim of rumors started by a thoroughly discredited group on the lunatic fringe. Things went haywire when a legitimate publication, *The Boston Globe*, reported an exchange in which a *Boston Herald* reporter asked Dukakis if there was any truth to the rumors. Instead of saying no, I don't beat my wife, the governor shrugged and walked away, and from that point on he was under suspicion.

We give our criminals more benefit of the doubt.

The Dukakis camp continued to deny the rumors, but those denials then became news stories. *The Washington Times* ran the headline "Dukakis Psychiatric Rumor Denied" on Tuesday and then followed up yesterday with this exclusive: "Dukakis kin hints at sessions." Well, if you read the story, you find it has nothing to do with the headline. In a real coup for enterprise reporting, a reporter interviewed Kitty Dukakis' sister, who said that her brother-in-law might have chatted informally with a family friend, who is a psychiatrist, in 1978, but (1) she doesn't know if that happened and (2) she doubts it. And she has no knowledge of him seeking professional help on a more formal basis during that time. This "story" was stripped across the top of a daily newspaper.

The Dukakis campaign has released a letter from the candidate's physician of seventeen years saying that he is in excellent health and physical shape, that he has had no significant illnesses in his lifetime, and listing medication he occasionally takes. The Bush campaign has responded to a *Detroit News* questionnaire, indicating that the candidate is similarly in fine shape, and Bush has said he will release all relevant medical records.

The public needs to know whether the candidate is in good enough shape to survive the rigors of the presidency. If we stop and think about it, we might realize that the candidates themselves have a stake in being healthy enough to survive the job. There's a certain natural selection process that's going to be at work here. Meanwhile, this obsession with the details and complete records and so forth of the candidates' medical histories robs them of privacy they are entitled to and the dignity they should have.

Dukakis and Bush have given the voters a note from the doctor saying they are fit for the work. That's enough, already.

Stand Up for Dignity
AUGUST 10, 1988

That cliff-hanger senatorial race in Virginia has taken a turn that might have been written by a "Saturday Night Live" scriptwriter after he dropped acid. In one corner, we have Charles S. Robb—ex-marine, ex-governor, ex-First Son-in-Law—and in the other, we have Maurice A. Dawkins—ex-Baptist minister, ex-presidential appointee, and current unknown—both laying claim to the title of Mr. Clean.

As in drugs.

Late last week, both candidates submitted to drug tests after Dawkins gave three samples of his blood to a hospital in Richmond for testing and challenged Robb to do the same. Within hours, Robb showed up at Arlington Hospital and produced a urine sample that the hospital declared was 100 percent organically pure.

The *Washington Post* story declared that it marked the first time that statewide candidates in Virginia had publicly submitted to drug testing. This proves, among other things, that the present contestants' predecessors have a lot more sense of dignity than do these two. Can one imagine what Senator Harry F. Byrd would have done if someone had challenged him to pee in a bottle? If someone had challenged Thomas Jefferson to submit to such an indignity, there would have been a duel.

No one in the great state of Virginia—at least no one with any brains—has ever suspected Robb of doing drugs. A lot of folks wonder whether he even does coffee. But that's not the point. The point is what on earth does he hope to prove by dashing off to Arlington to take a drug test just because some political opponent tries to jerk his chain?

This is leadership?

Dawkins, who set aside a vial of his blood for the media to test at the same time he said he wasn't doing this for publicity, said he was having himself tested to "set an example, to be a role model for a drug-free Virginia." Robb's people labeled this foolishness for what it was—gimmickry—but instead of dismissing it, the candidate then fell for it.

Robb's press secretary said the staff didn't want the campaign to turn into who took the drug test and who didn't. Robb is leading with 68 percent of the vote in the latest polls. If he can't control the dialogue of a campaign, and stay on the high road, with that kind of lead, then you've got to wonder what he'll do if he's elected. The tail is really wagging this dog.

Suppose that Dawkins next submits an affidavit saying that he has never had lascivious thoughts. Can we expect an affidavit twenty-four hours later from Robb to the same effect? Or suppose Dawkins appears some morning on the steps of the governor's mansion in Richmond and swears on his family Bible that he has never, ever told a lie? Will Robb appear in angel's wings at dusk with a similar claim?

Many of the seeds of freedoms we all enjoy were sown in Virginia, and it is a state with a proud political heritage. It has been mercifully free of the political corruption and shop-at-home principles that have flourished in Maryland. A contract of good faith exists between Virginia voters and their politicians, and a certain amount of dignity about the political process is expected on both sides. Good character is assumed.

Under the Reagan administration, drug testing and polygraphs became quick-fix solutions for embarrassing political problems. To his credit, Secretary of State George P. Shultz put the brakes on polygraphs for employees who had access to highly classified information when he threatened to resign if required to take a test. Shultz, according to news reports at the time, felt strongly that the tests were ineffective and misleading and implicitly questioned the character and integrity of public servants.

More recently, Attorney General Edwin Meese III tried to inflict a random drug-testing plan on the Justice Department. A group of forty-two department lawyers and other employees won a permanent injunction against the plan from U.S. District Court judge George H. Revercomb, who ruled that there was no evidence of a drug problem in the department that would justify such infringement on the constitutional rights of "trusted and apparently law-abiding employees."

The employees had argued that the testing violated their protections against unreasonable search and seizure.

Their case was argued by Stephen Sachs, former Maryland attorney general, who told Revercomb that "even if a war on drugs is a good idea—and every one of the forty-two plaintiffs agrees that it is—the Bill of Rights should not become a casualty in that war."

Nor should human dignity. If Robb had to stand up to Dawkins, he should have stood up for that—and not to take a drug test.

Marketing the New, Improved George Bush
AUGUST 17, 1988

I feel like I've walked into a marketing campaign like the one the American car companies put on when they introduce their new, sleeker, higher-powered, smoother-running, quieter-engined, latest-in-technology automobiles. The Republican marketing types are trying to make us believe that the heartbeat of America depends on electing George Bush.

Whether that's true is anyone's guess. What's not being left up to guesses, however, is the slick packaging of the new, improved

George Bush. The 1989 model got a tremendous amount of media exposure immediately after the Democratic convention when two things happened to Bush that made the Japanese import invasion look like minor glitches on the American car industry sales charts.

First, the Democrats took children, women and families out of the backseat of American politics and put them in the driver's seat, not only in speeches, but in very real, physical terms. They were all over the stage in Atlanta and all over the convention floor. Half the delegates to the Democratic convention were female. Second, and certainly related to the first, the gender gap hit the Bush campaign with the force of a Mack truck.

The campaign has responded with a multipronged strategy designed to win women voters back into the Republican sales tent at least long enough to listen to the pitch. Bush's handlers, who have access to some of the most in-depth, sophisticated polling about women voters that's ever been done, are putting on a marketing campaign that would be the envy of the marketing geniuses in Detroit. What Bush has that they don't is constant, free exposure in the media, starting with the extraordinary amount of convention coverage.

It's a free ride, and Bush's people are capitalizing on it. In a matter of weeks, George Bush is getting a massive overhaul of his public image. The question is, will women voters buy it?

Shortly after the Democrats folded their tents and went home smelling victory, the new George Bush emerged in Kennebunkport, Maine, surrounded by his family. We're not talking about his wife, Barbara, and a couple of kids. We're talking about a multigenerational, multinational genealogical triumph. George the Family Man was up to his kneecaps in grandchildren, and soon all of America knew that little George P. had, in his grandmother's words, a "special relationship" with his grandfather, who is known as Gampy to his grandchildren. For the record, Bush has five kids and ten grandchildren, but we won't need to learn all of their names or ages or occupations unless he's elected. Also, the family is very close.

The oldest grandson, George P., twelve, and his mother, Columba, will have their first fifteen seconds of fame tomorrow night, when he delivers the pledge of allegiance and she seconds her father-in-law's nomination in Spanish. Columba Bush met Jeb Bush when he was an exchange student in her hometown of Leon, Mexico. They married three years later.

Both Governor Michael S. Dukakis and Senator Lloyd Bentsen speak fluent Spanish. Bush has countered that with the fact that he has a Hispanic daughter-in-law and a half-Hispanic grandson. Give him points for planning. Not every candidate can produce a Hispanic daughter-in-law when needed.

Soon after George the Family Man emerged, out came George's Chicks. These are the women who have prominent positions in the Bush campaign, and while they may not be inner circle campaign positions, they are definitely Important Jobs. The women themselves, according to *The Washington Post*, refer to themselves with heavy irony as "chicks." If any of them harbor heretical leanings toward feminism, they are keeping it under a tight grip. These are the female engineers in the campaign—and while one of them may have helped develop his child care plan, the others want little or nothing to do with gender-specific marketing problems such as women's issues.

As a final touch, Bush has been showing up lately wearing less clothing. The man who looks like he was born wearing a blue business suit has been appearing in photo opportunities *au casual*. We have been hearing a lot about how fond he is of fishing and what a warm and caring family man he is. He wants to be known as the education president, and his campaign is going to stress leadership and experience. This is going to be a tough marketing job, however, so the campaign ought to select a theme that's got proven marketing appeal: The Heartbeat of America—Today's Bush.

Potty Parity
OCTOBER 19, 1988

Modern women have been divided on about as many issues as they've been united on, but finally an issue has come along around which all women should unite. Full-time homemakers and women who work outside the home, young women and old, black and white, married and single women, rich and poor, all of us can stick together on this one and we'd better because divided we stand, united we sit.

I am talking, of course, about the great restroom crisis that has personally hit every one of us who has ever attended a crowded event. What happens is this: you are having a wonderful time at a concert, athletic event or movie and you don't want to leave your seat for fear of missing something. Thus, you along with 10,004 other women in the complex wait until intermission to go to the ladies' room.

By the time you get there, there are several hundred other women waiting in line ahead of you. Because all public restrooms are built on the principle of adjoining plumbing, near you is a line of men leading into the men's room.

That's at the beginning of intermission. Halfway through it, however, you notice that the line of men has disappeared and they are all out in the lobby or back in their seats.

Meanwhile, back at the ladies' room, you've progressed from the end of the line to the middle of it. You start looking at your watch, wondering if you're ever going to make it back to your seat. And you start silently cursing every member of the sisterhood who is primping inside while you are steaming outside.

Some women have taken the law into their own hands. Several years ago, at the end of a sold-out basketball game at the Capital Centre, the traffic jam in the ladies' room was worse than in the parking lots. Finally, a group of women noticed that no one was waiting to get into the men's room. They promptly turned it into a multiuse facility and cut the line for the ladies' room in half. Beer drinkers in the line were eternally grateful for their brave act.

Travelers along the nation's highways routinely pull off to the rest stops to find lines of women and children waiting at the ladies' room while there is no one in line at the men's room.

Any veteran mother traveling with children figures in a ladies' room line delay time when she asks her youngest whether he or she needs to stop.

At least two studies have shown that women take nearly twice as long in the restrooms as men do. A Virginia Tech study done by Savannah Day, a professor of housing, and Sandra Rawls, who did the study as part of her doctoral dissertation, found that men took between 84 and 113 seconds while women took between 153 and 175 seconds. A study by Cornell University engineering student Anh Tran of two hundred men and women at highway rest stops found women took 79 seconds and men 45.

Rawls told *USA Today* that the delay time is caused not just by women taking excessive time in front of the mirror. Men do that, too, and they also wash their hands.

Women take longer for some obvious reasons, like the way we are designed and the way our clothes are designed. There are also 6.3 million more of us and more of us are elderly and a great many more of us are pregnant. Also, we are usually the designated hand-holder when it comes to taking small children to the restroom.

Delegate John A. Rollison III (R-Woodbridge) got the 1988 Virginia General Assembly to support public hearings on changes in the plumbing code that would increase by 50 percent the number of women's toilets in new buildings such as theaters, arenas and churches. Old buildings would be affected only if they are renovated. Rollison testified at the first hearing on Monday that the present regulations requiring an equal number of toilets in men's and women's rooms "is as out of date as the chamber pot." Eloquently put.

California is the only state that has passed legislation to correct what is coming to be known as the "potty parity" issue.

Rollison is saying that the only problem he has found is that people don't take it seriously. Whoever doesn't take it seriously has never waited in line or stood near the line waiting for the woman of his dreams to go to the bathroom.

I was at a country fair on Sunday with a friend who was in and out of the men's room in two minutes while I was waiting in line for at least ten minutes.

When I finally emerged, my friend, who'd been waiting nearby, took his life in his hands and asked a question men have been asking across the ages. He said: "What took you so long?"

Rollison, obviously a man of vision, should get support on potty parity not just from the sisterhood, but also from those who only stand and wait.

Steinberg's Excuse Works
FEBRUARY 1, 1989

Joel Steinberg has been found guilty of first-degree manslaughter in the beating death of six-year-old Lisa Steinberg. He faces a maximum sentence of eight and one-third to twenty-five years in jail. Had the jury convicted him of second-degree murder—the most serious charge he faced—he would be looking at a minimum of twenty-five years to life. Sentencing is set for March 8.

Michele Launders, the natural mother who gave Lisa to Steinberg, believing he would find her an adoptive home, told TV reporters after the verdict: "The only verdict that would be justice for Lisa is murder."

Lois Lee, director of Children of the Night, a Hollywood, California, center for sexually abused children, told *USA Today:* "You're not going to be punished as severely if . . . [the victim] is a child. There's still a lack of recognition of children's rights."

Jurors emerged from eight days of deliberations to tell reporters that they had been seriously divided from the beginning on several key points and, in effect, compromised on a first-degree manslaughter verdict in order to avoid a hung jury on the second-degree murder charge. The difference between the two centered on the question of whether Steinberg recklessly struck Lisa and then demonstrated a "depraved indifference" to human life by failing for twelve hours to get medical help that might have saved her.

This finding of depraved indifference would have led to the second-degree murder charge, but some jurors said they felt his use of cocaine for days before the killing and immediately after he struck the child had significantly diminished his awareness of what was happening. "We felt there was a lack of proof of his depravity," said juror Helena Barthell, thirty-six. "I feel sorry for him. He's gone through a terrible ordeal, even though he brought it on himself."

What utter nonsense.

From the very start, one of the most sickening aspects of this whole monstrous case has been the absence of personal accountability, the lack of intervention on the part of adults who came into contact with Lisa and the collusion between the state and its key witness to use victimization as an excuse for the most reprehensible behavior. Thus, Hedda Nussbaum, the former children's book editor who was Steinberg's lover for ten years, was effectively relieved of personal responsibility for not having blown the whistle on Steinberg when he started to abuse the child because she, Nussbaum, had been systematically abused by him for years.

Nussbaum was originally charged with second-degree murder, but the charges were dropped when she agreed to testify against Steinberg. Acting Justice Harold J. Rothwax told the jury in his instructions that Nussbaum was an accomplice in the child's death—she, too, did not seek help for the child until twelve hours after she was beaten—but these instructions were for the purpose of telling the jury that it could not rely solely on Nussbaum's testimony in reaching a verdict because it was tainted. The jury foreman later told reporters the jurors felt Nussbaum was "culpable in some sense."

Nussbaum and Steinberg were both allowed to take refuge in their extensive drug use. Nussbaum will never be tried in connection with Lisa's death or any of the other assaults against the child that she testified to seeing. And Steinberg, who apparently smoked crack cocaine the way other people smoke tobacco, had a jury excuse him from second-degree murder because some jurors felt his brain was too fried at the time to know what he was doing.

It doesn't wash. If Steinberg, who watched a football game at the hospital while his daughter was being diagnosed as brain dead, didn't exhibit a depraved indifference to human life, then it's hard to imagine what that term means. Drug abuse may lead to family violence, but society and its institutions are poorly served if drug abuse is allowed to be an excuse for savagery. Just to put things in perspective here, it is worthwhile remembering that Jean Harris had been deprived of tranquilizers prescribed to her by Dr. Herman Tarnower on the night she shot him. She was convicted of second-degree murder.

Crime and punishment in the Steinberg case has to be followed by a couple of asterisks denoting mitigating circumstances: Hedda Nussbaum was battered, that's her excuse; Joel Steinberg was a crack head, that's his. Instead of both of them doing a lot of long, hard time for the horrendous death of a defenseless child, he gets a weak-minded juror who feels sorry for him, and Nussbaum is talking about writing a book "to help battered women." There's talk of a lecture tour and personal appearances, with her doctor touting her as someone who can help others stand up for themselves. Give us a break.

Ins and Outs for the Nineties
JANUARY 3, 1990

This is the season of the year when everyone is publishing lists of what's in and what's out and, as happens with dispiriting frequency, half of the people who show up on the "In" lists are people

I've never even heard of. I'd like to think I'm ahead of the trend—that I've heard of these people and then forgotten about them—but the fact is, that's not true.

USA Today, for example, declared that Julia Roberts is In and Melanie Griffith is Out. This was not good news to the last surviving American working woman who had not seen *Working Girl* until we rented it over the weekend. All last year, I'd been wondering what people saw in Melanie Griffith and why her romance, pregnancy and marriage to a has-been TV star was such hot copy for every legitimate magazine, as well as the tabs, that provide reading matter in supermarket checkout lines. The movie, as everyone else knows, was wonderful and so was Melanie Griffith, and now I see why everyone is so fascinated by her. Too late, though. She's Out and somebody named Julia Roberts, according to *USA Today,* is In.

Who is Julia Roberts and what does she do?

That same list says that Janet Jackson is In and Michael Jackson is Out. I've read enough of these lists over the years to have a clue as to how they are put together. Michael Jackson is a singer so I'm going to assume that Janet Jackson is, too. These lists are nothing if not studies in symmetry. Beyond that, Janet Jackson is on her own. I've not a clue.

Which probably makes me a poor authority for predictions on the coming cultural upheaval that we are going to be calling the nineties. Being a poor authority on matters has never stopped a newspaper columnist before, however. I don't feel up to compiling a whole list, but I would like to add a few things that seem to have been overlooked by other list-makers. And like others, what I'm including is more of a wish list than hard-nosed prognostication.

Part-time work should be In for both men and women. Workaholics—especially those who put in sixty hours a week doing what they ought to get done in thirty hours—should be urged to go into treatment. So should supervisors who create corporate climates in which marathon work hours are equated with excellence and dedication rather than slowness and a dull outside life.

Children should be In as they have never been before. Children have been Out for a long time now. Having them at all was Out for a while, then having more than one or two was Out because the costs and hassles of juggling family and career were exhausting too many couples and they opted for the zero-sum solution. They stopped having kids, and a great many confessed in dozens of magazines and newspaper articles that they'd also stopped having sex.

Too tired.

What with the Cold War over, though, we should be able to redirect a huge chunk of our resources to kids: to having them, educating them, giving them the basic health care they need and aren't getting now, and to shoring up the structures of lower-income, single-parent families that are falling apart all around us. Messy divorces and custody fights that tear children apart ought to be as Out as child abuse.

Child care, which was the burning issue for working parents in the eighties, shouldn't be Out. It should be retired from active competition for a place on lists along with other cultural icons such as mothers, the American flag and sports. Elder care, however, ought to be In. Neglecting your parents ought to be Out.

Marriage, of course, is now so In that couples actually went ahead and got married in the last quarter of 1989, despite negative tax implications. Living together may not be necessarily Out, but when the chances are pretty good that one of the parties has custody of his or her children, it's not quite the same as when they lived together in the sixties with the person who may have become the First Wife. Middle age is hitting the baby boom generation with such force that middle age made *USA Today*'s In list, but along with middle age comes either a midlife crisis (which was briefly In) or the urge to find someone you can grow old with.

In that same spirit, friends will be back In. Family and career were all that people had time for in the eighties, and they lost touch with their friends. No one gave dinner parties anymore. Too tired for that, too. But kids are growing up and so, at last, are their parents. They are taking stock of what's important. They'll be making time for human contact, for making and keeping friends.

Finally, the baby boom generation is heading toward the peak earning years in this decade. Greed may be Out, but you can bet your bottom dollar that making money will be In.

Rooney and the Censors
FEBRUARY 16, 1990

No careful newspaper reader could miss the historical parallels that occurred between two incidents chronicled in last Friday's Style section of *The Washington Post*. The battles between individual liberties and censorship, private actions and public pressure, are not new, they are just heating up again.

The lead article told of CBS's suspension of Andy Rooney for remarks he allegedly made to a gay-rights publication. Rooney has denied making the statements and the reporter cannot prove him wrong because he did not tape the interview. One person's word against another's and CBS, in a monumental act of disloyalty and unfairness, hung Rooney out to dry. But, then, it was only borrowing a page from its own shameful past.

Inside the Style section, there was a review by Harrison E. Salisbury of historian William L. Shirer's autobiography, which tells how William Paley, then head of CBS, and Edward R. Murrow got rid of Shirer when he was attacked in 1947. Shirer, wrote Salisbury, blamed what happened on McCarthyism and commercial greed.

"He presided over one of the great radio audiences of his time," wrote Salisbury. "He was jerked from the air, March 20, 1947, by a shaving soap manufacturer and, after his name appeared on a blacklist of supposed communist sympathizers, he never found a major broadcasting niche again." Salisbury describes the firestorm that followed the dismissal: "thousands of telephone calls to CBS, pickets marching in the streets, mass meetings, front-page newspaper reports, petitions, editorials and articles from coast to coast, almost all inveighing against the violation by CBS of freedom of speech and of the press. But CBS and Paley stood like the Rock of Gibraltar. Within two years Shirer had vanished from the air, and by 1950 his family was thankful they had a large garden at their Connecticut place to eke out their food budget."

Shirer and his family were not the only people who lost out when CBS caved in to the McCarthyites. In the decades that followed, the generation of broadcasters who covered World War II has been replaced by people "selling little more than a voice and a blow-dried hairdo," as Salisbury neatly puts it.

Andy Rooney went against the mold. He is seventy-one years old and has been with the network forty-one years, as opposed to four years, which seems to be the average for the blonde-of-the-month anchors the networks keep trying to wake America up with. He is one of the few people on the air who actually have something to say: a thought, an opinion that is not the pablum that Dan Rather dishes out on his evening radio commentary. Another is Pat Buchanan. He may be the conservative liberals love to hate, he may offend you, you may disagree, but at least he has the courage to say what he thinks. If you don't like it, tune him out.

It is no accident that Buchanan and columnist Nat Hentoff have quickly come to the fore to denounce CBS's treatment of Rooney. Free speech is dear to both of them, and both have exercised it long and well.

People who work in the media are usually deeply troubled when they see any company cave in to a pressure group. They know that this year's pressure group can be next year's tyrants, and the following year's crazies. They remember the reign of terror left by the McCarthyites on the press. Some of the best—and wealthiest—news organizations in the country caved in to the kind of smears that brought down Shirer. Careers were ruined and families were left destitute.

Now, forty years later, if someone told a newspaper editor that someone on his staff had been seen at a Communist cell meeting, the editor would probably start thinking he had a potential star on his hands, or at least someone with a more exotic turn of mind than he usually sees.

What characterizes all of those movements is a self-righteous intolerance for others. Some movements wrap themselves in the flag, like the McCarthyites, while they steamroll over the individual protections enscrolled in the Bill of Rights. Others wrap themselves in human rights causes or equal rights causes while they violate the individual rights and economic rights of those with whom they disagree. The animal-rights activists who terrorize fur merchants and throw red dye on people wearing furs come to mind. So do the antiabortion activists who block access to clinics and bomb them.

We are a nation of laws, not of causes, a nation in which individual rights and liberties and freedoms of speech and the press are of paramount importance. Above all, we ought to be able to agree to disagree and not to be out for each other's blood. Tolerance and respect for one another's opinions—even those that offend us—are as essential to democracy as the intolerance we have seen in the past was anathema to it.

11

Life in the Nation's Capital

Parts of the nation's capital are among the prettiest places on earth. Drive down the George Washington Parkway on the Virginia side of the Potomac River, look across at the monuments to Jefferson and Lincoln and see the Capitol Dome in the distance. In the springtime you see tulips and daffodils bursting out of the ground, colorful reminders of Lady Bird Johnson and the program she undertook to beautify America. But not far from the tranquil grove that memorializes her and not far from the monuments and the majestic buildings of government people live in conditions that are appalling. Poverty, illiteracy, epidemic rates of drug use, Third World rates of infant mortality, homicide and school dropouts tell the story of a nation that is deeply divided along class and racial lines. Sadly, nowhere is this more starkly visible than in the capital.

The American dream which my generation was taught to speak of in reverential terms is mockery for far too many Americans who are trapped in the urban ghettos that have few emergency exits. As drugs have spread throughout the ghettos, they have

222

poisoned and destroyed everything they've touched. The most basic human instinct—that of a mother to protect, nourish and cherish her child—has been destroyed by crack cocaine, alcohol and other drugs. Mayor Marion Barry—for years the eye of his own political storm—told me in an interview shortly after he completed seven weeks of in-patient treatment for alcohol and drug dependence that Washington's urban ills are no different than those of other major cities. He is undoubtedly correct, but if we are ever to have a racially and economically stable country—a land with freedom and justice for all—these problems must be resolved. Humanity aside, we cannot afford to have huge segments of our community crippled and defeated by drugs, teenage pregnancy, illiteracy and economic impotence.

We know enough now to understand that these destructive patterns replicate from generation to generation, just as alcoholism and drug dependency do. In that same interview, Barry spoke about the need for us all to understand more about the nature of addictions and how to treat them. You've got to treat the whole person, he said. Of course you do. But this is a luxury that only middle-class addicts with health insurance can afford. Expensive in-patient treatment centers are not an option for the addicts in the ghetto who are unemployed, have no insurance and are not employable as long as they are incapacitated by addiction and a host of other problems that make them unable to function economically.

We have to give people something to live for. The capital of this nation ought to be an exemplar of the best that democracy can provide in the way of opportunies for our citizens. How can a free society that has captivated the imagination of the world endure an infant mortality rate in its capital city that would cause governments to topple if it occurred in Western Europe? We are a nation of enormous natural resources and vitality. We are a young nation, still full of promise. Yet minutes away from the heart of democracy, people are living in conditions that break your heart. They are a drain on themselves, their families, their communities and the public treasury. They are an affront to the conscience of America. They take, they do not build and create. Young black men are killing each other and themselves. Homicide is the leading cause of death in young black males in America. Young black women are having babies just to have someone to love and be loved by. But they pawn their own futures in an attempt to dilute the agony of the present. The conditions in our cities will fatally poison our country unless we give the people who are trapped in this nightmare underclass a way into the economic mainstream. That's more than just something to dream about: it means providing people a way up and out. Too many of our citizens have just heard the promises. There are many promises to keep.

Child Hunger, Infant Mortality
FEBRUARY 6, 1987

There was a story in *The Washington Post* last week that was about as stunning an indictment of our social service systems as anything to come along in a long, long time. The story was about how schools decide whether to close because of snow. At least, that's how the story started out.

"The decision to close," wrote reporters Marc Fisher and Leah Y. Latimer, "has very little to do with education. In the suburbs, the decision has much more to do with safe transportation of the children. In the District, it has to do with hunger."

Yes, here in the nation's capital.

"On Tuesday," wrote Fisher and Latimer, "when snow closed all area schools except the District's, eight of the 32 teachers at Bruce-Monroe Elementary School in Northwest never made it to work. But Gladys Gartrell's cafeteria crew was there, on time, in full force."

"For a lot of these children, this is the only meal they will have today," said Sadie Jackson, a counselor at the school.

No breakfast, in other words, and no dinner. We are talking about children living on one meal a day. In the nation's capital. Do we expect a kid living on one meal a day to learn anything in school?

The story went on to note that 85 percent of the children in this city qualify for free or subsidized meals. And the story reported the incident of a boy going into the cafeteria at 11:00 a.m., asking for food. He hadn't eaten anything that day.

On Monday, the Children's Defense Fund issued its annual report on infant mortality. Here again, in the grim portrait of poverty, the nation's capital was out in front: when ranked against states, it had the worst infant mortality rate in 1984; when ranked against cities, it was second only to Indianapolis in black infant mortality. It ranked last in the total amount of early prenatal care visits and forty-ninth out of fifty-one in terms of late or no care.

The report put the matter in stark terms: "A black infant born within five miles of the White House is more likely to die in the first year of life than an infant born in Trinidad and Tobago or Costa Rica."

Mayor Marion Barry, at a news conference, said he was "shocked" that Marian Wright Edelman, the head of the Children's Defense Fund, would "say that." Then the peripatetic mayor offered this analysis: "I've been to Trinidad. Babies are born in the hills, away from the towns, nobody even knows that they are there."

Having thus dismissed the baby-counting abilities of the folks in Trinidad, the mayor went on with this thought: "The responsibility for infant mortality rests with the parents. The mothers are the ones who bear children and mothers ought to take care of their bodies long before they get pregnant. Government does not get women pregnant, men do, and men have a responsibility to try to help the one they got pregnant to stay healthy, eat the right kind of food, to stop drinking alcohol, to stop taking drugs, and stop eating all this crappy food."

Well, at least the mayor knows it takes two to tango.

The nation's capital has had the worst or among the worst figures on infant mortality of any large city for more than two decades. Every year, about two hundred babies die before their first birthday; the death rate is twice the national average.

The Children's Defense Fund, in an analysis of why this is happening, said poverty is perhaps the single greatest factor. "The barriers to adequate prenatal care include long waiting lists at public health clinics, lack of health insurance and resources to purchase care, lack of transportation and lack of child care." *Post* reporter Margaret Engel recently wrote of instance after instance of bureaucratic disincentives ranging from long office waits to computers programmed to generate repeated billings to women who can't pay.

Only half of the eligible population is getting supplemental food through the federal program designed to improve the nutrition of pregnant women and babies. Engel found that the city is paying a private contractor $375,000 to hire four to six workers to find pregnant women and tell them about prenatal services. That comes to about $62,500 per worker. The city is paying out only $58,000 to the Visiting Nurses Association to make home visits to high-risk patients.

The Department of Human Services has a $541 million budget this fiscal year, which is supplemented by $316 million in federal grants. That's close to $900 million. For that, the nation's capital has hungry kids and one of the worst infant death rates in the country.

What is going on here?

A Deep and Lasting Grief
NOVEMBER 13, 1987

Every so often, you come across a book that is so profoundly moving that it permanently alters your understanding of things. Such a book is *Shrapnel in the Heart*, a collection of letters and remembrances from the Vietnam Veterans Memorial. It is a book about love, loss and sorrow and reading it was sad beyond words.

Laura Palmer, the author, is a journalist who, as she writes in the introduction, grew up in the sixties and worked in Saigon in the early seventies. She first went to the memorial on New Year's Day in 1986. "I had no inkling this book was in the offing. I went alone and spent six hours at the wall, mesmerized and moved. The names seemed to go on forever; it felt eternally sad.

"I was moved simply as a mother. Name one child, your own, and each of the 58,132 names on the wall [it was raised to 58,156 this week] will break your heart.

"I was fascinated by what was happening at the memorial: one by one, without anyone suggesting it, people were silently crossing over their moat of grief and leaving a letter, poem, or other offering at the wall.

"This rite of remembrance began with the plunk of a Purple Heart into wet cement. As the foundation of the memorial was being poured, a man asked construction workers if he could drop his brother's medal into the concrete. He saluted as it slid beneath the surface. There have been more than six thousand similar salutes since the memorial was officially dedicated on Veterans Day, November 11, 1982.

"It was then that America finally turned to embrace her own. Engraved on the wall's black granite panels that pry open the earth are the names of every man and woman who went to Vietnam and never came back. In dedicating the memorial, America finally acknowledged that we lost more than the war in Vietnam; we lost the warriors."

The letters, poems and other mementos that have been left at the memorial are being saved by the National Park Service for a museum. Some are addressed simply to Daddy and signed with nicknames such as "Your baby girl always Peanuts." The anonymity of the note in no way reduces its poignancy. Others are addressed to the dead by name and signed with enough specificity that Palmer was able to track down the bereaved survivors and find out what prompted them to leave the letter or poem and how their loss had altered their lives. There are letters and poems from parents, lovers, high school friends, siblings and there are letters and poems from the men and women who served and survived. These are among the most wrenching. The pain of loss and of surviving is almost palpable.

"Courage is the common thread that runs through these stories," Palmer writes. "*Shrapnel in the Heart* brought me, quite literally, to the doorsteps of the quietly courageous. I have always been struck by the savagery and randomness of the blows that lacerate some lives. I am in awe of the courage it takes to go on."

She has included pictures of some of the dead men in her book, along with the letters written to them, and she tells the story of their brief lives and the relationship they forged with the bereaved. It is stunning to remember how young the men were. The average age of the men who fought there was nineteen years old, Palmer writes, seven years younger than the average age of the men who served in World War II.

Palmer writes that the survivors were grateful to tell their stories. "Sequestered so long with grief, each survivor seemed to think he or she was the only one who continued to mourn so deeply. Time after time, I saw smiles of relief when I told someone about someone else I'd interviewed whose sadness remained intense, even after 15 or 20 years.

"People, I found, not only want to talk about the person they lost in Vietnam, they need to talk. It is a deep yearning in many, suppressed because of the wildly erroneous notion that by now they should 'be over it.' "

Yvonne Sherman's brother, Allan John Dyer, died when his helicopter was shot down. She discovered that people do not understand how deeply siblings, as well as parents, feel the loss. She kept her grief to herself for many years, and left a poem at the wall. "I feel like there's a void within my heart because a piece is gone," she told Palmer. "I would say the shrapnel entered my heart and took a piece of it."

The stories come out of the small towns and the cities of America, just as the soldiers did. They are the stories of lives and families that were forever altered by the war. For them, as it has been for so many, the memorial became a part of the healing process. What *Shrapnel in the Heart* does is tell us how deep their pain was, and how long it has lasted.

Citizen Uprising Needed
SEPTEMBER 15, 1989

Few stories in this newspaper have provoked more reader reaction in recent times than the two series about children who have been neglected, abused and plain-out abandoned because their parents are crack addicts.

The children are living in squalor and danger. The series about six-year-old Dooney Waters told of how his mother had turned her Prince George's, Maryland, apartment into a crack den to support her own habit. She let users take over Dooney's bedroom to trade sex for drugs. The plumbing was backed up, there was usually no food and there were violent fights over drugs. He begged his teacher to let him sleep on his classroom floor.

In a series on children affected by crack in the District, reporter Marcia Slacum Greene wrote: "Children of crack addicts are entering the [child welfare] system at an alarming rate. Consumed by drugs, the parents are not feeding, clothing or supervising their children, many of whom are being discovered during police drug raids." And she quoted Thomas Wells, a social worker, who said: "When we define tragedy, it is not a child's failure to thrive. It is either they are maimed to the point they will never recover or they are dead."

The situations Greene chronicled are appalling. They are the kinds of things one expects to read out of the poorest Third World country, not the capital of the most prosperous nation that there has ever been.

But it is happening here, and the public agencies responsible for those children have a great deal to answer for. Those youngsters have been neglected by their parents and by the agencies that are supposed to help them. Instead of moving heaven and earth to get the children out of those places, social welfare bureaucrats have thrown up their hands and stuffed hundreds of complaints and investigative files in drawers with the shabby excuse that they don't have enough manpower to investigate reports of kids living in abominable conditions.

Tragically, there is nothing new in that attitude. More than fifteen years ago, when I covered the miserably managed Human Resources Department in the District for this newspaper, half the slots for protective service workers were empty and the social workers in the Family and Child Services divisions were carrying caseloads that were more than double what they were supposed to carry. They couldn't find foster homes or shelters for neglected or abused children. On occasion, they broke department regulations and took the children home with them because there was no other place for them to go.

Despite a billion-dollar budget, nothing has changed—except the number of neglected and abused children, which reached eight thousand in the District in 1988. Half the 113 social worker slots in the Family and Child Services divisions are vacant, wrote Greene, and there hasn't been a division chief for two years.

Mayor Barry turned down a request for 150 more social workers in May.

Social workers in Prince George's County told reporter Michele L. Norris that they too have backlogs and cases worse than Dooney's. Investigations take months and it can take years to remove those children from their parents.

Crack is a far more dangerous drug than anything this society has had to deal with. Addicts are a menace to themselves and others, and it is imperative that social workers and youth division officers be empowered to remove children from crack-contaminated environments swiftly. Too often, laws protect parental rights and not children's lives.

Communities with a crack crisis must insist that their elected officials allocate enough money in their budgets to develop foster homes and other placements for these youngsters. The District currently pays a little over $300 a month to a foster family for a child. That's not much. If the city were to double its payments, it would surely find more families willing to help. Given the alternatives for these kids, that would be a great bargain.

Hundreds of volunteers have responded to the stories of those children. Much more is needed, however. Residents of Prince George's and the District ought to be outraged that their elected officials and the welfare bureaucrats have allowed those situations to deteriorate so badly, and they ought to demand swift action to rescue children who are imperiled.

It will take money, well-trained, tough-minded social workers, and it will take an aroused citizenry demanding action and accountability from public agencies. It will take a great deal more than the usual talk about children being the future of the country.

These kids won't have a future unless we radically change the way we care for them now.

A Culture Made Sick by Drugs
DECEMBER 8, 1989

The conviction of Rayful Edmond III for cocaine trafficking and the life sentence he automatically receives removes a cancer from the city's streets, but the fifty-six-day trial showed how deeply the drug organism has taken hold in a culture that has no viable, permanent, legitimate economy.

And it showed how the sociopathic behavior that such a culture inevitably breeds has now passed from generation to generation in Washington's streets. The numbers runners and heroin dealers of the sixties and seventies have reproduced and given their offspring the same antisocial values they had. Law enforcement officials have said that the Edmond family had old ties to the city's drug and numbers rackets. It is not unusual for cousins, brothers, fathers and sons to do time simultaneously in Lorton, the District's finishing school for thugs.

But what was so stunning about the Edmond family was the pervasive acceptance of the drug business and the reach of criminal activity within the extended family structure. There was no one, it seems, who could just say no.

When Edmond was arrested in April, so were three sisters,

two brothers, an aunt, a cousin, two brothers-in-law, one common-law brother-in-law and, topping it all off, Edmond's mother. Among those convicted in this first batch of ten defendants were his half-brother, his aunt, a sister, a cousin and a brother-in-law. The jury heard a tape-recorded conversation in which Edmond's mother said that his father had started him out selling drugs "a long time ago." Royal Brooks, Jr., a childhood friend of Edmond's, told the jury that he had bragged of being "raised bagging stuff." Law enforcement officials have said his father started him out with a kilogram of cocaine.

Said the mother on the tape: "And like when he started out, it was just like, you know, like he was doing hand-to-hand . . . on the corner and they was selling." Then, she said, "it just got too big, he just up and went out on his own."

Junior, in other words, set up his own dealership.

Prosecutors repeatedly portrayed Edmond as the CEO of a tightly managed family business that at its peak employed more than 150 people. It was an effective portrayal that obtained convictions on forty-three of forty-four counts, but the blurring of lines between legitimate and criminal activity probably did nothing to demystify Edmond and his gang in the eyes of young hero worshippers. At twenty-four, he was running one of the most lucrative businesses in the city. He showed up in a stretch limo to pick up a summons from the cops who wanted to chat with him about a murder. He was a legend among kids and not just because he could play basketball. It was because he had lots of money and let everyone know it.

Edmond's conviction for heading a continuous criminal enterprise carries a life sentence, with no possibility of parole, and he thus becomes the most visible example so far of the tough federal antiracketeering legislation. The price extracted from major dealers is no longer up to some weak-minded judge who might go misty-eyed over the prospect of sentencing a young man to spend the rest of his days in the slammer. Law enforcement officials hope—and so should everyone else—that Edmond's sentence will deter others.

Norton J. Wilder, the top Drug Enforcement Administration official for this area, made that point memorably: "The message that this kind of case sends to the Washington community, especially to the youth, is this: That it is better to earn a slow, honest nickel than to earn a fast, dishonest dime."

That ought to be out on bumper stickers and plastered on banners across cafeterias and stuck up on the walls of restrooms in every school and gathering spot for youngsters in the city. It's probably the hardest lesson for any kid to learn, even when it is being drilled into them by parents who are setting that example.

There is no point in empty sloganeering, however. The hard truth out of the Edmond trial is that there are lots of parents setting a malignant example, and that a culture has now evolved over generations that is so stymied by the hopelessness of its condition that it turns to drugs as an escape and a business as a matter of course. As long as those cultural conditions exist, there will be people who prey on it, who hire and destroy their own, not for the honest nickel but for the fast thousands they can make in a day.

The real war on drugs is going to be won when the people who did business with Edmond have a way of earning the slow, honest nickel, a way to spend it on a decent home, and a decent chance in life for their own children. The illegal drug economy, with its violence, fast money and multigenerational sociopathic families, will flourish for as long as there is no alternative.

Using Racism as an Alibi
JANUARY 24, 1990

Racism has become a central theme in the downfall of Mayor Marion Barry. It was a theme he played for all it was worth in his desperate attempts to elude responsibility for his own actions and now misguided friends and supporters are taking up the chant.

Benjamin Hooks, executive director of the NAACP, became the most prominent black leader to make the charge when he strongly suggested on Monday that Barry was a victim of selective law enforcement aimed at black elected public officials. He said the NAACP has "felt that there has been undue emphasis on harassing black elected offficials. . . . To that extent, the Barry case might fit into it."

The most meritorious point Hooks made was that "we haven't found all the people who've stolen all the money from the savings and loan associations and are driving Rolls-Royces and Jaguars. So obviously, many of us in the black community will have some peculiar feeling" about the Barry arrest.

If the full force of the legal system had come down on the rogues who turned the S&L industry into their own private bank accounts, the Justice Department and the Republican administrations that oversaw this deregulatory debacle would be on much firmer ground to answer Hooks's allegations.

Unfortunately, white-collar crime—which could also be known as crimes committed by whites because that is usually the case—have never been dealt with as harshly as street crimes. Thus, the heads of drug companies that knowingly market products that maim or kill people don't do time in jail. A kid who holds up a convenience store may do more time than a guy who robs an S&L of its assets, taking thousands of small investors down with him and costing the taxpayers billions in bailouts.

In that sense, Hooks is right: there is selective enforcement of the law. But the difference between the way white-collar crime and street crime are treated is something that has been going on since the first enterprising pillar of the community got caught with his hand in the cookie jar. It is an argument for another day, and Hooks should make it. Another day.

During his long downward spiral, Marion Barry kept trying to hold on to power by blaming public embarrassments of his own making on some plan by the white establishment to unseat the black home rule government. Sadly, some of his constituents bought this line and they are still buying it. Listen to the talk shows on the radio.

But what nobody seems to be asking in all of this is: to what point? Why would some mythical white establishment want to bring down a black home rule government? What's the prize for harassing Marion Barry?

The truth is that no one has anything to gain by racist attacks against blacks or by racist attacks against whites. Perhaps the most destructive thing that Marion Barry did in this whole sordid episode was to use the rallying call of racism as a shield, an us-against-them defense that acted as bellows would to fan the dying embers in a fireplace.

The Justice Department, in response to Hooks' allegations, issued a statement that pointed out that nearly 5,100 federal, state and local officials have been convicted of corruption charges brought by the department during the last five years. That's an astonishingly high number of crooked politicians that ought to give every taxpaying citizen pause. But, beyond that, it shows that at the very least the department has been a vigorous pursuer of wrongdoing by people on the public payroll. Given that, and given the long, gloomy history of allegations against Mayor Barry, the Justice Department would have been completely remiss had it done anything less than mount a thorough investigation of possible criminal transgressions four blocks down the street from the FBI building.

The sympathy spin is in full gear for Marion Barry. He is being portrayed as a victim. At the end, he was at his most self-serving: "I have had to look my human weaknesses straight in the eye, had to realize I have spent so much time caring about and worrying about and doing for others, I have not worried about or cared enough for myself."

Nothing could be further from the truth. While he was out performing functions of a nonmayoral nature—how's that for a euphemism?—young black men were getting killed in record numbers, black babies were dying or being abandoned in record numbers, young black men and women were dropping out of schools and out of their futures at devastating rates. It is the black people of the nation's capital who suffered because of a besieged and incapacitated leader who could not or would not put their interests above his own. The real racism would have come had legal authorities ignored the various goings on at City Hall.

Fame and Fortune for D.C.'s Newest Femme Fatale
JANUARY 26, 1990

Move over Donna Rice, Jessica Hahn, Paula Parkinson, Fannie Foxe, Elizabeth Ray. There's a New Kid on the Block.

If the precedents hold, Rasheeda Moore is about to go from obscurity to megacelebrity in the space of about forty-eight hours. She has all the attributes: This is a thirty-eight-year-old woman who has not, by most accounts, lived a life of abstinence and she still looks spectacular. So much for all those Hollywood beauty queens who tell women's magazines that they keep their youthful complexions by drinking eight glasses of water a day, exercising four hours a day and abstaining completely from alcohol, cigarettes, caffeine—and no, not that. Rasheeda Moore has been around the block and doesn't look it. This is not a woman we can all look up to, necessarily, but we can certainly envy her genes.

She has had, as best anyone can make out, a checkered employment career. Her previous modeling experience paid off handsomely in her first public appearance since the rendezvous at the Vista. That was a nice outfit she wore to the grand jury, good earrings, very smart hat. Black hats are always good for going to court. Leona Helmsley didn't wear hats and look what happened to her. She lacked mystery. If she'd worn a hat, she'd have looked like a woman of substance and dignity instead of a rich witch. Rasheeda Moore understands hats. She looked elegant and mysterious in her first day in the spotlight, and that whetted the public's curiosity about her more than any combination of other "looks" (sex kitten, career girl, pharmaceutical entrepreneur come to mind) could have.

The bet here is that Moore will be able to milk this burst of publicity into some significant fame and fortune. The first talk show she's appearing before, of course, is the grand jury and the legal folks probably have an exclusive on her right now. But once she is through, she's going to be a hot property, and if she doesn't have an agent yet it's because she's not returning phone calls. Swifty Lazar? Take a message.

Moore's biggest problem is that she's got to avoid overexposure. She can't do just any show, and she'll have to think carefully which show to do first. "Nightline"? "Today"? "Good Morning America"? Whoever gets her will have a ratings triumph, especially if she can start soon.

Then, she's going to have to decide which talk show to do. Oprah? Donahue? Larry King? If she did Carson first, the whole country'd be late for work the next day, but think of the dialogue:

CARSON: My next guest has been in the news a bit lately; she's a very lovely lady whom I've never met; would you please welcome RASHEEDA MOORE. [Studio audience goes wild, lots of whistles, applause. Moore appears in elegant black cocktail dress—no hat this time. She shakes hands with Carson, waves to crowd, smiles shyly, sits.] So, Rasheeda. May I call you Rasheeda? You've been in the news as a close friend of Marion Barry, mayor of the nation's capital. How long have you known the mayor?

MOORE (speaking softly): Oh, years.

CARSON: You worked for him for a while, too, didn't you?

MOORE: Yes, I worked in the summer job program along with my sister. We helped young people with their self-esteem.

CARSON: Self-esteem's very important, isn't it?

MOORE: Yes, it is.

CARSON: Now, the papers have identified you as a close friend of the mayor, but I'm never sure just what they mean by that. How close are you?

MOORE: Very close.

CARSON: But then you set him up. You were the bait in the FBI sting operation that led to his arrest in a hotel room. What made you do it? What made you set up your close friend?

MOORE: I had a religious experience.

CARSON: A religious experience! I think my ex-wife had one of those, too. What kind of religious experience?

MOORE: I found God just a few days after I got stopped by the police out here in L.A. and they charged me with DWI. I said to myself, Rasheeda, this is no way to be living. You'll end up dead or in jail.

CARSON: You'd already done a little time, hadn't you?

MOORE: Well, yes, but that's not something I care to talk about.

CARSON: All right, we don't want to bring up bad memories. Tell us, though, were the FBI agents part of this religious experience?

MOORE: No. They came before I had the experience. They said they needed my help with the mayor. I knew in my heart of hearts that Mr. Barry needed help and that's when I had the religious experience. I knew it was time for me to stop thinking of myself and start thinking about others. I knew I had to help Mr. Barry and that's why I did it.

CARSON (visibly moved): That's really very moving. Very moving. Rasheeda Moore, folks. Just giving a little help to her friends. We'll be back after this break.

12

Memorable People

They have little in common, these people, except that each stands
for something and each was an inspiration. One was a teacher, a
man who had enormous influence on me and what I believe in.
Another is a child. Another was one of the tiniest people I've ever
known, and certainly the bravest. She is Ida Nudel, the woman the
refuseniks called the guardian angel of the prisoners of conscience, who spent four years in one of the harshest labor camps in
Siberia. One is a Mormon, a mother of ten, a widow and a staunch
Republican. She is one of several people I have interviewed over
the years who have multiple sclerosis, a disease that is as mysterious in the way it afflicts its victims as it is in its origin. For a brief
time, the disease was a factor in one of the most riveting legal
entanglements of our time, the Baby M case. Dr. Elizabeth Stern,
the woman who wanted to adopt Baby M, claimed that she could
not have children herself because pregnancy and birth could
exacerbate her multiple sclerosis. By contrast, Sheila Olson, the
woman I interviewed and who left such an impression on me, had
five children when she was diagnosed as having the disease, and

she subsequently gave birth to five more. That took grit, determination and courage. Those are the qualities that bind these memorable people together, and each of them has enriched the human community.

Madam President of Engineers
APRIL 15, 1987

"Nobody ever told me girls weren't supposed to be engineers," says Nancy Fitzroy, who has been one for more than thirty years. "Once in a while, you'd have a professor who'd say, why don't you stay home and save your father's money? But it wasn't all that hard."

Fitzroy is a pioneer and her list of accomplishments is breathtaking. She is the first female president of the American Society of Mechanical Engineers, serving a one-year term that ends in June. She pilots airplanes and helicopters, and until two years ago, owned her own twin-engine plane. She has been an engineer with the General Electric Company for thirty years, working in corporate research and development, the company's center of advanced expertise. Her specialties include heat transfer, gas turbines, nuclear energy and space vehicles. She holds three patents, including one on the design of a thermal protection system for early warning radar to protect it against a nuclear event.

She is a warm, articulate and thoughtful person who came from the rough-and-tumble of a large family in which curiosity was encouraged. So was fun, a word that pops up repeatedly in her conversation. As in, "I said I would work as long as it was fun, and I'm still there."

Her father, a building contractor and self-taught engineer, had a glider in the backyard. That prompted her interest in flying, and by the time she was a teenager, she could pilot a plane. While her sisters went ice skating, she went skiing with her brothers and her father. "Nobody told me you can't do it." Her father was a ham radio operator, and when she decided she wanted a record player, he bought her the parts and a wiring diagram. "So I made myself a record player. Some people are challenged more than others to do things they haven't done before."

She didn't want to go to college. Only 10 percent of her high school went on to college, and most of the women who did went to Skidmore and studied English. Her celestial navigation and calculus teacher suggested she study math. "I didn't want to teach. So we hit on engineering." She ended up getting a bachelor's degree in chemical engineering from Rensselaer Polytechnic Institute. "Women could be chemists."

She believes engineering is "an exceptionally" good field for women, although only 4 percent of the country's engineers are women. That is changing: about 16 percent of the engineering students now are women. "I tell students make sure you take your math and science courses even if you don't like them. By skipping those courses, you cut off your options." She says it is "mothers and aunties" who think girls are not as good in math as boys are. "They think engineers drive choo-choo trains. Our image is dull and unexciting. But you can have a quiet, plodding job or an exciting job. Engineers are the ones who transform ideas into practical reality. People forget that." The microwave oven, for instance.

Other advice for young people: "When you think about things you want to do, don't restrict your thinking just to things people before you have done. Look at what everybody's doing and see what might be fun for you.

"The secret when you're a kid is to put all the things on the list. Girls should make sure they put everything on the list without preconceived notions" about what girls can do and boys can do.

Fitzroy, who is married to an engineer, has a way of making engineering sound like fun. With the U.S. Patent Office as her source, she cites past engineering successes of women. The first two patents granted to a colonist were to a Philadelphia man for two of his wife's inventions. The cotton gin was conceived by Catherine L. Greene. Eli Whitney helped build the prototype. Martha Coston invented a flare that earned her $20,000 during the Civil War. In 1888, a black woman named Ellen Eglui of Washington, D.C., invented a clothes wringer. She sold the design for $18. During World War I, a woman invented an automatic pistol, a railroad torpedo and a submarine mine. More recently, a woman invented Scotchguard, and a woman invented a triggering device for underground nuclear tests.

"Engineers used to be people who were the big heroes," says

Fitzroy. "Edison and so on were great figures. We've gotten away from that to business as usual."

She wants to change that, and one of her recurring themes in professional association meetings is that with America's growing industrial problems, engineers have to change. "I'm saying to the engineer, how can I do my job better? Assume the responsibility. Don't figure somebody's just assigned you a job."

It's a call to excellence from somebody who has been there.

Immortalizing the Constitution
AUGUST 12, 1987

The brown envelope arrived in the mail a couple of weeks ago. The return address showed that whatever was in it was from Simon Korczowski, and that name provoked a lot of wonderful memories. If you're very lucky in this life, you might have a teacher like him.

Inside the envelope was a beige booklet and stapled to it was this photocopied message:

"With compliments from a former teacher who believed that no student should leave his class without having been thoroughly familiarized with one of the most important documents in our American history—the Constitution of the United States.

"So, during this bicentennial celebration of the writing of this great document, please accept this copy of The Constitution of the United States of America. Again, with my compliments.

"Mr. Korczowski."

Simon Korczowski taught American history at Washington-Lee High School in Arlington County, Virginia, for thirty years, before retiring in 1981. In the late 1950s, as the United States tried to respond to the perceived educational superiority of the Soviet Union, he was selected to teach the experimental advanced placement history course at the school, then widely recognized as one of the best public high schools in the country. Those early courses were limited to fifteen juniors. We used college texts and were taught at that level. The attrition rate was high, but those of us who made it through never forgot the class or the teacher. And he did not forget us. He was at our twentieth reunion, a strong, very kindly man who had held his own against time.

He now has leukemia and has been in Georgetown University Hospital for the past five weeks. His wife, Marian, who taught nutrition at Georgetown's school of nursing for thirty years, also has been very ill. Yet Korczowski is sending out copies of the Constitution

"That's my contribution to the bicentennial," he said during an interview from the hospital. "I must have sent about 250 of them out. The response has been beautiful. I sent them to former students that I could remember, family members, friends, and I even sent them to small children to get them started. I don't know how many people at the hospital have gotten them.

"It's one of the three most important documents we have: the Declaration of Independence, the Constitution and the Bill of Rights. It's a guide as to how we should live. It's a written guide and it's there where we can go to it, read it and interpret it. It is such a profound piece of writing in such a small space. You don't have to wade and wade and wade through it. It's there.

"I always tried as best as I could to get my students to relate their own personal activities, their own personal living to the things they study and the things that they learn. I'm very much afraid that after September [when the bicentennial takes place], that it's going to fade out of existence again and my idea was to get people to have something they could hang onto and read. Some of my friends said, 'I haven't read this thing for a long time and now every so often when I'm sitting around doing nothing, I pick it up and read it for a bit.' That's the idea.

"What was the big thing in 1976? The anniversary of the Declaration of Independence. Do we ever think about it? What I'm trying to do is to make the memory of this bicentennial last a little bit longer. Maybe three or four years from now somebody will put out that copy and say, 'Here it is. Mr. Korczowski sent me this.'"

Korczowkski left the Army in 1945 and received a high school equivalency certificate while working in Akron, Ohio. He enrolled in Ohio State and got his master's in history in 1951. He heard through a friend that Arlington County was hiring teachers. He was hired and that summer he and his wife were married. "That's where we've been ever since."

The first essay question on every one of his final exams was this: State fully what Thomas Jefferson said about the nature of man, the nature of man's right and the nature of man's government.

"He said the nature of man is that man is created equal, that man was created with certain inalienable rights coming from his creator, and that governments are set up with the purpose of protecting those rights and get the power to protect those rights from the people. Whenever any form of government becomes destructive of those rights, the people have the right and a duty to change or abolish that government and set up one that will do the job for them and use plain words."

Simon Korczowski loves his country, its history and what it stands for. He gave that to his students, and from one who was profoundly touched by him, in plain words, thank you.

A TV Evangelist with a Mission
AUGUST 19, 1987

Larry Jones is the kind of fundamentalist preacher who could help us all forget what's-their-names. He is a television evangelist based in Oklahoma City who uses the airwaves to raise money to feed hungry people, not to line his own pockets. And he knows a sin when he sees one: like having huge government food surpluses when there are hungry people all around.

Jones has a couple of other things going for him. He gets things done, and he is smart enough to hire Hill and Knowlton, the public relations firm, to help him distance himself from the PTL scandals. At a meeting with reporters and several Washington ministers last week, he was refreshingly blunt. Fund-raising was off 25 percent. "When the PTL thing happened, I looked at positioning and image harder than I ever had in my life. With the kind of budget we have, in a three-month period we were down $1 million. We knew we were going to need some help."

Jones is heading a project to bring a million pounds of food to Washington to be distributed through the churches to food centers and needy families. About six hundred Washington area churches, of various denominations, are involved in the effort that will include a three-day event on the Mall during the Labor Day weekend, with the actual distribution of the food taking place on September 8.

Jones found a special calling in feeding the hungry when he was in Haiti in 1979 and was profoundly affected by the plight of a hungry child. "It is a crime for us to have all this surplus grain and children 650 miles from here are starving," he says. He founded Feed the Children, and got grain from farmers in Oklahoma to ship overseas. Since then, however, farmers in the Midwest have been hit with bankruptcies and Feed the Children has developed assistance programs for needy families here as well. "The Larry Jones Ministries" has its own trucking line, and since last August it has delivered 215 truckloads of food to ninety-five distribution centers in forty states, according to Jones. That includes delivering three truckloads of food to churches in this area, which inspired Jones to develop the Labor Day event in conjunction with local ministers who have been active in feeding the hungry here.

"We have 13 billion bushels of surplus grain and people are going hungry," Jones said. "The Bible tells the church to feed the hungry. Food wasn't made to be stored. We should take the surplus and the hunger problem and put them together and the one to do that is the church." Jones says it is costing the American taxpayers $9.6 million a day to store surplus grain.

"My concern is to help the hungry and the farmer and get rid of the surplus," he says. "Until you get rid of the surplus you're never going to get a fair price" for farm products. "The government would be much better off to get rid of the food and save on this enormous cost of storing it."

Jones has raised $100,000 to buy and transport surplus food for distribution in Washington. Six truckloads of canned goods have been donated. In the past, Continental Can has donated ninety-one truckloads of Progresso soups to his ministry and Heinz has donated baby food. Zayre has given the ministry $2 million worth of new clothing. This spring, the ministry arranged for ten truckloads of free seed corn to be delivered to North Carolina farmers who were affected by last summer's drought.

The ministry is audited by Coopers & Lybrand, which found that more than 89 cents of every dollar raised through the airwaves is spent on relief programs, with the rest spent on administration and fund-raising.

"It's difficult to understand what's going on" in the farm states, Jones says. But he tells of meeting a man whose wife had committed suicide because her third-generation farm was facing foreclosure, and of meeting another man who was worth $3 million one year and looking for an apartment the next. He told of a farm family that sorted through garbage for food and shared what they found with six other families.

The Labor Day effort is the first to target an American city. Phoenix is next. Jones wants the government to cut the red tape so that surplus food can be distributed to those who need it and he wants the churches to get more involved with helping to get food to the nation's hungry and malnourished. He's trying to help the hungry and the farmers and is quite passionate in his condemnation of policies that have us storing surplus food while people are going hungry.

We've spent much of the spring and summer seeing the worst of televangelism. Jones is an example of what it can be at its best.

With Only Courage for Company
DECEMBER 11, 1987

The tiny gray-haired woman looked out of the dining room of the Capital Hilton and watched the screaming motorcade of black Soviet armored limousines race toward the Soviet Embassy. The woman watched and then she turned and said rather pensively: "They are so fearful."

Ida Nudel has a profound understanding of the dark side of the Soviet system: it tried to destroy her and failed. Since 1970, she has been one of the most prominent Jewish activists in the Soviet Union and was known in the movement as the guardian angel of the prisoners of conscience. Until her arrest in June 1978, she badgered Soviet officials to provide humane treatment for imprisoned Jewish activists. She sent them food, pictures, reading material, chocolates and clothing. She gave them, and their families, hope, and that was unforgivable. An economist, she lost her job and was repeatedly detained for fifteen-day stretches by the KGB. After she held up a sign on the balcony of her Moscow flat— "KGB, give me my visa"—she was sentenced to four years of internal exile in Siberia.

It was a descent into hell that began with a forty-day train ride to collect prisoners bound for Siberia. She was given a room in a male barracks. "It was an old building with wooden walls," she says. "It was so cold because the wood was so thin. It was 50 degrees centigrade under zero. You cannot breathe, it is too cold."

The barracks housed hardened criminals, many of whom had served sentences but been unable to return to their homes because their families had rejected them. They worked in the village on a project to drain the marshes. "I lived among them, a woman alone. They were very primitive. Their mentality was if you are a woman alone, you belong to them. I went through an experience that was very difficult to make them understand that I was not for them. I needed to protect myself. I behaved toward them like they were human beings. They were not accustomed to being treated that way. In the Soviet Union, punishment is very cruel. The goal of the punishment system is to break you as a human being, to break your spirit. I needed to explain to these men that they are human beings like me. I succeeded. I lived in this men's barracks a year and they began to respect me."

Later, the police allowed her to buy a one-room peasant hut. "They understood I could not survive in the men's hostel. My life became a little better." She grew vegetables in the short growing season and raised chickens, which surprised the villagers, who knew she was from the city. "I put all my heart into this. I read books. I shared my knowledge with the village women. In this way, I earned their respect."

The townspeople knew she was a political prisoner and they avoided her. Police pressured anyone who had contact with her. She had a collie, however, that played with the village children and they told their parents "who began to feel more warmly to me." Gradually, she was able to establish some human relationships. Her plight became known internationally after an activist visited her and smuggled out a 16-millimeter film about her exile. She received twelve thousand letters from people in fifty-one countries before she was released in 1982.

Her ordeal after that was far from over. The Soviet authorities would not let her live in Moscow. They would not let her be registered as living anywhere else, and for months she wandered homeless. "They said, you did not change your behavior. This is why they did not want me back in Moscow to be active. I was an outcast from society."

Without a registration stamp on her passport, she could be arrested at any moment. She knew that anyone who helped her would be harassed by the KGB. Finally, she was able to settle in Bendery, in the Republic of Moldavia. She lived there until she was allowed to leave the Soviet Union on October 15 after industrialist Armand Hammer appealed for her release. She and her collie flew out to Israel on his plane.

She endured nine years of loneliness, ostracism and deprivation. "I had no choice. It is my character. I cannot go left, right. I felt myself in a tunnel as wide as my shoulders. It is straight. I believe that my people have the right to be equal among all nationalities. I believe that now that Jews have our own homeland we have the right to be resettled there. We paid a terrible price to be a nation."

Nudel, who is fifty-six now, gives meaning to the word "courage." "I was saved by working with the earth. The more emotionally I was drained, the more time I spent working with plants and flowers. But sometimes even this work doesn't help." She spoke of her loneliness. She never spoke of fear.

The Future Is Our Children
DECEMBER 21, 1988

Marian Wright Edelman, president of the Children's Defense Fund, has seen the bleakest poverty and hunger of the Mississippi Delta. She was one of the few to emerge with a victory—it was the Food Stamp program—from the quagmire of the Poor People's Campaign and Resurrection City. After a quarter-century of exposure to the plight of poor families, a letter from a child named Herbie can still move her to tears.

Edelman was invited to address the National Press Club last week, and her remarks were excerpted from the fund's coming *Children's Defense Budget,* a comprehensive and sympathetic overview of the plight of poor children that the Children's Defense Fund releases annually.

For years, Edelman and the fund have been trying to warn the nation that we are risking and losing millions of children to all the familiar plagues of drugs, crime, illiteracy, ignorance and unemployment that accompany poverty and hopelessness. Finally, during a campaign in which candidates at every office level were looking for day care centers to show up at, there are signs that politicians are finally listening.

Edelman knows that they, like the rest of us, hear about the children whose tragic circumstances are unusual enough to put them on the front pages—children such as Lisa Steinberg, who died violently, and whose illegal adoption was not detected by authorities, and Jessica McClure, who fell into an open well shaft at an unregulated family day care home. Edelman wants political leaders, and the rest of us, to hear about eight-month-old Shamal Jackson, who died in New York City "from poverty complicated by low birthweight, poor nutrition, viral infection, and homelessness." He never had a home.

"He had slept in shelters with strangers, in hospitals, in welfare hotels, in the welfare office, and in the subways which he and his mother rode late at night when there was no place else to go."

Children of all races are growing poorer, Edelman warned, with the poverty rate of white children growing the fastest of all. If trends are not reversed, she said, one out of every four American children will be poor by the year 2000, for a total of 16 million, or 3 million more than today.

"By the year 2000," she said, "the total number of minority children will increase by over 25 percent and will constitute one-third of all children; the number of white, non-Hispanic children will increase by two-tenths of one percent.

"Demographics do not dictate destiny. Attitudes, leadership and values do." To compete economically and morally in the future, she said, America has to reject its racist past and recognize that its "ideals, future and fate are as inextricably intertwined with the fate of its poor and nonwhite children as with its privileged and white ones." America needs to acquire the discipline "to invest preventively and systematically in all of our children now in order to reap a better-trained workforce and more stable families tomorrow."

Edelman outlined in stark detail the numbers of children who are abused, homeless each night—100,000—or in various institutions. "The rage and pain of these homeless, hopeless, abused, alienated children will continue to explode in our faces in communities all over America," she warned.

"At a time of massive deficits, America cannot afford to waste resources by failing to prevent and curb the deficits which cripple our children and cost billions in later remedial and custodial dollars. At a time when future demographic trends guarantee a shortage of young adults who will be workers, soldiers, leaders and parents, America cannot afford to waste a single child, not even the poorest, blackest one."

She called on citizens to join in a national effort to make

preventive investment in children and families a cornerstone of domestic policy—pointing out that if citizens lead in a reordering of our investment priorities, politicians are sure to follow.

And at the end, she read the letter from *Children's Letters to God*. "Dear God," wrote a child named Herbie. "My Sunday school teacher told me yesterday that you lost your Son. I'm sorry to hear that you lost your Son. Mommy and Daddy have one son too—that's me. I'm six years old. I'm not very strong. I don't have any money. But I'm writing this letter to you to say to you . . ." And here Edelman could not go on. And when she resumed a minute or more later, you knew why. "I don't really understand what you're doing in the world," wrote Herbie. "But whatever it is that you're doing in the world, count me in on it."

Which must have been something Marian Wright Edelman vowed long before she ever took Senator Robert F. Kennedy on a guided tour of the most harrowing poverty in the Mississippi Delta.

A Testament to Courage, Tenacity and Teaching
JUNE 2, 1989

Katie Gardner was eight years old when a mysterious bump appeared on her right leg. It was summertime and the bump looked like a bruise she might have gotten from banging her leg on the side of the pool. Within a couple of weeks, however, the bump had gotten bigger. So had her leg.

An X ray showed what appeared to be a benign bone cyst. Katie's parents, Jane and Leland Gardner of Columbia, took her to a pediatric orthopedic specialist at Georgetown University Hospital. "He felt that's what it was, too," says Jane Gardner. "It wasn't until they went into surgery that they found it was a very rare form of cancer. It was so rare that they'd never seen it before. They phoned around the country to find out how to treat it.

"They hoped to save the leg by taking out the malignancy and then doing chemotherapy," she says. For four horrendous days, they waited to find out what doctors would recommend. "Amputation was the cornerstone of treatment," says Jane Gardner. "The surgeon told her in a very gentle way that she would have the amputation. She was silent the whole time. Then she just leaned over to me and said, 'I don't want an artificial leg.' That's the only thing I remember about when he told her that day."

Katie's leg was amputated just above her right knee on September 26, 1983. At first she was fitted with a heavy, awkward prosthesis. Later, she was fitted with a lighter prosthesis which she covers with a cosmetic stocking. She had to learn to walk again. She had fourteen months of chemotherapy and spent much of her third grade at home with tutors instead of at Bryant Woods Elementary School. Katie's doctors at Georgetown told her she would eventually be able to do everything she had done before, except the one thing she loved to do most: roller skate. She met Ted Kennedy, Jr., who also lost a leg to cancer, at an event at Georgetown and, she recalls with a smile, "he told me that was probably the one thing I could not do because of the loss of ankle control."

Enter Jane Vaccaro, the physical education teacher at Bryant Woods Elementary, who got in the habit of making small miracles happen by teaching orthopedically impaired students enrolled in a program there. Vaccaro, who also works in the cardiac rehabilitation unit at Children's Hospital, has published a number of papers in health journals on pediatric rehabilitation. To Katie Gardner, she was a godsend.

When Katie returned to the fourth grade, she started observing in gym classes and talking to Vaccaro about what she could do. Often, during recess or lunch periods, Katie would go to the gym and practice something she wanted to do. Usually, her three best friends, Carrie Gingras, Amanda Burns and Shana Weinberg, went with her. Later, she would do it in front of the class. In gym classes, rules were sometimes modified so Katie could participate. "If kids want to try something, you can fix it so they can," says Vaccaro.

In the fifth grade, Katie confided to Vaccaro that she wanted to try to roller skate again. Vaccaro and her husband had seen amputees on ski slopes. They put together a device using a shoe tree that they hoped would help Katie skate. It didn't work. "We went from the shoe tree to just pure hard work," says Vaccaro. Katie started off with a clamp-on skate on her left foot and a shoe on her right. Her three friends and Vaccaro took turns holding her hand while she practiced. "Then we added the second skate," says Vaccaro. "She's very determined, but we didn't know if it would work.

"She kept practicing, all through the fifth grade at lunchtime. She was finally able to do it." A video, prepared by Vaccaro for a physicians' conference on rehabilitation, shows Katie skating in the gym, and holding Vaccaro's hand, and then skating on her own for the first time since her operation. It is a testament to tenacity and courage.

"She would not have been as determined if it hadn't been for Jane," says Jane Gardner.

"It showed me that doctors weren't always right," says Katie. "And it showed me that if I put my heart and head into something, maybe I could do it. If you just sit there and don't try, you won't accomplish it. But if you try, there's a good chance you can."

Katie is fourteen years old now, and an eighth grader at Harper's Choice Intermediate. Her prosthesis is often uncomfortable and walking too much tires her. Each year she gets a CAT scan to see if the cancer has recurred. Each year that it does not is a milestone. She is bright, very articulate and wise beyond her years. She wants to be a nurse and she wants to work with children. She would be very good at it.

Jane Vaccaro taught her well.

A Mother's Triumph Over Adversity
JUNE 28, 1989

Sheila Olsen was pregnant with her fifth child when she was found to have multiple sclerosis, an incurable disease of the central nervous system that is often progressive but whose course is difficult to predict.

Olsen's first symptoms were tingling sensations on her right side. "It was like somebody had drawn a line up and down my back. For years, it was just my right side that was affected." She had no feeling in her hands. Then she lost vision in one eye. The presence of a nodule on her optic nerve confirmed the diagnosis. The year was 1967. The loss of her vision was, she says, "the scariest thing." Treatment with a drug reduced the swelling and her sight returned. For many years, she was able to remain mobile with a walker or cane.

Olsen, who lives in Idaho Falls, Idaho, was married to a successful lawyer, Dennis Olsen, a former state Republican party chairman. The family belongs to the Mormon Church and it is clear when she talks of her illness and how her family has managed that her faith has been a bulwark against self-pity and despair.

"We decided at the beginning," she said, "not to focus our lives around my illness. Dennis was adamant in insisting I get my rest and that the children would help me. It sent the clear message to me that I was a competent person who could manage. And I do."

She had five more children. She has continued to be active in state Republican politics and founded *The Trumpeter*, the Idaho GOP newsletter that she writes and edits. She was a delegate to the last Republican National Convention and was on President Bush's Idaho steering committee.

"No doctor has ever told me what I could do and couldn't do. I knew what I could handle. I didn't do it to prove a point. I did what was right for me. The children have enriched my life."

Dennis Olsen dropped dead from a heart attack while shoveling snow four years ago. Sheila Olsen says he left her well provided for, and she and her younger children have remained in the family's six-bedroom home. There were six children living at home when her husband died, and now there are four. She has a mother-and-daughter team who come in and clean the house once a week, but the rest of the time she and the children manage alone. Her disease has progressed significantly since her husband's death. She no longer can walk, and uses a tricart to get around. She recently bought a van that had been owned by and equipped for a paraplegic, so she can continue to drive. She has used her organizational skills to compensate for what she cannot do physically.

Her children, she says, have days when they are in charge of cooking and cleaning up in the kitchen. The house is divided into sections and each child is responsible for that section for three months at a time. "When that section includes the utility room, they are responsible for the laundry," she said. Thus, Jon's chore list for January 28, 1989, printed on her computer, was headlined: "No TV until these chores are done!!" The first paragraph read: "This page is valuable! When all the blanks are properly filled in, it is redeemable for a full allowance. . . ." Among the items on Jon's list: "Gather dirty clothes from all over house, sort, wash, dry, fold. Straighten up utility room. Vacuum utility room when everything is off the floor. Wipe off appliances in utility room so they look nice. Clean your bedroom thoroughly. Vacuum. Feed and water Charlie."

Jon was ten.

"We've done what we had to do to live around the MS and above it, and at the same time acknowledging it. It's like AA: Accept the things you can't change and change the things you can. That's the balance.

"I think that every person in life has their own set of challenges that they face. I honestly believe some of the things you see are easier to bear than the unseen heartaches. I get all kinds of help and understanding. What about the person who is having real heartaches with a child or a spouse? They don't have the support system I have," through her church, political allies, and friends. "So I have never felt sorry or bitter.

"That is not to say it isn't a challenge. I've walked and it is better to walk."

Last Friday, Sheila Olsen, fifty, went to the White House to receive a plaque from Bush honoring her as the MS Mother of the Year. Her ten children were with her. She is enormously proud of them. "The thing you practice in a family is unconditional love," she said, "and you keep the circle of love regardless.

"I am the support and mother to those children. I determined when Dennis died that we would go on as a vital, happy family and that has been my goal," she said.

"And I think we've achieved it."

MS: "The Best and Worst Thing"
NOVEMBER 29, 1989

Debra Norby is a thirty-six-year-old sculptress from Portland, Oregon, who came to town this week to give, rather than to receive. Her mission was to launch the National Multiple Sclerosis Society's annual "Thank You" week, in which the health agency expresses its appreciation to the volunteers, donors and other supporters who sustain it the other fifty-one weeks of the year.

This is public relations at its most positive and the society couldn't have picked a more positive personality for its campaign. Norby was discovered to have MS six years ago, and she has subsequently established herself as a painter and sculptor of considerable whimsy. Her clay figures of people frequently depict them with pleasantly goofy faces and elongated shapes. Her work was selected for inclusion in this year's "Project Rembrandt" at the IBM Gallery of Science and Art in New York.

The juried art show featured works by twenty-three artists who have MS, a devastating disease of the central nervous system that strikes about 10,500 people a year. It is most frequently diagnosed in people aged twenty to forty, and the incidence among women is substantially higher than among men. There is no known cure and no known cause. It was only after the relatively recent development of the magnetic resonance imaging machine that lesions on nerve endings caused by the disease could establish a definitive diagnosis.

MS travels a course as varied as its victims—one of the reasons it was formerly so difficult to diagnose—and it is still difficult to predict how it will affect the patient. Some patients became severely crippled, others have debilitating episodes and then go into remission. Numbing of the hands, arms and legs and double vision are common symptoms, which makes Norby's career as an artist using her hands all the more extraordinary.

"I try to make myself laugh," she says. "I wanted to be productive in some way. I turned to clay. It was great therapy physically and emotionally. You have to move with clay and I work out all sorts of emotional problems I go through with the clay."

She'd always shown an interest in art, but she followed her mother's advice and went to the University of Nebraska, where she got a teaching degree. She got back into art, however, and was an art director for an advertising agency in San Francisco, where she met her husband, Jerry Haworth, an illustrator. Once in San Francisco, her hands went numb. She figured it was a circulation problem. She moved to Ithaca when she went to work as a graphics designer for Cornell University. Her left leg went numb once while she was there. She moved to Omaha to join an ad agency and her symptoms got worse.

"You know there's something wrong with your body, but you can't get a confirmation of that," she says. She was also suffering from depression caused by a chemical imbalance in the brain that is part of her illness. She and her husband sold their house in Omaha and headed west to try something new. They ended up in Portland.

"I sort of saw this as the beginning of pulling myself out of this thing. I started taking clay courses. Then I got a residency at the Contemporary Crafts Association." That was 1983, the year her illness was finally diagnosed. "Jerry decided to stay home and do commercial illustrations so he could help me." Since her balance is dodgy, he puts her big pieces in the kiln for her and spends a lot of time driving her places.

Norby is a member of an MS support group in Portland whose members share tips and information about how to cope with the illness and she team-teaches an aerobics class for the handicapped with a woman who has cerebral palsy. She is taking antidepression medications that cost her $200 a month. She has become keenly aware of the high cost of medicine. While in town, she planned to talk to members of Congress about health issues, including the need for more home health care and the need for better access to psychiatric counseling for people with handicapping diseases. MS patients, she points out, frequently can't work and thus have no health insurance. When they apply for Medicare, they are frequently turned down initially. "They understand if you are blind or in a wheelchair. But with MS, it's a hidden disability."

She cannot carry a full ice cube tray or cup of coffee without spilling. She has to use a catheter, and has bouts of clinical fatigue. She has to pace herself very carefully. Her eyes can't judge distances, yet she says she feels very fortunate. "MS is the best and the worst thing that's ever happened to me," she says. "I've met people and done things and steered my life in a direction I never would have thought of going. There are those painful times, too. God gave me art to help me deal with the MS."

13

Family Ties

A friend who works at a hospice in Washington put it as well as I've ever heard it said. She has helped a lot of people die—cancer patients and young AIDS patients. "I've never heard anyone say I wished I spent more time at the office."

Family. In the end it is what really matters. No amount of money on earth can replace a lost child or a lost parent. Family is what makes you—and it should always be there for you. You draw from the family members who preceded you in this life and you pass on the legacy of those men and women to your children. No woman really grows up until she loses her mother. For then, after that she is truly the mother. And her own mother lives on in the daughter's admonitions to her own children—"My mother used to say . . ." Or, "I remember the time my mother . . ." The echo of these women's voices, their standards, their values are heard down through time.

Early in my career, women were asked to choose between children and careers or they were asked by younger women which had been more important to them, their children or their careers. In those days, the newspapers I worked for presumed that women

255

were cut from the same cloth newspapermen were, and that they
put their careers first. I never did, and I never had any questions
about which gave me more reward and more fulfillment. The joy
that comes from a child's simple embrace, a child's personal
success, a child's complete trust is something that touches the
heart the way nothing else does. When a child is badly hurt, it
sears the soul. I cannot to this day talk about the evening that my
son was hit by a car. It was too close a call.

For six years—almost the whole period of time these columns
cover—I was a single mother with three children. During most of
this period, my mother was in declining health and my father cared
for her. Their home is about eight minutes from mine and both of
my siblings live in other parts of the country. So it fell on me to do
as much of the care for my elderly parents as I could, at the same
time that I was caring for my children.

It was brutal. It was emotionally and physically and psycho-
logically exhausting. It is the crucible for more and more American women and the country must do something to help them.
When I hear the term "sandwich generation," I want to stuff it in
the speaker's mouth. The phrase trivializes an ordeal that makes
boot camp look like a summer outing.

And I had the best of it. Columnists have more flexible
schedules than most newspaper people do. My father was able to
supervise my mother's care and pay for it. My former husband has
never missed a child support payment, he is involved with his
children's welfare and lives and was a strong shoulder for my father
to lean on when he desperately needed it. My brother and sister
and sister-in-law came to town for as long and as often as they
could, and all of us spent hundreds of hours on the phone with
each other, keeping each other informed and trying to sort out what
to do. We have never been closer in our lives. But the long decline
of an aging parent is one of modern medicine's most dubious
blessings. We are only beginning to talk about these problems,
much the way we talked about child care problems twenty years
ago: these were private agonies and we sought private solutions.
We must begin to talk publicly about elder care the way we do now
about child care. Women cannot continue to be stretched between
aging parents, jobs and children without breaking.

"Cross that bridge when you come to it." That may have been
the best advice I got during those years and it came from my new

husband, whom I married in September of 1989. He was a source of enormous strength and support during those years when I was trying to sort out what could be done for my parents and their equally venerable housekeeper, who has been with the family since I was six years old. My husband had been through a similar decline with his mother and he understood better than most people what we could reasonably hope for and what we could not. He was a rock for me at a time when I badly needed it.

We are combining families—and we try to be mindful of all the different sensibilities that are involved in this delicate proposition—and we are entering the next stage of our lives with the kind of enthusiasm and joy that people have when they are truly happy and have a marriage that works. It is very nice to have someone who is a hundred percent behind you, and it is very nice to be able to give that to someone you love. It took us a long time to achieve it, but we have something we appreciate profoundly.

Test of Faith
DECEMBER 28, 1983

One evening before Thanksgiving, I went out and left my son the seventeen-year-old in charge of his brother the eight-year-old and his sister the four-year-old. This, I can assure you, was an act of faith; not long before that, when I left him in charge and said leave the door open, he had done precisely that.

I am a firm believer, however, in giving everyone a second chance; I am also a firm believer in having everyone assume certain household responsibilities and I see nothing wrong with having an older sibling baby-sit on occasion. On this particular occasion, the chore was made somewhat less onerous by the presence of his girlfriend, who had surprised him by coming home from school for the weekend. I left with complete confidence that the older children would do a wonderful job of baby-sitting the younger children and the younger children would do a wonderful job of chaperoning the older children.

About an hour later, however, I discovered that complete confidence was the last thing I should have left home with.

I had decided to return home earlier than planned so that my son and his girlfriend could go out. I called home with this happy news. But instead of hearing his cheerful, grateful voice on the other end of the line, all I heard was the sound of a telephone ringing.

It was, I should point out, after ten o'clock, when the two younger children should have been in bed.

It was, I should also point out, after ten o'clock, when the two older children should have been answering the phone.

Obviously, I had dialed the wrong number.

I dialed home again. Very carefully.

No one answered.

I started to panic.

One of the problems with having a seventeen-year-old is that you can never be sure exactly how responsible or irresponsible they are. When they are younger, you can be relatively sure that if they have an option of being responsible or irresponsible, the odds are that they will choose the latter. When they are eighteen, you can figure they will choose the former. When they are seventeen, however, it's a toss-up.

"I'll wring his neck," I said. I decided that they must be outside. Why they might be outside at 10:30 on a wintry night I had no idea, but it was the only explanation I could come up with for their failure to answer the phone. I waited a few minutes and dialed again. Still no answer. "I'll kill him," I said.

Finally, in desperation, I called his girlfriend's house. That phone rang a lot, too, but after a few moments, a miracle occurred: his girlfriend answered the phone. "Yes," she said brightly, "he's right here."

He came on the phone. I was not my usual calm, rational self. After all, one of the rules of survival for modern parents is that you can't trust modern teenagers. "Where are the children?" I said. He allowed as how they were with him. He also allowed as how all my terrible thoughts about what trouble they had gotten into with the younger children were quite out of place. They had not gone out joy riding, they had not set the house on fire, they had not overdosed on drugs, alcohol and rock 'n' roll. They had not behaved like typically irresponsible teenagers, at all.

They had taken the younger children over to his girlfriend's house to have ice cream and cake.

This is the kind of thing teenagers haven't done since the *Saturday Evening Post* went out of business. This was too wholesome to be believed.

Well, it turns out that I shouldn't have believed it. It was only part of the truth.

Saturday evening we were at my parents' home celebrating (actually, I was merely commemorating) my birthday. I received some lovely gifts and I received some funny gifts—that is, if you, like my brother and his wife, happen to think vitamin E, Oil of Olay and wooden canes are funny.

And then my oldest son gave me the children's gifts. Mounted and framed were a series of fabulous color photographs of my children, dressed in their best clothes, and wearing their most wonderful expressions. Between Christmas and my birthday, I received formal portraits of my children together and of my children individually, of my children looking funny, of them looking happy, of them hugging each other and mugging for the camera. They are pictures to treasure a lifetime, all taken by the father of my son's girlfriend. That is what they had really been up to the night they went over to her house for ice cream and cake.

And that was the most precious gift of all.

Real Mother Talk
JULY 16, 1986

There we all were in the parking lot of the swimming pool, about fifty members of the swimming team, looking healthy and vibrant and young, and ten or so mothers, looking awake. It was 7:30 in the morning and the delineation was clear.

Some of us were going with the swim team to Kings Dominion.

Some of us were not.

"So, I'm being a real mother today," said one who was going.

"I've got a class," said one who was not.

"Sure you do," said one who was going.

"I've got to work," said one who wasn't.

"Hey, I've got a career, too," said one who was.

"Yeah, but you're not just starting out," said one who wasn't.

What was really happening was that the four mothers who were going had younger swimmers—six, seven, eight years old— who could not have gone on the swim team trip by themselves. The older swim team members got onto a school bus and the four mothers and their five younger children got into a van and by eight o'clock we had pulled out of the parking lot and were on our way to the amusement park.

Real men may talk about killing ducks.

Real mothers talk about rearing children.

Before very long, being real mothers at least for the day, we were talking about our children, whom we've all known for years, and we finally got to the question of guilt and responsibility. As in: If my oldest son did something truly dreadful, would I feel responsible? To which I offered a theory recently developed by another mother, who is a lawyer in New York. She calls it "no-fault parenting."

Caroline, who was driving the van and who is married to a dentist, decided a very long time ago that she was going to be a mother. She had been accepted to graduate school in psychology, but she worked and put her husband through dental school instead. She handles her husband's business accounts, but she is first and foremost a full-time mother. She has four children, two in college, one in high school and one who is seven. She doesn't believe in no-fault parenting.

"I think," she said, "that people who take up parenting, whether you do it full-time or simultaneously with other things, to do it well, it's a full-time attitude. If my child turns out to be an ax murderer, I would take the blame.

"I'm teaching my children moderation, to take the center of the road, not trampling on other people for your own pleasure, for your own profit, not taking risks with other people's lives." Her oldest son is twenty-one years old. "I still want to be an operational force in his life philosophically."

She told of an acquaintance who had what she referred to as a "bad incident" with one of her children and was wishing she had done things differently. "The foundation she has laid is different from the foundation she wishes she had laid."

Which, of course, got us talking about our own mothers, and one of the other mothers in the van said: "Why don't I like my mother? I love my mother, but I don't like my mother. She's never let go of me. Whenever I go back home, it's a put-down: You can't do that, you can't afford this." Which got us to thinking what our own children would say about us.

"You have to have the ability to treat each child as an individual person," said Caroline. "If there's one thing I think I've done well with my kids is they all know who they are. They may not know where they're going, but they all have a sense of their own uniqueness."

She believes that one of the problems we've developed in this country is the tendency toward "mass production of kids," with the result that they have lost their sense of uniqueness, and, thus, their sense of self-worth. She told of going to one of Washington's toniest private schools, which she hated, and going off to one of the country's finest women's colleges. "Mother wanted only the very best for me." She returned home in six weeks. She believes she went off to college with no sense of her own self-worth. She enrolled in another well-known college and ultimately majored in psychology, met her husband and married him.

"I consciously chose motherhood as a full-time career. I had graduate school in my pocket. I chose to marry instead. In my heart, I knew I wanted to be a mother. I didn't know if I'd do it well, I still don't know if I've done it well, but I knew that's what I wanted to do."

What's been nice, of course, is that she has been able to do it. What was also nice was that mothers with careers and mothers who had made motherhood a career were able to kid each other, learn from each other, talk about the various choices we had made, with no one passing judgment. Real mothers understand.

White Picket Fence Inequality
JULY 11, 1986

There you are, trying to plan the summer for your children, and you are calling other parents to find out what arrangements they have made. You call the other soccer parents to find out about soccer camps, and the other basketball parents for tips on basketball camps, all in the spirit of sharing information, and with any luck, transportation. For working parents, coordination and car pools are the twin pillars of summer survival. So, you dial the phone and whom do you ask for on the other end of the line?

Little Ernie's mother?
Little Ernie's father?
Either one?

There was a time, of course, when there was no question whom you would ask for: little Ernie's mother was the only one in the household who would have a clue about his summer schedule. If you had the follies and asked little Ernie's father what camp his kid was going to, chances are he'd say: "Hold on, let me get his mother. I'm not sure he still lives here anymore. Didn't he graduate this year? Or was that Engelbert who graduated?" Or words to that effect.

But times have changed. Little Ernie's father might still not have a clue about what his kid is doing, but he knows he's supposed to and there's a good chance that he'll take umbrage at the suggestion that he doesn't. Thus, it is probably poor form to call up and say, "This is So-and-so. Is your wife home? I want to find out what soccer camp little Ernie's going to." The new etiquette might have you say: "Hi, this is So-and-so. Who is the best person to talk to about plans you've made for little Ernie this summer?" The ball then is in the court of whoever answers the phone.

What brings the new etiquette to mind are the continuing tribulations of a male friend who is becoming more and more convinced that the women in his neighborhood may be thoroughly modern in their dealings in the workplace but they are hopelessly traditional in their dealings over the white picket fence. He says this doesn't really bother him—but in point of fact it's been bothering him for a year and a half.

Ever since his wife went back to school.

What happens is this: She goes to classes in the morning and early afternoon and then takes care of the children; he takes care of the children in the mornings and early afternoons and goes to work in the late afternoon and evening.

He runs the household. He does the marketing and he puts together the summer schedules for their children and he takes them to the recreation center and to the swimming pool.

But then what happens is this. "The phone rings and I answer it and they'll say, Is Anita there? I say, No, she isn't, is there something I can help you with? And they'll say, I just wanted to check with her about the recreation center schedule, and I'll say, Well, I can tell you about that. I know more about that than Anita does," he says.

"I can tell you what row the beans are on in the Safeway. She can't. I'm becoming more of an authority on the little things than she is. She's preoccupied with getting through her course work. She's a mother when she's home, but the first part of the day I'm in charge. Most people go shopping in the morning so she hasn't mastered the Safeway yet. People call with inquiring questions in the morning so they can get the day going." And they reach him.

But the women in his suburban social network, he believes, "have trouble accepting me as the parent. We're part of a baby-sitting co-op. They ask for her for the baby-sitting co-op. I'll say, Bring them over, I'm here. They say, Uh, uh, okay. They fail to see me as equal as far as the organizational responsibilities of the family. They don't think I'm supposed to know these things, or maybe I'm supposed to, but probably won't.

"There's an interesting observation to be made here," he says. "In the business world and the corporate world everybody's treated as an equal." But not at the swimming pool or the super-market. "I don't think I can talk to the ladies at the pool like I would like to. You know, talk about things like the progress of the kids' swimming lessons. Casual friendship is neat, but for some reason I get the impression they're on guard.

"It's a very subtle thing. At first I asked my wife, am I doing something wrong? Am I coming across as wanting to have an affair or something crazy like that?"

His wife told him that there was more of that going on than he realized.

But that's not what he has in mind. He is a man who is splitting the household responsibilities down the middle—sharing, not just helping out. Perhaps, this time, the new woman needs to catch up with the new man.

Soccer Dynasty Lives On
MAY 28, 1986

There are, I have concluded after extensive research, soccer families, baseball families, football families, swimming families and some families who do some of each. Little brothers emulate big brothers and cycles get started and before you know it you have mini-dynasties going, as in: "All the Smith children are terrific soccer [or fill in the blank] players."

Thus it was that my son the ten-year-old started playing soccer when he was six (his brother the goalie, by then, was playing in high school) and a few years later, their sister the six-year-old signed up for her first season. Both had spent hours of their toddlerhood on the sidelines of soccer games and the presumption was that they'd picked up a little of the idea through osmosis. Lesson number one turned out to be that you can't depend on osmosis.

My daughter's debut on the playing fields of McLean was memorable. Her coach started her at fullback. He emphasized the importance of staying in one's position.

My daughter is a very literal person.

The ball came back to her and passed a few feet away from where she was standing.

She did not move.

My son the college student, sitting on the sidelines, put his head in his hands. He said: "I don't believe what just happened."

That was last fall.

There are always a couple of little children who know what they are doing and the rest of them have to get the hang of it. While my daughter was trying to get the hang of it, I was trying to remember whether the boys had been any better at that stage. I knew one thing for sure, which was that they had not skipped across the field. The season ended with my daughter talking retirement. It ended with me talking about the merits of girls participating in team sports.

The discussion ended in a draw, which goes to the parent. I signed her up for spring soccer and she agreed to play one more season.

There's a certain amount of pathfinding being done on the part of parents who encourage girls to participate in team sports. There's not a whole lot of practical literature available yet on the business of unisex child-rearing, so you are often left wondering whether a child is doing something because that's what girls (or boys) do or because it is simply her nature, or whether there are external influences that are stereotyping her into certain behavior.

A friend, whose daughter is thirteen and a good soccer player, believes that girls come into their own once they start playing with other girls. Her theory is that a lot of the coaches have lower expectations for the girls, thus they play them at fullback and the girls never have the chance to develop all their abilities. Also, she says, they get bored.

Our coach, however, believes in rotating players. As the spring season progressed, more and more of the six-year-olds were getting the hang of the game. More stars emerged. No girls had scored. My hopes of keeping my daughter involved in a team sport—one of the cornerstones of my child-rearing theories—were disappearing.

"I'm not going to play next fall," she announced on the way home from a recent practice. "Soccer is boring and, besides, girls don't play soccer." To which I gave her a list of girls she knows who play, including three who played all the way through college. "I don't care," she answered. "I'm not going to play next fall. I want to do gymnastics."

My son the college student paid a surprise visit home that weekend and went to her game. About ten minutes into it, he said: "Gymnastics."

Soccer registration came and went and I did not sign her up. I was going against the tide.

Last Saturday she played fullback the first quarter and sat out the second. The coach started her at forward at the beginning of the second half. In a tied game. At one point, I simply covered my eyes. On the bright side of things was the fact that I wouldn't be going to two soccer games every weekend next fall.

A couple of minutes later, however, one of my daughter's teammates kicked the ball across to the center of the field, about five yards out of the goal.

My daughter was there.

My daughter kicked the ball. It went up in the air. It came down on the ground. It went into the goal. The crowd went wild.

The smile on her face could have lit up a night game.

She sat out the final quarter and came over to sit with us. She accepted all sorts of congratulations and hugs. Then her brother said, "So, Katherine, do you want to play soccer next fall?"

To which she replied happily, "Yes, I'll do soccer and gymnastics. I am going to play soccer next fall."

Grand Expectations
DECEMBER 5, 1986

There is something about the Thanksgiving holiday that seems to trigger an automatic response in my children: as soon as the word "turkey" enters the household discourse (as in "Thanksgiving turkey"), so does the word "Christmas." Within moments, Christmas gift catalogues appear (bootlegged from their grandparents' house) and their annual creative writing effort gets under way.

This is known as their Christmas list, and each year these Christmas lists evoke a series of automatic responses from the person to whom they are addressed, and I'm not referring to Santa Claus. There is one lecture entitled "I'm Not Made of Money, You Know." There is also the lecture about "The True Meaning of Christmas," in which emphasis is placed on the religious nature of the holiday, in an effort to maintain an equilibrium in my balance of payments to the Japanese, Taiwanese and Koreans who have spent the past year fabricating toys that no American child is complete without. I've given up on the "It's More Blessed to Give Than to Receive" lecture because the sight of children looking at me as though I'd lost my mind is simply too disquieting.

This Christmas has been made all the more challenging by a relatively new development in my daughter. It began a couple of months ago when one of her schoolmates came over to play. The schoolmate is taking piano lessons. She discovered a little toy piano that I'd given my daughter two Christmases ago in hopes of kindling some musical interest in at least one of my children. The piano had, however, spent much of its life on a shelf and was even more out of tune than the day it arrived.

I am a firm believer in not trying to pursue your own failed ambitions through your children, and I am also a firm believer in not pushing children when it comes to such things as musical interests. It simply doesn't work, as I quickly learned during my only previous attempt to develop the musical side of a child whose idea of having a musical side is knowing how to turn on his stereo.

Thus, I did not go to pieces when my daughter failed to turn into a piano prodigy at the age of five. I looked at the bright side of this turn of events, which was that I would not have to buy a piano or find a place in the house for one—which is no easy matter when you have already filled up your house. That was before my daughter's friend the pianist arrived.

Before the afternoon was over, my daughter had also discovered the piano. She had mastered one complete tune and was well on her way to others. She had also taught her older brother to play the tune. In the weeks that followed, she has learned more and more tunes from her friend the pianist. For the first time in recorded memory, her brother has been awestruck at something his sister is doing, and she has been showing him how to play, too.

For the first couple of weeks after she discovered the piano, I took some solace in the notion that children have short attention spans. This passion might soon give way to something we already had, like dolls. This has not occurred. What has occurred is that the toy piano has become too small for her. Thanksgiving evening, we went to her grandparents' house and she effortlessly transferred her toy piano techniques to their grand piano. What has also occurred is that at some point before Thanksgiving she peered up at me, with her hands held prayerfully, and her eyes lit up like sparklers, and she said, "Please, Mommy, can I get a piano for Christmas?"

And I said: "I would love to buy you a piano for Christmas. Let me see what I can do."

What I did, of course, was to promptly call her grandfather and apprise him of the musical talent that was flourishing in yet another generation of the family. I figured a decent used piano was going to cost around $500 (that's before I started shopping), but by then I'd rationalized this by figuring I'd start playing again. He rose to the occasion magnificently: "I'll help," he said (which was a great deal more than he said when I floated my yearning for a mink coat by him).

My daughter is aware that my purchase of a family piano for Christmas is going to limit the resources available for other gifts. Meanwhile, however, the creative writing exercise is blooming and her list is pointedly positioned on the refrigerator door. I can only hope she is not thinking what her brother thought one year. He gave me his Christmas list, and then a few days later I found him writing yet another list. There were no duplications. I reminded him that he'd already given me his list.

"I know," he said. "This one's for Santa."

Parents' Pangs Over Pain
MAY 8, 1987

Over the years of rearing children, I've fancied myself as becoming something of an expert in distinguishing between routine illnesses and those requiring medical attention. I've dealt with sprains and I've dealt with broken bones. I can hold my own in a discussion about growth plates. I can tell an inner ear infection from an outer ear infection, an allergy attack from a common cold, a legitimately sick child from a con artist.

You learn a lot about illness and medicine as a parent. Besides, it is one of my theories that working mothers exercise extreme caution in these areas in order to protect themselves against seizures of guilt brought on by even the remotest appearance of child neglect. The possibility of serious problems, such as broken bones, for example, has led to innumerable visits to pediatricians and emergency rooms. I am not cavalier about broken bones.

Several weeks ago, my son the eleven-year-old hurt his thumb playing basketball. We put it on ice, but it wasn't looking good. As the evening progressed, it got worse. The next morning, we visited the pediatrician. He thought it was a bad sprain but wasn't sure. Off we went to the X-ray place. About $100 and three hours later, the diagnosis was that he had a bad sprain. The advice was not to play basketball for at least another twenty-four hours.

He did not play in the game the next morning, but he had a miraculous recovery in time for the game that afternoon. It did nothing to bolster my belief in the merits of getting immediate attention for minor injuries. I resolved, henceforth, to do my part in reducing America's health care costs.

I mentioned this during the game to my friend Lynn, who has three sons. Every working mother should have a friend like Lynn. She is warm and wonderful, but if she'd been in charge of the Normandy invasion we'd all be speaking German.

She said the same thing had happened to her oldest son, Brendan. "It was awful. He was playing basketball and jammed his finger. We never did a thing. He was complaining a lot but we never paid that much attention to him. And then this neighbor, who's a doctor, came by and he dropped his kids off because Brendan was going to baby-sit. And he just happened to look down and he saw Brendan's little finger. It was purple. And he said he was pretty sure it was broken, and Brendan said he thought so, too, but his parents didn't pay any attention. And the doctor looked at me, and he said, 'Lynn, when it turns purple, then it's a pretty good clue that it's broken.'"

On a recent Thursday evening, my son came into the house and called out: "Hi, Mom. I broke my finger at soccer practice." This news didn't exactly cap my day. We examined his little finger and he described how he had injured it. We put ice on it and about fifteen minutes later he went outside to play. This did very little to convince me that we were dealing with a major injury. It still hurt the next morning, but so had the sprained thumb. It was swollen, but then the sprained thumb had been swollen. His finger certainly wasn't purple.

By the time I got into work, there was already a message from the school clinic. He couldn't write and he'd been in for ice. I called the doctor and he advised keeping it on ice and taping it to the adjacent finger and seeing how he did over the weekend. This, said the doctor, would probably be the treatment even if it were broken. I made the mistake of mentioning this turn of events to my editor, who, as the mother of two young children, is something of a kindred spirit in these matters. She commiserated. Saturday morning, a friend who was over for coffee looked at my son's finger. He said it looked like it was jammed. I said I'd never had a jammed finger.

"Of course you haven't," he said. "Girls don't get jammed fingers."

By Sunday, I noticed the finger was looking a little gray. Maybe even a little purple. By Monday, we were at the pediatrician's office. He sent us for X rays. That afternoon, the diagnosis was in: the finger was broken and had to be set.

Shortly before noon on Tuesday, I mentioned to my soulmate, the editor, that I was giving her my column early because I had to take my son to the orthopedist. As I spoke, her eyes got wider. Finally, she burst out: "His finger's broken? How many days has this poor child been walking around with a broken finger? Five?"

This is a woman who knows how to do guilt. I said: "Don't do this to me." I tried to explain about broken fingers and how they are generally just taped, anyway. She didn't buy a word of it.

So I told her about my friend Lynn.

Gifts for the Season and Beyond
DECEMBER 25, 1987

Christmas lists, I have decided, are signs of life's passages. The day after Thanksgiving, I suggested—as I do every year—that my children start poring through the various catalogues at our house and their grandparents' home to see what they want for Christmas. The idea is for them to select items that can be purchased over the phone, which will spare their mother and father trips to the malls. Last year, my daughter the eight-year-old had more than forty items on her wish list. If she were ever nominated to be secretary of defense, I'd testify against her. That year, I suggested that she contrive some way of letting us know what items were essential to her well-being at Christmas and what she could do without. It was also the last year that I was able to blame the anticipated shortfall on Santa's logistical problems. He will be missed.

This year, the lists were briefer. At first glance, I thought the reason for that was that my children had finally realized that they were not born into a wealthy family. But that's not what happened at all. There were fewer items, but they were more expensive—as in tennis rackets. As any parent of a twelve-year-old knows, tennis rackets now come in an infinite variety of designer names, shapes and prices. This means that tennis rackets are now like tennis shoes: an investment.

As children get older, it gets harder and harder to give them something meaningful at Christmas. They want clothes, sports equipment, machinery to produce various kinds of sounds, electronic gadgets, home furnishings. Every so often a parent might still find the word "books" on a list.

If I could give my children anything, it would not be any of those things.

I would give them the gift of integrity to take into a world that seems to have forgotten the meaning of the word. With it, they could sleep at night and wake up and look at themselves in the mirror in the morning. They might not get rich, but with it they won't be poor.

Integrity would protect them against greed in a world that is consumed by it, and driven by it. I would give them the gift of independence—so that they can leave home complete and whole and strike a course of action that is dictated by their will and heart and mind, and not by fashion. I would give them the wit to be critical, to see greed for the unseemly, selfish and antisocial thing it is and to despise it, not embrace it.

I would give them the true sophistication and good taste to be able to distinguish between that which is fine and enduring and that which is trading on the fickle fancy of the moment. With those gifts, they will be able to appreciate great music, food, literature, architecture, theater—and they will be able to nurture a culture worth preserving and passing on to future generations.

To do this well, they will need the gift of passion. They will need the ability to care deeply about the things that move them and the people they love. This, too, takes courage, for it takes a great deal of courage to care.

Humor—I would give them each at least two boxes' worth of humor to take into a world that takes itself infinitely too seriously. They will need ready supplies of humor in school, when they go to work and when they deal with their true loves and their children, not to mention their mother. I would also give them patience, but not too much.

They will need tolerance, as well. There's an oversupply of intolerance right now and of dreary self-righteousness that is causing all manner of conflict. I would wish them the self-confidence to be tolerant of others' views and to respect them. Someday, they could be your own.

A love of peace is another gift I would give them, along with a hatred of violence. I would want them to be sensitive to violence in all the forms it takes around them and not to be insensitive toward it. This is not easy for children who are exposed to it from the headlines in the morning paper to the last show of the night on television. I would want them not to be dulled by it, but to be attuned to it, whether it is the violence of one nation toward another people, or the violence of a single person toward another human being.

And I would give them the gift of friendship—to give it and to receive it. I would give them the sensitivity to care about their friends, the energy to cherish them and the selflessness to give of themselves to others for the pure joy of the human connections. And, if I could, I would give them the joy of love. For that is what life is all about.

Merry Christmas.

The Christmas of the Red Car
DECEMBER 30, 1987

There is a red car in my driveway.

It has been there, off and on, since the late afternoon of the day before Christmas. That day, in a monumental triumph of bad timing on the part of my parents, also happens to be my birthday, and the arrival of the red car did not make me feel younger.

Christmas holidays, especially those that involve big family reunions and family passages, earn their place in the memories of all the family members and they get shorthanded in subsequent years with phrases such as: "That was the year Grandpa got drunk and pinched your mother." The resident grandpa in our family hasn't done anything quite so daring in years, however, so we are reduced to remembering Christmases in more mundane ways such as where we hid various bikes, or knocked over Christmas trees, or got stranded in subzero weather on the way home from Grandma's. This year, however, may well be remembered as the year the red car appeared.

The appearance of the red car coincided with the return of the twenty-one-year-old. He has been working and going to college in Manhattan and has taken, of late, to calling home to have brotherly conversations with the resident twelve-year-old. I do not mean to suggest that he doesn't also call and have conversations with me or his little sister, but it did come as a shock when he started calling his brother to converse exclusively with him. It's the kind of thing that makes you feel ever so slightly irrelevant. Especially when the twelve-year-old appears in the kitchen after one such marathon episode and says that his big brother said to say hi. Twenty-one years of sacrifice, not to mention $1.5 billion in outlays, and all you get is a hi?

A couple of weeks before Christmas, I came home from work to discover that one of these phone calls had been under way for some time. I was told that the topic du jour was Christmas presents. In the spirit of the occasion, I got on the kitchen extension and told Joe Manhattan what I planned to get for him and gave him a brief list of things that he could get for me, if he was so inspired (I have learned over the years that people who are shrinking violets about their gift list get forgotten). My main recollection of the conversation is that the first five minutes were on my son's dime and then he had his little brother call him back so that the rest of the summit was on mine. He said he was coming down on the twenty-fourth, and I told him not to come too late in the day so I could pick him up at the subway station, and he would not turn my birthday dinner into a fire drill.

By late Thursday, I had heard nothing from him about his travel plans. I decided I wasn't going to worry about it. This is, after all, a grown man in the eyes of just about everyone in the world whom he doesn't call Mother. Shortly after 5:00 p.m., however, the grown man hadn't called to let us know whether he was even on the way, and I was busily concluding that underneath the surface of the grown man is yet another irresponsible college student.

Suddenly, the door from the carport opened. My daughter screamed. We all looked around, and he made his entrance into the family room, looking very much the grown man, and very pleased with himself. We had a loud and happy reunion, and after things settled down, I asked the burning question, which was not "How are you?"

It was: "How did you get here?"

He said: "I drove."

I said: "You drove? What did you drive?"

He said: "My car."

I said: "Your car? What are you talking about? Your car!" I used to live in New York, too.

He said: "I bought a car."

I said: "Without me? You bought a car without telling me? Without asking my advice?"

His little brother was gloating. "You knew!" I said. It turned out that the proud owner of the newly acquired car had bought it two weeks earlier and had told his little brother the night of the marathon phone call and sworn him to secrecy. When the little brother helps his big brother keep a secret instead of spilling the beans, you know the balance of power within a family is subtly shifting.

We all went out to the driveway. There sat the biggest, reddest 1972 Pontiac Le Mans I have ever seen. We went, of course, for a ride, during the course of which he told the story of how he got the car, and more relevantly, how much he paid for it and how much he subsequently had to put into it. I had to admit that he seems to have made a pretty good deal. Even without my advice.

Then we got home. Suddenly it hit me: "What about insurance?"

"It's all taken care of," he said.

After all, he's a grown man. Even in the eyes of his mother.

House Cleaning Still Women's Work
MARCH 9, 1988

It is well documented that no one since the dawn of time has ever liked to do housework. People like to cook, they enjoy gardening, they get a big bang out of doing things with their children, but they do not like to vacuum, dust, wash the kitchen floor, clean the bathrooms, do the laundry, clean the oven, defrost the refrigerator and do the marketing. The list alone is exhausting.

So it should come as no surprise that early on in the distribution of labor between the sexes housework was assigned to the female of the species, who was then known as the "weaker sex." Women did the housework while men went off and hunted for food. Later they hunted each other. Women also were assigned the principal tasks of caring for children. In return, women got food and shelter and animal furs in which to wrap themselves, which is more than most of them get today.

This arrangement, or some variation thereof, went on for thousands of years, resisting most challenges. There was a period of time when some women had servants to do the housework—la belle epoch, as it was known—but that didn't last long and didn't affect most women. Housework became something of a barometer of character. Women who had dust-free houses and sparkling kitchen floors were known as "good housewives." The underlying assumption was that their husbands and children would have sparkling clean souls. Conversely, a filthy house was a surefire sign of a family headed straight to ruin.

Then came the mid-1960s, when a confluence of events upset the apple cart. This included widespread use of the birth control pill, the easing of divorce laws and the publication of *The Feminine Mystique*, all of which helped launch the second phase of the women's liberation movement in the United States. (Historians have placed the first phase as the period leading up to and including winning the right to vote.) Women postponed or forsook childbearing, they divorced or didn't marry, and they went to work outside their homes, entering the professions in record numbers.

Two great philosophical questions were asked all across America. One was: "Who's minding the children?" and the other was: "Who's doing the housework?"

Two of society's most precious assets were imperiled: one was its future and the other was its real estate.

Could studies be far behind?

No. Hard on the heels of women's march into the labor force came the studies that showed that as soon as they marched home at night, they had to do almost as much housework as they had to do before they sat down on the sofa that fateful day and read Betty Friedan's book while munching bonbons. Microwaves, self-cleaning ovens and no-frost refrigerators have helped compress some household work, but most working women are still swamped.

In its January issue, *Psychology Today* published the results of a University of Florida study of 1,565 married couples. Overall, the study found that wives spent almost thirty hours a week doing housework, compared with about six hours done by their husbands. Wives who work full-time do about 70 percent of the housework, compared with 83 percent done by housewives. High-powered career women and other working women both do about three times as much housework as their spouses.

This study was followed by a recent *New York Times* survey of 1,870 people that showed that 90 percent of the married women are responsible for doing most or all of the cooking in their households. Eighty-six percent of those who worked did most of the cooking, while 93 percent of those who stayed at home did most of the cooking. And 90 percent of the women employed full-time did most of the shopping.

Progress, in altering the division of labor, is obviously coming in the tiniest of increments. Getting husbands to share in housework simply has not worked.

Into this valley of dust have come two men with a single dazzling thought: do less.

In response to the *Psychology Today* article, Anthony Belcher of San Antonio wrote: "The basic problem is not that men are unfair or lazy, but that women often have excessively high standards for which they will sacrifice their free time, relationships and careers."

Hank Bullwinkel of Baltimore wrote in his letter: "House-keeping is 'women's work' only because women in dual-career households choose to do it, while men like myself feel that dusting is only necessary after someone writes his or her name on the table."

These gentlemen obviously don't realize that a family's entire moral character is at stake. But the whole housework controversy might be diffused if it weren't.

Coping with Convenience
JANUARY 25, 1989

It is no longer enough to be a safe driver, adequate cook, capable seamstress, practical nurse and ever-ready friend and counselor to qualify as a competent mother. You also have to be an electrician. Or at least a very high order of handyperson.

Otherwise, all those terrific household appliances that have been devised to make our lives more fun and less complicated won't work.

There is no such thing as a simple telephone that you plug into a jack anymore or a simple television set that you plug into the wall. That's an exaggeration, of course: these quaint devices do exist, but they don't seem up to the needs of modern suburban households. A phone that doesn't record messages is the path to social oblivion. A television that isn't wired to cable, videocassette recorders and video games and isn't run by two remote controls is a sign of emotional deprivation.

Ever since the old TV in the family room started smelling like rubber was burning inside it, my children have been playing Nintendo on a thirteen-inch black and white TV their older brother acquired in a dormitory sale at the end of his freshman year in college. Those sales make garage sales look like estate sales. When you turn the set on, a picture wiggles across the screen.

The verdict from the repair shop was that it would cost $110 to fix the vertical-something on the old TV, and the picture tube didn't look too good, either. The choices came down to disconnecting the children from their major Christmas present, letting them go blind, or disconnecting the Nintendo from the black and white set and hooking it up to a new set.

About the same time that the television in the family room died, so did the phone in the kitchen. The dishwasher wasn't draining properly and the disposer stopped altogether. The clothes dryer wasn't drying the clothes. My daughter the nine-year-old, who has a way of getting to the heart of matters, threw up her hands when the kitchen phone line went dead and cried out in total exasperation: "NOTHING IN THIS HOUSE WORKS!"

I have in the past managed to get disposers started up again and dishwashers drained, but the upshot of my home remedies was that a pipe connecting the disposer to the drainpipe broke and water started pouring onto the floor. I called the plumber, who made a house call that afternoon. He was a big psychological help. He didn't cost me a fortune or tell me I needed two new expensive appliances that would cost hundreds more to install. Moreover, a couple of things started working again in the House Where Nothing Works.

Hope springs eternal on the home-repair front, and I decided to see what was wrong with the dryer. It turns out that a bunch of things had fallen onto the hose leading out of the house. I liberated the hose and that seems to have helped. Buying a new dryer is not my idea of a fun way to spend $400.

Much encouraged by this success, I decided to fix the kitchen phone. Have you looked inside a phone lately? It looks like the insides of a computer and there is no clue whatever as to what tiny piece of metal does what. I knew my limits.

Saturday afternoon I went to my favorite discount store to get a new TV for the family room and a new phone for the kitchen. I figured the money I saved on not having to buy a new disposer and dryer and dishwasher could be used to improve the kitchen phone to an answering machine so that our family would not be left completely behind as we headed into the age of total-convenience homes.

Installation books for those appliances have a perturbing way of describing what you're supposed to do in a foreign electronic language. By late afternoon, my daughter was standing in front of the new TV, saying: "The new TV doesn't work." By dinnertime, I was in deep dialogue with an extremely patient woman at our cable system. We got the TV working and my daughter's faith in her mother was fully restored. When I got the Nintendo hooked into it and resurrected Super Mario in living color, she was ready to send me to the Mothers Hall of Fame.

Energized by that, I decided to hook up the new phone in the kitchen. That took much of Sunday afternoon. You can't just plug a phone that does thirteen different things into a jack. I finally got the batteries installed and I finally found the hidden button that you have to press to tape outgoing messages and I finally got the phone secured to the wall. We taped a message and my daughter went to the phone in my home office to make the call launching us into the age of total phone convenience. I was starting to believe in Supermom again. And that's when we found out that our new phone that does everything doesn't do one small thing: it doesn't ring.

The Highlight of a World Odyssey
FEBRUARY 24, 1989

Last June, my older son left his job in New York, moved his belongings back home and left the United States to see the world. If this sounds simple, it was not. The invasion of Normandy was probably conducted with less upheaval.

For one thing, he left his big red jalopy in my carport, making the house look like a self-contained suburban slum, which is not the look I've been striving for. The plus side of this, however, was that it guaranteed that I would think of him at least twice each day: when I pulled out of the carport in the morning and looked at the car and when I pulled into the carport in the evening and looked at the car.

Armed with a backpack and a tent, and accompanied by his best friend, he left on a plane bound for Paris with plans to return in a year. I figured his money would run out by the end of the summer. He was twenty-two. "When I was twenty-two," I told him that afternoon, "I already had you." In my generation, seeing the world meant going to Manhattan. In his generation, seeing the world means going to Cairo. His generation sees Cairo in its youth; mine may see Cairo in our retirement.

I took considerable comfort in the fact that his friend had spent her junior year in France, the two of them had already had some experience traveling abroad and, besides, there wasn't much point in worrying. Fatalism can be useful at times like this. I repeated all the good advice the State Department gives American travelers about not carrying strange packages across borders and resolved not to think about young travelers vanishing off the face of the earth without a trace. Besides, the other mother left behind in this adventure had extracted a promise that the adventurers would call one of us once a week.

My daughter took the first call that came to our house and the message she delivered was that her brother was on some island and having a good time. He called a week or so after that with the news that they'd fled the high cost of living in Paris after less than two days and had headed south. He also wanted the phone number for a college classmate of mine who now lives in Geneva. I didn't hear anything after that for several weeks. My father, however, got a call and so did my brother. So did the people at my son's former office in Manhattan. The world traveler had turned into a world-class telephoner.

It turns out the adventurers had taken up residence at my friend's home in Geneva and were helping her remodel her kitchen in return for lodging. That struck me as extraordinarily resourceful. I realized not long after that that my son was not going to run out of money before the end of the summer and that he was infinitely better at coping than I'd given him credit for. Admiration replaced worry.

He resumed traveling in the fall. We got cards and phone calls from Yugoslavia and Crete, Italy and Greece. His best friend returned home at Thanksgiving. My younger children hoped their brother might be back at Christmas, but I knew he would not. When he didn't call over the holidays, however, I started to worry again. On December 31, he called from Jerusalem. He said he'd been on a boat in a terrible storm. I got the feeling I wasn't the only person who'd been worrying. He said that he and a friend he'd teamed up with were headed to Cairo. He planned to be home around April 1 and was looking forward to spending time with the family.

Several weeks ago, we received a long, wonderful letter. He described living for a week in a Bedouin village and he described Cairo. We all realized how much we missed him. This week was particularly hard because February 24 is his birthday. We had no way of calling him.

Wednesday evening, I called his best friend to see if she could take care of my children Thursday evening. Her mother said her daughter wasn't home, but she thought she could. We caught up on family matters and she said the latest they'd heard from my son was that he would be home around the first of April.

I finished the dinner dishes and started to make my daughter's lunch. Suddenly, there was a loud knock on the front door. It was 10:15 p.m. I went to the door with a sandwich bag in my hand. "Who's there?" I asked.

"Collecting for *The Washington Post*," came the reply. It was a deep man's voice.

I didn't like the sound of that at all. "It's a little late for that," I said. I glanced to make sure the door was locked. Then I saw the upper half of a man's face in the window at the top of the door. I opened the door and there was my son. I remember hearing his best friend say "Surprise!" and while there have been some moments in my life when I've been as happy as I was right then, there have been none when I've been happier.

Watching a Parent Slip Away, a Little at a Time
APRIL 21, 1989

For more than a decade, this column has shared some of the joys, triumphs and simple passages of life that have occurred within my family, not because they were unique, but because they happen, in one form or another, to so many families. It is in that same spirit that I share now the greatest sorrow that my family has known, for this too will happen to all of us.

Early in the evening of March 28, I received a call from the Powhatan Nursing Home in Arlington saying that my mother had died. Her name was Margaretta Warden, she was eighty-seven years old, and she had been living in the shadow of death for more than a year. As anticipated as that call was, there are no words to describe the sense of loss I felt then, and feel to this day. The closest physical sensation I can think of is having the wind knocked out of you, again and again and again.

There were a number of themes that ran through my mother's long and productive life, and one of the most constant was that of teaching. Mother's heritage reached deep into the earliest days of the Society of Friends in Chester County, Pennsylvania, and from those roots she brought forth an enduring appreciation of education, productivity, frugality and, above all, a gentleness and sense of courtesy toward her fellow human beings that guided her every action. Mother was a classmate of Margaret Mead's at Barnard College and delighted in reminding us from time to time that she, Margaret Mead and someone whose name long ago dropped out of the story were the only three students exempted from their anthropology final exam. After college, mother taught at and later ran the first Arthur Murray studio in New York. Years later, she taught French, and she was a stickler for correct grammar.

Mother would not have scripted her final years the way they occurred. One of the enduring lessons she taught us in the end is that there are some things we simply cannot control, and we simply must do the very best we can. Mother was independent and self-reliant—she prized those qualities highly—and they were taken from her mercilessly. I can remember her saying fifteen years ago, when the debate over life-support machines first surfaced, that she did not want to be hooked up to any kind of artificial machine. "Just let me go," she said firmly. But for most of her last year the only nourishment she could get was from a feeding tube and for much of that time she received assistance in breathing from an oxygen tank.

A great deal of attention is being paid now to the problems of aging parents, who cares for them, and the pressure this puts on their sons and daughters who are working themselves and also raising children. To call this the "sandwich generation," the current term, trivializes the crushing emotional, physical and financial stress that takes place when a family is caring for an aged, incapacitated member. Our family was far more fortunate than most: my father, Charles Warden, was torn apart by grief and worry during the years of Mother's decline, but he was there to oversee her care. He was there to hire the health care aides and physical therapists, to take her to the doctors and specialists who, in the end, ruled out Parkinson's disease as the cause of her problems but came up with no alternative diagnosis, or, more to the point, no way of helping her recover.

My father, their housekeeper and several home health care workers took care of my mother at home until a year ago, when she got pneumonia. By then she was bedridden almost all the time and eating was a terrible ordeal. She had lost a great deal of weight.

On St. Patrick's Day 1988, their housekeeper called me and told me Mother was dying. I had been at their home the night before and realized then how heartbreakingly close the end was. When I went to their home the next day, I knew she had pneumonia and I knew her death was imminent and that her wish to die at home could soon be fulfilled. My father knew on one level how grave the situation was, but in his heart he could not admit it, and his heart always ruled where my mother was concerned.

I could have made the decision then not to call my mother's doctor and not to call the ambulance and not to have her taken to Arlington Hospital. But I could not do that. These quality of life arguments become meaningless when we have to make the decisions for those we love. I felt a year ago, and I feel today, that she deserved every chance to live that we could give her. With the agreement of my father, however, I told her doctor in the emergency room that we wanted no heroic measures and no code blue lifesaving procedures to start her heart if it stopped. That is a terrible decision to have to make.

Mother had no chance to fight the pneumonia without nourishment. My father and I agreed that a feeding tube should be inserted through her nose, if it could be done without causing her pain. She began receiving antibiotics, but within days the doctor gave Mother twenty-four hours to live. My brother and his wife arrived from Massachusetts. Their daughter and my older son spent the night in Mother's room with their grandfather. My sister and her husband came from Michigan. My younger son spent the next day by his grandmother's side, instead of going to school, and urged me to bring his little sister to the hospital so that she, too, could be with her grandmother. There were times during her struggle when Mother woke, and when she saw her grandchildren she smiled and reached for their hands.

We made decisions about what funeral home would handle arrangements, and the cemetery plot, and my brother and sister-in-law selected the casket. We spent the hours comforting my father, who was inconsolable, and ourselves, and we made sure that Mother was never without a family member by her side. The hours passed into days. Mother's lungs began to clear. We brought in heart and lung specialists and began respiratory treatments to help her. Mother had survived double pneumonia, but it left her weakened beyond measure. The hospital was ready to discharge her.

We made the hard decision to put her into a nursing home because she needed the skilled nursing care and physical therapy that could never be managed at home. My father could tolerate the idea only by thinking that it was for a short period of time to help her regain her strength so she could come home. She never did. For the last half year of her life, she was at Powhatan, which is close to my home and that of my father. He saw her every day. The two home health aides who had helped her at home continued to care for her while she was in the nursing home.

The last day that I saw her when she was awake was New Year's Day. My father and I visited her, and when I saw how alert she was, I went home and returned with my daughter. Mother's face lit up when she saw her granddaughter. That smile and the way they held hands are a memory I will always cherish.

I will not deny that this past year has been hard on my father and hard on all of us. We ran headlong into the staggering costs of nursing homes and the patchwork of Catch-22 federal health care and private insurance regulations that often seem more designed to save money than lives. We explored every possible medical hope. We also discovered the kind of love and care that exists in a good nursing home. We saw genuine respect for human life.

And we saw a love affair that lasted nearly sixty years. Toward the end, when Mother seemed to be sleeping most of the time, my father visited her every afternoon and read her poetry. He took her roses. He spent the last evening with her. My family and I have taken comfort in the idea that the last year was a way of letting us prepare for Mother's death. Father could not have handled it a year ago. He was not ready to let go until a couple of days before the very end. We think of the last year as her final gift, her way of giving us time to get ready.

But we were not.

A Close Brush with Near Tragedy
MAY 3, 1989

It was the call that every parent dreads. It came at 5:40 in the evening of April 21, three weeks after the death of my mother, and

I was sitting in my living room, feeling emotionally and physically depleted. Ten minutes before that, my son the thirteen-year-old had phoned to say he was riding his bike home from his friend David's house. I had noted the time and was looking forward to seeing him.

"Mrs. Mann?" said a male voice on the phone. "This is Mr. Newman. Your son has been hit by a car."

I said the hardest thing I've ever had to say: "Is he still alive?"

"Yes, he's conscious and a nurse has been with him since it happened." He told me my son was at 1703 Great Falls Street, a major road near our home in McLean. Somehow I had an image of Jeff in a living room with a nurse beside him. I was dismayed to see that traffic had backed up on Great Falls Street because that would delay my getting to him. Then I saw ambulances and police cars stopped at a curve about three blocks up the road. It was moments before I made the horrendous connection, and then I put my hand on the horn of my car and opened my windows and went around cars and got as close as I could before pulling the car over to the curb and getting out.

My son was lying in the street, blood pouring from underneath a compress on his forehead. Paramedics were kneeling over him, checking him over and asking him questions such as where he went to school, how old he was, where he lived, what day it was. They were trying to keep him conscious, trying to keep him talking. I crouched down next to him and told him I was there, that he was going to be all right. He wanted to know what had happened and then he started asking for his older brother, a request he would repeat frequently.

I watched as the paramedics put a neck brace on him and then cut away his clothing and strapped him down on a board to immobilize him. That he had a head injury was obvious. I knew that he could also have brain damage, spinal injuries and damage to his internal organs. He looked heartbreakingly helpless. He was still talking, but he was confused. My next-door neighbor appeared and said she would take care of my daughter and tell their father what had happened. I rode in the front of the ambulance to Fairfax Hospital, where they admitted Jeff into the shock-trauma unit. I will not forget the calm professionalism of the McLean rescue unit that cared for him, nor the kindness of the ambulance driver who tried to reassure me.

Jeff was wheeled into a large room where members of the shock-trauma team began examining him. I was taken to a consultation room across the hall, where there was a phone. I called home and talked to my daughter and I called my father's home and talked to my sister, who had just returned to town. I asked her to help find my older son. The doctor who was in charge of the shock-trauma unit that evening appeared in the room to tell me what they were doing. He returned repeatedly to tell what the various specialists were finding. The news was relatively good: there would be lots of X rays done to confirm the preliminary examinations, but there appeared to be no broken bones, or neurological or internal damage. There were two large, bone-deep gashes going from his eyes up to his hairline, which would require extensive plastic surgery that evening. An X ray later showed a hairline fracture in the forehead. His right eye was swollen shut but there was no permanent damage to his sight. Around 9:00 p.m. we were told that a CAT scan showed no brain damage.

My family, Jeff's father, several very close friends of mine and my oldest son came to the hospital, as did his closest friend. Two people were able to be with Jeff in the emergency room almost all the time until he actually went into surgery later that night. A tube had to be inserted into his stomach to stop him from vomiting blood. I was grateful to be able to be with him, and I was grateful to the doctors and nurses, who were immensely reassuring. I was moved beyond measure at the closeness I saw between my two sons, as my older son, who is twenty-three, sat by his younger brother, comforting him and trying to get him to lie still. My older son is helping coach Jeff's lacrosse team, and one of Jeff's recurring questions that night was whether his season was over.

The police officer who investigated the accident came to the hospital and told me that Jeff had apparently ridden his bike out between cars and had not seen the car coming around a bad curve in the road. The driver had swerved to avoid hitting him head-on and his head had hit the side mirror of her car. I asked the officer to call her and tell her that Jeff was going to be all right and to tell her how deeply grateful we were for her swift reaction. I talked to her later that night, and after Jeff came home on Monday, she and her daughter came to visit him.

The Consumer Product Safety Commission says there were 525,027 bike injuries in 1988. Fifty-seven percent of those were to youngsters ages five to fourteen. According to the National Coalition to Prevent Childhood Injury, at least one child under the age of fifteen is killed every day in a bicycle crash, and more than 75 percent of them suffered head injuries. Most, according to the coalition, could have been saved if they had worn bike helmets. Had my son been wearing an approved helmet, he probably would not have been as badly hurt as he was.

The plastic surgeon has told him that his lacrosse season is over, that any damage to his forehead would be disastrous. He will have scars, but he knows how lucky he was. And my family, grieving the death of my mother, is feeling profoundly grateful and blessed that on that Friday evening we were given the gift of Jeffrey's life.

Support for Cycling Safety
MAY 17, 1989

Over the last decade or so, we have seen a number of campaigns mounted to increase safety on the road, and they have worked. People are wearing seat belts, they are restraining infants in car seats, and drunk drivers are doing hard time. Those public awareness campaigns have changed attitudes and laws, and the result is that lives are being saved.

This week, the National Safe Kids Campaign is trying to do the same thing for bike safety that earlier efforts did for car safety. The campaign is sponsored by the National Coalition to Prevent Childhood Injury, and its goal is to make parents and youngsters aware of the increased dangers of bike riding and of the importance of wearing approved helmets and following safe cycling practices.

As the mother of a child who narrowly escaped devastating injury when his bicycle hit a car recently, the fervent hope here is that the Safe Kids Campaign will do for young cyclists what the car seat campaign did for infants and toddlers.

The lesson of past public awareness campaigns is that when the public becomes aware, it becomes aroused. Surveys done by the National Highway Traffic Safety Administration showed that in 1981, only 40.4 percent of the infants observed in nineteen cities around the country were buckled into car seats. By 1988, that figure had soared to 81.9 percent. A spokesman for the agency said that in 1987, child safety seat use by children under the age of four saved about 200 lives and prevented about 28,000 injuries.

A 1981 survey of seat belt use in nineteen cities showed that only 11 percent of the drivers were using them. By March of this year, that figure had risen to a record 47 percent. NHTSA estimates that from 1983 to 1988, safety belt use saved 15,200 lives.

All fifty states and the District now have laws requiring child restraints and thirty-three states and the District have seat belt laws.

The campaign to reduce accidents attributable to drunken driving has also had some solid results: the number of drunk drivers killed in accidents dropped by 23 percent from 1980 to 1987, and the proportion of drunk teenage drivers who were involved in fatal crashes dropped from 28 percent in 1982 to 19 percent in 1987.

Meanwhile, the number of accidents involving cyclists has risen 27 percent over the last decade as the sport has soared in popularity, as traffic has increased and as bikes have gotten faster. The Safe Kids campaign cites these statistics: every day, at least one child under the age of fifteen is killed and one thousand are seriously injured in bike crashes. More than 75 percent of the children who died suffered head injuries.

The NHTSA, which includes adults in its data, says that each year about twelve hundred bicyclists are killed and more than half a million end up in emergency rooms. About 10 percent of the irreversible brain injuries that occur each year are caused by bike crashes.

Yet, according to NHTSA, fewer than one in ten bicycle riders wears a helmet.

By far the most vulnerable bike riders are school-age boys, who are five times more likely to be killed than school-age girls. This is the age group that is more vulnerable to peer pressure than to the most basic instincts for survival.

This is the group that the Safe Kids Campaign has to reach, and it's not going to be easy. The campaign is mounting public service announcements on television, urging youngsters to wear helmets that are approved by the American National Standards Institute or the Snell Memorial Foundation. There is still no uniform national standard for helmets, which is something the Consumer Product Safety Commission ought to have done years ago. The CPSC and the NHTSA announced this week that they have signed a memorandum of understanding to work together to improve safety, and that includes developing ongoing programs to teach youngsters how to ride more safely.

There's no great mystery about how to do this. Shortly after my son's accident, I received a copy of a booklet published by the Fairfax City Optimists Club that was based on NHTSA research. The booklet was designed to help police officers educate kids on bike hazards. A similar booklet was developed for parents and youngsters. Community groups across the country could publish booklets that could be distributed through schools, fire departments and the rescue squads that are all too often called to the scene of biking tragedies.

In the end, peer pressure for wearing helmets will do more than anything else, and it may take designer helmets to start the trend. For once, however, parents could take comfort in knowing that the money they spend on a designer item is a very, very small price to pay.

To Renovate or Move: The $40,000 Question
SEPTEMBER 13, 1989

This was the year for deciding whether to renovate or move. That monumental question was influenced by a number of outside factors, not the least of which were interest rates and the real estate market that, as everyone knows, was comatose if not actually dead.

We ended up making the decision in stages, which is definitely not the way to go about it. The kitchen, we decided, had to be transformed into a thing of beauty whether we sold the house and moved or stayed and expanded. From that point on, each decision about the kitchen—and I think there were roughly three hundred—had to be weighed on whether we liked it or prospective buyers might like it. Fortunately, I like white.

The kitchen renovation began in March with my oldest son doing most of the work in exchange for funds that would allow him to reestablish himself after his travels abroad. That meant, in a word, getting his car working. It meant insurance. It meant new shocks. It meant work on the front end, and the rear end, and just about everything in between. There are certain lessons in life that people can learn only by experience and one of those is not to buy used old macho cars because they cost as much to support as another child. When my oldest son thinks about buying another car, I suspect he will think about stripping sixteen kitchen cabinets to the bare wood and painting them white, a process that took weeks.

Meanwhile, the kitchen descended into a state of chaos. It was impossible to find things. A simple dinner took a couple of hours to make, not because of any gourmet touches, but because it would take a half hour to find a frying pan. A stock pot is still missing to this day.

While my kitchen was descending into a state of chaos, the real estate market was going down the tubes. Furthermore, it became apparent in looking at houses and discussing heady mortgages with real estate agents—who have miraculous ways of stretching your money—that simple transfer costs of buying and selling a house were rapidly surpassing the equivalent of a new Jaguar. Real estate agents traditionally collect 6 percent of the sale cost of a house. On a $100,000 house—which was a nice middle-income property around here not so long ago—that would have netted the agents $6,000. That $100,000 house is a $300,000 or $400,000 house these days, and the agents are pulling out $18,000 and $24,000. If the agent sells you the house of your dreams and then turns around and sells your house so you can afford a down payment on your move up (that's real estate talk), the agent is making a killing. What with settlement costs, agents' windfall fees and various other legally sanctioned homeowner ripoffs, we figured we'd be spending upward of $40,000 to move.

You can do a lot to a house with $40,000.

You can also avoid moving.

Thus, the next phase of the interior renovation got under way.

This involved developing a grand plan of expanding the master bedroom into an adjoining sitting room and building a walk-in closet. It involved moving children into other rooms and it involved putting a better egress window into a lower-level bedroom. This, in the grand plan, was the first step. My middle son would move into that area, my daughter would move into his room, her room would become a study and everything would fall neatly into place in a matter of a week or so.

The custom window ordered by the nice lady at the lumber company arrived last week from Minnesota. It was a few days later in coming than we expected and it was twice as large in structure as we had ordered.

This kind of disaster, I am told by survivors of remodeling, is to be expected.

A contingency plan was swiftly devised. Suffice it to say that my younger son is a very good sport.

When we moved thirteen years ago, I resolved never to move again. This made remodeling enormously appealing. It was also a huge delusion. I have spent weeks throwing my past away and weeks trying to get my children to clean their rooms so they could move. They have spent weeks pretending I was talking to someone else. Finally, this last weekend, with painters scheduled to show up on Monday, they had no choice. Nor did I. I had to help my daughter, the resident pack rat, clean her room. She does not deal with separation well. If she ever becomes a famous writer, her biographer will have plenty of material. Her most primitive works from elementary school are safely preserved.

I have been tempted at various points to lock up the house and sell it "as is." I have fantasized about genies. As for the move-versus-renovate debate, there's probably only one answer: you save money by renovating, but in the end it's better to start out by being rich.

Curate That Collection, It's a Mess
OCTOBER 25, 1989

At our house, we have been moving rooms. We have also been moving people's histories and discovering that they have all manner of secret collections, hobbies and treasures with which they cannot bear to part. They've been acquiring property at a rate that makes Donald Trump look like a minor player. Unfortunately, he acquired real estate and my children acquired junk.

Moreover, the real estate they live in isn't large enough for their holdings. Getting them to divest, however, is like telling Trump to sell. For some people, the instinct to collect is as atavistic as the instinct to make money. Trump has made a fortune collecting. So far, my kids have made a mess. I'm told, however, that this can ultimately be a productive thing.

I am discovering that my children are hardly unique in this regard. Conversations with various friends in recent months have yielded the finding that none of them recall having nearly as many possessions in their youth as the children living in their households do now. Put another way, they say: "My kids have a lot more junk to put in their rooms than I ever did."

Meanwhile, modern homes may have big master suites, but the children's bedrooms are ten by eleven feet—barely enough space to house a teenager and his stereo, clothes and schoolbooks, let alone his skis, trophies, posters, weights, lacrosse equipment and back issues of *Sports Illustrated* and the *Sporting News*. (We all know where he puts his back issues of *Penthouse* and *Playboy*: under the bed.)

We began moving rooms when my oldest son moved out, liberating his bedroom for occupancy by his younger brother. Over the years, I have heard numerous horror stories from friends I thought were nice people about how they disposed of possessions their grown children left behind for their parents to store in perpetuity. My oldest son was happy to take his current portfolio of possessions with him and equally happy to leave his classic collection of thrift shop clothes, records, books, scholastic works and other items of historical interest behind. Unfortunately, this took up space needed by his younger brother, who made it clear that he was not interested in becoming the curator for his brother's museum. We have now boxed a collection of hand-me-downs that has as much chance of being used as I have of making a big score in commodities futures.

My younger son got the family award for cleaning his room and getting it ready to move. A certain amount of duress was involved in this evolution, which occurred early one Friday evening. What was at stake was the rest of that Friday evening.

His little sister, who was destined to move into his room, was an entirely different matter. She cannot bear to throw anything away. She has a stuffed animal collection that occupies every inch of a floor-to-ceiling bookcase. Suggest that she part with one of those and she will look at you as though you are Attila the Hun. She also has an extensive collection of stamps, foreign coins, cards and letters, artwork, art supplies, jewelry, toys, stickers, puzzles and playing cards, books and you-name-its, which are generally all over the floor.

"Aside from just being fun," writes Jody Gaylin in the October

Parents magazine, "collecting affords a child a sense of orderliness and mastery that can carry through to adulthood." She quotes Kenneth Brecher, director of the Children's Museum in Boston, as saying collecting helps a child develop a sense of control of his life. "Collecting is need-fulfilling," Brecher said. "It can take you to another place, create internal harmony, or satisfy whatever your particular need is at the time." Brecher collected postcards when he was a child. Now he has twenty thousand of them. This is control over your life?

I suspect from reading the article that I've gone about this business of dealing with my children's possessions in entirely the wrong way. Over the years, I have cajoled, threatened and bribed them to get their junk off the floor and clean their rooms. I've posted signs telling them that the rooms have been condemned by the health department. I've begged them to throw things away. This is obviously behavior that stems from a deprived childhood, in which I—like so many of my friends—had a lot less junk than our children.

What we should do is treat their junk as valuable collectibles so they would get a sense of orderliness and mastery that would carry them into adulthood. Instead of hollering at them to clean their rooms, we should tell them to go curate their collections. It sounds much more elegant and much more in control of your life. It sounds almost as though you have at long last achieved a sense of orderliness and mastery in your own adulthood.

Be Prepared—for Cookies
JANUARY 12, 1990

A neighborhood child came to our door the other evening—the one who I thought was born only a couple of years ago—and she arrived in the company of her father, who was escorting her on one of the all-time great American missions: she was selling Girl Scout cookies.

I always go to the door when the Girl Scout cookie girl comes. This is not a task you can delegate to children or husbands. This is a task that requires firm resolve and good character.

I do a lot to avoid solicitors. They invariably come at inconvenient times—like when I'm on the phone or getting out of the shower or trying to find something I've lost—and a rap on the door from someone soliciting for some disease research or social cause is guaranteed to escalate the irritation level to outright hostility.

Furthermore, there are enough creeps walking around loose these days that when you hear an unexpected knock at your door, you've got to wonder whether you can go right up and open it like you used to be able to do in the fifties, or whether you should hit the deadbolt and chain lock and start interrogating the person on your front steps like he or she was the leading suspect in the unsolved crimes generally attributed to Jack the Ripper.

Never mind that most rapists, burglars and other malevolent sorts generally don't approach their victims by knocking on the front doors of suburban subdivisions. You can't be too careful, and anyone who approaches her front door without a tiny bit of trepidation hasn't been watching enough trash television.

So here it was on a Monday evening, sometime after 7:00 or so, when I was in the kitchen trying to think of thin food to fix; my son was at basketball practice, my husband was on his way home, and my daughter was allegedly doing her homework, when there came this knock on the door and I went to answer it. The next generation of Girl Scout cookie pushers had arrived.

I do not know why the Girl Scouts sell cookies so soon after the holidays, when everyone is trying to shed their ill-gotten gains, but they do. And you can hear firm resolves being shelved across the land as soon as the first neighborhood child shows up on the doorstep to sell her cookies and test your willpower.

What willpower?

One of the things about Girl Scout cookies is that they have a way of making thin people who don't eat sweets start behaving like compulsive eaters. It is a well-known fact that Girl Scout cookies disappear faster than any consumer good that enters private homes. I know people who hoard those cookies so they'll have enough to last for a couple of months. I know people who hide boxes of Girl Scout cookies in their bedrooms, in dresser drawers, in the darkest corners of their closets so that they'll still be able to get a fix in May. And I know people of rigorous intellect who are capable of going through half a box of chocolate mint cookies while sipping skim milk and doing the Sunday crossword puzzle.

I used to try to hold some kind of a line on Girl Scout cookie acquisitions. There was a time when I thought four boxes was a major binge. Then my children revolted against their mother, the tightwad, and began buying their own. This was partly in response to the fact that whatever child got home from school first, which is invariably the oldest one, got a disproportionate share of the family's cookies. Thus, we'd get four boxes for the family and various children put in their own additional orders, which they then hoarded. Girl Scout cookies do not create an ambiance in which sharing is considered the highest virtue.

This system kept the peace for a couple of years and the family budget remained relatively balanced through the first quarter of each year. Then one year I was on the telephone when the Girl Scout child arrived at the front door. It was on a weekend and my oldest son—by then technically an adult—was home. "I'll take care of it, Mom," he said grandly, "you stay on the phone."

So I did. The other children appeared in the living room out of nowhere. I heard some murmuring, but I was grateful that someone else was handling something and I could continue whatever business I was involved in, without interruption.

Somebody else was handling something, all right, but not the way I would have handled it.

That year, our family placed what may have been the largest order for Girl Scout cookies ever made on the East Coast. My son the heir apparent blew the cookie budget for about four years in the space of fifteen minutes. We didn't run out of cookies for months that year. "I knew what I was doing," he said the other day. "I knew the chance that I had and I had to go for it."

And that's why I always go to the door now when the Girl Scout cookie moppet comes to call.

Match and Set
SEPTEMBER 22, 1989

On Sunday, if all goes according to plan, I shall be leaving the ranks of single mothers and returning to what I hope will be the comfort, joy and unity of marriage. It has been six years since my former husband and I separated and I hope that I will bring to my new marriage the hope and wisdom that comes from having lived through difficult times.

I have learned some things about being a single mother and about how not to be a single mother. Some mothers use the occasion of being single to fall apart and others use the occasion to become superwoman: to do everything, and to show your former spouse, family members, neighbors and colleagues that you can keep everything going by yourself without missing a beat. This, I submit after some empirical experimentation, is folly. One parent cannot do what two parents could do and to think otherwise downgrades the contributions of the absent parent, often deprives children of the other parent's talents and company and is probably a leading cause of single-parent burnout.

It is human nature, unfortunately, to label the other party in a divorce a worthless so-and-so, no matter whether everyone else thinks he or she is an absolute gem. All the books tell parents not to criticize the former spouse in front of the children, and they are right. It is absolutely destructive. What they don't emphasize enough, however, is the value of working hard to perpetuate the involvement of the former spouse in children's lives.

This means making sure that copies of report cards and athletic schedules are sent to both parents, that both parents are invited to parent-teacher conferences and school events, that both are involved in the celebrations of birthdays and significant holidays and that both are present when a child enjoys triumph or is hit by hardship and loss. It means trusting the other parent to take the children shopping, to doctor's appointments and on vacations. The operative word here is "trusting." Divorce, by its very nature, implies a breach of trust and of faith. The healing process divorced parents go through involves rebuilding that trust so that it can be a foundation and bulwark for their children's lives.

I found—as have other women—tremendous comfort and help from my friends. When you are married, your spouse is also your best friend and the person you lean on the most. Friendships can wither from lack of use. I rediscovered how wonderful good friends—male and female—can be. One of the great joys of maturity is having mature friends who have been through enough that they can give you good advice. Often they are going through the same difficulties with children, aging and ill parents or romantic entanglements, and you can give each other solace, if not solutions. They can also give you the courage to take chances—to do something you don't think you can do—and to finally take control of your own destiny. I hope when they need me that I can be as good a friend as I have had.

My intended has taken to referring to Sunday as the day of our impending doom. Already, I see where this merger is going to require compromise. My idea of an appropriate ceremony is something romantic and elegant—at, say, Versailles. His idea of an appropriate ceremony is something brief with a justice of the peace. A colleague lent us a book titled *The New Wedding*, which is a guide to scripting your own marriage ceremony. One, "the anarchist-feminist" wedding, is the most appropriately titled, but it involves rather tedious denouncements of the state. We have yet to write the ceremony.

Decorating is going to be another challenge. He is a minimalist. I go for baroque. We may end up with "His" and "Hers" sections of the house. Mine will have the flowery wallpaper and balloon curtains and his will be done in white. Then, too, there is the matter of pets: our cat and his small poodle. He assures me they will learn to coexist.

A few years ago, a friend who is divorced told me that friends of hers who had been separated for two years or more did not want to get remarried. "They value their independence too much," she said. I have grown to value my independence, and I know that I have gotten into the habit of making decisions unilaterally and doing everything myself—from fixing machinery around the house to opening windows that were painted shut, which I was struggling to do the other night while he was installing a light fixture in the new clothes closet.

"Here," he said, "I'll do that." I struggled with the window for a moment and then realized he was there to help me. It was a wonderful feeling. I stepped away and he took over and I understood in that minor moment how very major a change was coming about. I was not alone anymore.

Index

297

About the Author

Judy Mann, a prizewinning columnist for *The Washington Post*, has been writing about women, families and the politics of the women's revolution for more than a decade. She has covered the most far-reaching social changes of our times as a journalist, and she has lived them as a working mother. She has written for a wide range of magazines, including *Ms.*, *Working Woman* and the *Reader's Digest*, and she has been a guest on numerous radio and TV programs, "Nightline," "Good Morning America," "Primetime Live," "Inside Edition" and "The Larry King Show" among them.

A native of Washington, D.C., Judy Mann attended Barnard College and holds an honorary doctorate from Grinnell College. She is the mother of two sons and a daughter, and is married to Richard T. Starnes, editor of the *Journal* newspapers in Virginia.

Additional copies of *Mann for All Seasons: Wit and Wisdom from The Washington Post's Judy Mann* may be ordered by sending a check for $19.95 (please add the following for postage and handling: $1.50 for the first copy, $.50 for each added copy) to:

MasterMedia Limited
16 East 72nd Street
New York, NY 10021
(212) 260-5600
(800) 334-8232

Judy Mann is available for speeches and workshops. Please contact MasterMedia's Speakers' Bureau for availability and fee arrangements. Call Tony Colao at (201) 359-1612.

Other MasterMedia Books

THE PREGNANCY AND MOTHERHOOD DIARY: Planning the First Year of Your Second Career, by Susan Schiffer Stautberg, is the first and only undated appointment diary that shows how to manage pregnancy and career. ($12.95 spiralbound)

CITIES OF OPPORTUNITY: Finding the Best Place to Work, Live and Prosper in the 1990's and Beyond, by Dr. John Tepper Marlin, explores the job and living options for the next decade and into the next century. This consumer guide and handbook, written by one of the world's experts on cities, selects and features forty-six American cities and metropolitan areas. ($13.95 paper, $24.95 cloth)

THE DOLLARS AND SENSE OF DIVORCE, by Judith Briles, is the first book to combine practical tips on overcoming the legal hurdles with planning finances before, during and after divorce. ($10.95 paper)

OUT THE ORGANIZATION: How Fast Could You Find a New Job?, by Madeleine and Robert Swain, is written for the millions of Americans whose jobs are no longer safe, whose companies are not loyal and who face futures of uncertainty. It gives advice on finding a new job or starting your own business. ($11.95 paper, $17.95 cloth)

AGING PARENTS AND YOU: A Complete Handbook to Help You Help Your Elders Maintain a Healthy, Productive and Independent Life, by Eugenia Anderson-Ellis and Marsha Dryan, is a complete guide to providing care to aging relatives. It gives practical advice and resources to the adults who are helping their elders lead productive and independent lives. ($9.95 paper)

CRITICISM IN YOUR LIFE: How to Give It, How to Take It, How to Make It Work for You, by Dr. Deborah Bright, offers practical advice, in an upbeat, readable and realistic fashion, for turning criticism into control. Charts and diagrams guide the reader into managing criticism from bosses, spouses, children, friends, neighbors and in-laws. ($9.95 paper, $17.95 cloth)

BEYOND SUCCESS: How Volunteer Service Can Help You Begin Making a Life Instead of Just a Living, by John F. Raynolds III and Eleanor Raynolds, C.B.E., is a unique how-to book targeted to business and professional people considering volunteer work, senior citizens who wish to fill leisure time meaningfully and students trying out various career options. The book is filled with interviews with celebrities, CEOs and average citizens who talk about the benefits of service work. ($9.95 paper, $19.95 cloth)

MANAGING IT ALL: Time-Saving Ideas for Career, Family, Relationships and Self, by Beverly Benz Treuille and Susan Schiffer Stautberg, is written for women who are juggling careers and families. Over two hundred career women (ranging from a TV anchorwoman to an investment banker) were interviewed. The book contains many humorous anecdotes on saving time and improving the quality of life for self and family. ($9.95 paper)

REAL LIFE 101: (Almost) Surviving Your First Year Out of College, by Susan Kleinman, supplies welcome advice to those facing "real life" for the first time, focusing on work, money, health and how to deal with freedom and responsibility. ($9.95 paper)

YOUR HEALTHY BODY, YOUR HEALTHY LIFE: How to Take Control of Your Medical Destiny, by Donald B. Louria, M.D., provides precise advice and strategies that will help you to live a long and healthy life. Learn also about nutrition, exercise, vitamins and medication, as well as how to control risk factors for major diseases. ($12.95 paper)

THE CONFIDENCE FACTOR: How Self-Esteem Can Change Your Life, by Judith Briles, is based on a nationwide survey of six thousand men and women. Briles explores why women so often feel a lack of self-confidence and have a poor opinion of themselves. She offers step-by-step advice on becoming the person you want to be. ($18.95 cloth)

THE SOLUTION TO POLLUTION: 101 Things You Can Do to Clean Up Your Environment, by Laurence Sombke, offers step-by-step techniques on how to conserve more energy, start a recycling center, choose biodegradable products and proceed with individual environmental cleanup projects. ($7.95 paper)

TAKING CONTROL OF YOUR LIFE: The Secrets of Successful Enterprising Women, by Gail Blanke and Kathleen Walas, is based on the authors' professional experience with Avon Products' Women of Enterprise Awards, given each year to outstanding women entrepreneurs. The authors offer a specific plan to help you gain control over your life and include business tips and quizzes as well as beauty and lifestyle information. ($17.95 cloth)